The Pullman Strike and the Crisis of the 1890s

The Working Class in American History

Editorial Advisors
David Brody
Alice Kessler-Harris
David Montgomery
Sean Wilentz

A list of books in the series appears at the end of this book.

The Pullman Strike and the Crisis of the 1890s

Essays on Labor and Politics

Edited by

Richard Schneirov, Shelton Stromquist, and Nick Salvatore

University of Illinois Press
Urbana and Chicago

© 1999 by the Board of Trustees of the University of Illinois
Manufactured in the United States of America
1 2 3 4 5 C P 5 4 3 2 1

♾ This book is printed on acid-free paper.

Library of Congress Cataloging-in-Publication Data
The Pullman Strike and the crisis of the 1890s : essays on labor
and politics / edited by Richard Schneirov, Shelton Stromquist,
and Nick Salvatore.
    p.   cm.
Includes bibliographical references and index.
ISBN 0-252-02447-8 (cloth : acid-free paper)
ISBN 0-252-06755-X (pbk. : acid-free paper)
    1. Chicago Strike, 1894—Congresses. I. Schneirov, Richard. II.
Stromquist, Shelton, 1943– III. Salvatore, Nick, 1943–
HD5325.R12 1894.P85   1999
331.892'8523'0977311—ddc21   98-25404
                                      CIP

Contents

Introduction

Richard Schneirov, Shelton Stromquist,
and Nick Salvatore

THE STRIKE OF PULLMAN CARSHOP employees and the subsequent boycott that disrupted rail traffic throughout the territory west of Chicago in June–July 1894 marked the culmination of nearly two decades of the most severe and sustained labor conflict in American history. Yet until very recently little new scholarship has focused on the meaning of the Pullman strike and its historical context. By offering a close reading of contemporary perceptions of the strike and by examining the organizational and political continuities and discontinuities the Pullman conflict reveals, these essays resituate the strike in its historical context. They demonstrate that Pullman played an important role in defining the crisis of the 1890s, shaping a changing legal environment, spurring the development of a regulatory state, and fostering a new politics of progressive reform.

On September 23–24, 1994, more than two hundred scholars, students, educators, labor activists, and interested members of the public gathered at Indiana State University in Terre Haute to reconsider the Pullman strike in the light of new historical scholarship in labor history. The conference featured public addresses by the historians David Montgomery and Nick Salvatore and Jack Scheinckman, the president of the Amalgamated Textile Workers' Union (now UNITE—the Union of Needle Trades, Industrial and Textile Employees). Scholars delivered thirty-six papers at thirteen sessions that focused on various dimensions of the strike and its meaning. This edited collection contains revised versions of key conference papers addressing the significance of the Pullman strike in its wider historical context.

The Crisis of the 1890s

The Pullman strike was a central event in a broader "crisis of the 1890s," which scholars continue to regard as one of the important watersheds in American history.[1] The events of that decade had their roots in the Gilded Age, a period of accelerating and bewildering change as a northern agrarian society, composed largely of independent proprietors living in loosely connected small towns and rural areas, decisively entered the urban-industrial age , in which the majority were wage earners.[2] During this period small to middling family farms and shops producing for regional markets became integrated into national and world markets, subjecting farmers and small manufacturers to periodic gluts, price swings, and the dictates of railroads, Wall Street bankers, and the country merchants. In the old South a rural social structure dominated by large landowners strengthened its hold over newly freed slaves and reduced many white independent proprietors to the position of debt-ridden tenants and permanent laborers.

Even as the number of acres under cultivation doubled, for most Americans urbanization, industrialization, and immigration constituted the most compelling and remarkable drama of the time. The number of urban places increased from 400 at the start of the Civil War to some 1,737 at the end of the century, and the percentage of Americans living in cities almost doubled, from 19.8 to 39.1. The vast majority of urban residents worked for wages, but the nature of industrial wage work was changing. Although mass production technology was not yet dominant, many craftworkers found their autonomy, traditional skills, and working conditions threatened by the reorganization of work processes, mechanization, and new forms of business organization, though many other workers were able to parlay old knowledge into new skills that allowed them to survive and prosper in the new industrial workplace. Increasing numbers of workers, especially the bulk of operatives, helpers, and laborers, worked in large impersonal factories run by regional and national firms. By 1890, 3,000 large firms employed 125,000 of Chicago's 360,000 wage earners. Sixty-six of these firms, each averaging over 500 employees, gave employment to approximately 75,000 of these workers. Meanwhile, the continuing influx—dating from midcentury—of immigrants from Germany, Britain, Ireland, and Scandinavia made nonnative heritages and ethnic diversity distinctive features of the country's urban working class.[3]

Traditionally historians of Gilded Age politics have stressed the way that political machines won elections by engaging in corrupt practices while avoiding "the real" issues of industrial abuses. The "new political historians" of the 1970s, however, argued that conflicts among ethnic and religious groups defined voter loyalties and that such cultural issues as temperance mobilized party faithful. Recent work by political and labor historians has seriously undermined older characterizations of Gilded Age politics and has complicated the ethnocultural thesis. Historians now recognize that Gilded Age parties and the municipal and state governments they controlled, as well as nonpartisan reformers of both sexes, dealt substantively with such economic issues as the tariff, the currency question, and the curtailment of child labor and fought for the establishment of compulsory education and reform of the civil service. Corruption, it appears, was exaggerated, and state and municipal governments achieved significant structural reforms and expanded administrative apparatuses.[4]

Further evidence of the dynamism and importance of Gilded Age politics lies in the fact that large minorities of Americans, especially in the South and West and urban areas, expressed grave concerns that the social basis of a producers' republic was endangered by the appearance of railroad corporations, industrial and commercial "monopolies," ubiquitous urban poverty amidst new riches, mass violence during strikes, and urban mores, such as heavy drinking, that seemed to mock the work ethic. The constitution of the Knights of Labor referred with moral indignation to "the alarming concentration of wealth." Women temperance reformers crusaded against "demon rum." Even before the Populist Omaha platform of 1892 propelled the farmer alliances into politics, political unrest had generated a number of third parties, including the Greenback-Labor, United Labor, Prohibition, and a variety of rural antimonopoly parties that had considerable success at the state and local levels.[5]

The crisis of the 1890s appeared as the culmination of a quarter of a century of volatile socioeconomic development and growing social and political unrest. The crisis was triggered by the financial panic of 1893, which became a full-blown depression lasting five years. Unregulated market competition produced a surplus capacity in plant and equipment and endemic overproduction. The economy responded with falling prices and wages, a wave of bankruptcies, and a rate of profit below the level necessary for the reproduction of capital. The depression precipitated a national political crisis by undermining the ways party leaders had managed and contained the new issues and unrest of the previous two decades. The crash of July 1893 found a Democrat, Grover Cleveland, in the White

House. Elected less than a year earlier at the head of a precarious coalition composed of regional, class, and ethnoreligious elements, Cleveland responded to the depression in ways that greatly energized the simmering insurgencies of southern and western farmers and urban workers, groups that threatened to bolt the Democratic party in favor of the newly minted People's (Populist) party.[6]

Cleveland tried to restore business confidence, which banking and commercial leaders told him meant maintaining gold as the basis for international exchange. That in turn required repealing the Sherman Silver Purchase Act of 1890, a piece of legislation that had barely satisfied agrarian advocates of a bimetallic currency. Cleveland's well-orchestrated repeal only exacerbated currency deflation, deepened the depression, and outraged Democratic farmers, many of whom believed that the demonetization of silver in 1873 had caused their troubles.

The 1890s crisis also had an important labor dimension. In business downturns in 1873–79 and 1883–85 industrial employers had reacted to cutthroat competition and overproduction by increasing their scale of production, concentrating capital, and joining cartels and vertical and horizontal combinations to regulate production, prices, and investment so they could cut costs and restore profitability. When industrial employers cut labor costs, they often undermined the viability of existing bargains made with craft unions. In response skilled workers during the "great upheaval" of the mid-1880s began to ally with lesser skilled laborers and operatives in more broadly based, inclusive organizations, notably the Knights of Labor. Workers of different skills, races, nationalities, and sexes also adopted more militant and effective forms of collective action, such as the boycott and sympathy strike, and turned en masse to the movement for the eight-hour day. Though durable trade agreements had a precarious existence in the late nineteenth century, the aftermath of the great upheaval witnessed the first experiments by organized workers and employers to regulate and stabilize markets by taking wages out of competition.[7]

The Pullman strike of 1894 culminated almost a decade of labor unrest punctuated by episodes of spectacular violence, such as the Haymarket tragedy of 1886. The first three years of the 1890s witnessed the strike of Homestead Steel workers against the Carnegie Corporation, the miners' strikes in the coal mining regions of the East and hardrock states in the West, a longshoremen's strike in New Orleans that united black and white workers, and numerous railroad strikes. Particularly on the railroads both capital and labor experimented organizationally in regulating market conditions. The nation's railroads established patterns of management cooperation in labor matters through the tightly disciplined General Managers' Association (GMA), capable of directing the interests of the major transcontinental lines in a period of labor crisis. In the meantime railroad workers searched for the means to unify the disparate crafts. Despite resistance among craft brotherhood leaders, railroad workers joined the Knights of Labor in large numbers in the 1880s, and by 1893 many embraced the American Railway Union (ARU), a fledgling industrial union capable of challenging the GMA.[8]

The Pullman strike and its crushing defeat through intervention by the federal judiciary and the U.S. Army greatly exacerbated President Cleveland's political difficulties. Urban working-class constituents of the Democratic party joined southern and western farmers in their outrage and sense of betrayal at the hands of the Cleveland administration. In addition the strike coming amidst mounting unemployment—dramatized by the march on Washington of Coxey's Army—raised new fears among the nation's upper classes that a revolution of the dispossessed was at hand. The off-year elections of 1894 registered this discontent in a resounding Democratic defeat and set in motion an electoral realignment that reshaped the nation's party system by the end of the decade. In the aftermath of the Pullman strike rural-based Populists and segments of the labor movement sympathetic to the ARU hoped to create a labor-Populist alliance that might counter the growing power of monopolies, bankers, and industrialists. To their dismay significant numbers of urban workers instead switched from the Democratic to the Republican party. Republican William McKinley's 1896 victory over William Jennings Bryan, the neo-Populist candidate of the Democratic party, cemented the transition from the third-party system to the fourth-party system and secured national Republican party dominance through 1928.

The new Republican-dominated party system created the political climate for a resolution of the social and economic crisis of the 1890s. The decline of two-party competitiveness in different regions and a consequent decrease in the high levels of voter turnout that had characterized Gilded Age politics limited the political system's ability to register discontent. This was especially so in the South, where the defeat of the People's party and the legal disfranchisement of black voters eliminated any alternative to the Democratic party, the self-described "party of the white man." National turnout levels fell continuously from the high 70–80 percent range in the

1890s to a low of 49 percent in the 1924 presidential election. Strong parties with voter loyalties defined by ethnoreligious ties gradually gave way
to weak parties; issue-oriented, nonpartisan progressive politics; and interest group lobbying in a greatly expanded regulatory state.[9]

A dramatic corporate merger wave between 1896 and 1904 that accompanied these changes extended corporate business organization beyond
the railroads and restructured the nation's manufacturing economy that
had earlier been under proprietary ownership. Republican ascendancy
allowed for the progressive legitimation of the corporation in law and its
regulation by federal commissions affiliated with the executive branch,
developments that by the Woodrow Wilson administration suggested an
accommodation between big business and the country's democratic and
liberal traditions. The triumph of a new corporate economy created the
"seedbed of a new social and economic order." The new corporations'
growing ability to centralize investment decisions, regulate production,
and manage the demand for its products greatly restricted the cutthroat
competition and the length and severity of the crises of overproduction
that had characterized the late nineteenth century.[10]

Corporations had proved themselves capable of brutally crushing
unions, as they had done at Pullman, when they deemed labor organization incompatible with their fundamental interests. But the Pullman strike
proved to be an important moment in the development of new thinking
on the relations between labor and capital. The efforts of the Civic Federation of Chicago to mediate the conflict, the critical appraisal of the
strike by the U.S. Strike Commission, and Attorney General Richard
Olney's new thinking on labor relations, despite his prosecution of the
ARU strike leaders, signified acceptance by some corporate leaders and
their reform allies of the need to recognize responsible unions of their
employees. The Erdman Act of 1898 codified provisions that promised an
expanded role for government and an era of labor peace on the railroads.
The formation of the National Civic Federation in 1899 created a new
institutional framework for enlisting the nation's largest corporations in
a program designed to ensure stability in labor relations. These developments prefigured further expansion of efforts to legislate labor peace that
would culminate in the path-breaking labor legislation of the 1930s. The
Pullman strike of 1894, then, stands at the intersection of formative developments that have determined the shape of labor relations in twentieth-century American society.[11]

The Pullman Strike and Boycott

The significance of the Pullman strike lies not only in the larger patterns of labor conflict and national crisis it revealed but also in the visibility of the town, the company and its founders, and the ways a local conflict grew into a strike of national proportions. In 1880 the pioneer manufacturer George M. Pullman constructed Pullman as a factory town south of Chicago.[12] The town was not simply a site for manufacturing railroad sleeping cars; it was also an experiment in urban living and social reform. In contrast to Chicago's unpaved, grimy streets, its paucity of public services, and its ubiquitous shacks and crowded tenements that served as wage workers' homes, Pullman town boasted clean, paved streets; pure air; beautiful parks and playgrounds; an indoor arcade containing retail stores, a theater, a bank, and a library; neat homes with indoor plumbing; and no saloons. By removing his workers from the city, Pullman hoped to insulate them from crime, intemperance, poverty, labor riots, and trade union–inspired strikes that mugwump reformers of the Gilded Age so deeply deplored.

Despite scattered labor unrest Pullman's experiment in planned living appeared to most observers a stunningly successful demonstration that philanthropy and reform could be a "paying proposition" and thus compatible with large-scale corporate enterprise. Its living conditions appeared particularly ideal for wives. Only a few observers commented on the coercive paternalism in the service of moral uplift and social harmony that lay at the core of Pullman's experiment. Pullman expected residents to live and shop in the town, but they could not buy their own homes and had no democratic self-government. Nevertheless, Pullman's shop employees engaged in a long battle over piece rates and through periodic strikes expressed resentment over arbitrary treatment from foremen.

The 1893 panic glaringly exposed the underside of the Pullman experiment. The industrial depression that would last five years forced the company to produce cars at a loss. In response Pullman reduced his work force, cut its wages on average by a third, and declined to reduce prices at his company store or the rents on his homes. By December 1893 the *Chicago Times* reported that "great dissatisfaction and suffering prevails in Pullman."[13] Meanwhile, to the north, Chicago was inundated with "tramps" and unemployed and homeless men, many of them building workers thrown out of work by the completion of the World's Columbian Exposition. Following a dreadful winter workers at Pullman, who had joined the ARU, decided to turn to their union for support.

Founded in 1893 by Eugene Victor Debs, an ex-official of the Brotherhood of Locomotive Firemen, the ARU had grown out of the persistent efforts of railroad workers as far back as the great strikes of 1877 to find an organizational vehicle to achieve unity across skill lines and protect their pay and working conditions against the encroachments of railroad management. Mutual scabbing (strikebreaking) by members of the Knights of Labor and the craft brotherhoods during the mid-1880s (in strikes on the Gould railroads in 1885–86, the Reading Railroad in 1887, and the Chicago, Burlington and Quincy Railroad in 1888) had continually stymied labor organization. Following defeat in the Burlington strike of 1888, the brotherhoods experimented with federations for several years, but eventually some brotherhood leaders and thousands of rank-and-file members turned to a new industrial union. The ARU sought to transcend divisiveness by enrolling railroad operatives, laborers, and skilled craftworkers of all trades in a single organization.

The Pullman strike originated in the aftermath of the electrifying April 1893 victory of the ARU on the Great Northern Railroad. On May 10 a committee of Pullman workers presented a petition of grievances to the company; the next day three members of the committee were fired. The Pullman affiliate of the ARU called a strike at once.

At this early stage of the dispute Pullman workers won wide public support in their pursuit of an arbitrated settlement. The Civic Federation of Chicago and John P. Hopkins, the city's mayor, as well as an ARU delegation, attempted to mediate the dispute without success. Chicago's press disapproved of the company's intransigence. Referring to Pullman, the national Republican party leader Marcus Hanna exploded with exasperation, "A man who won't meet his men half-way is a God-damn fool."[14] But Pullman remained adamant. Just as important, the GMA saw the opportunity to crush the fledgling ARU before it reached maturity. When the union's first convention in June 1894 declared a boycott of all railroads using Pullman sleeping cars, the GMA appointed its own strike manager and resolved to discharge any railroad worker who participated in the boycott.

Despite significant scabbing by members of the craft brotherhoods, which prevented the strike from spreading east, the ARU boycott soon brought the nation's rail traffic to a virtual standstill from Chicago to the Pacific Coast. In response the GMA worked assiduously to federalize the conflict. U.S. Attorney General Richard Olney, himself a railroad attorney, appointed Edwin Walker, a legal adviser to the GMA, as a special U.S. attorney for Chicago. Meanwhile, a series of minor riots and confrontations with the militia became the occasion for the press to decry a breakdown in law and order instigated by "dictator Debs." On July 1, six days after the start of the boycott, Walker applied for, and the following day received, a federal court injunction declaring the strike a violation of the Sherman Anti-Trust Act. The next day, despite an absence of violence, Olney convinced President Grover Cleveland to dispatch federal troops to Chicago over the strenuous protests of John Peter Altgeld, the first prolabor governor in Illinois.

The events of these few days represented a fateful turning point in the strike. The presence of federal troops, which permitted strikebreakers to be employed by the railroads, and the demoralizing effect of the injunction, which led to the arrest of Debs and other ARU leaders on contempt of court charges, combined to facilitate the movement of trains by July 9. The blatant partiality of the federal government outraged organized Chicago workers, and sentiment grew for a general strike in support of the ARU strikers. Although 25,000 local unionists eventually struck in sympathy, most of the labor movement held back while Samuel Gompers and other American Federation of Labor (AFL) leaders met at Briggs House in Chicago on July 12 to consider Debs's plea for a general strike. Mindful that the strike was virtually defeated and fearful that a direct confrontation with the federal government would jeopardize the rest of the labor movement, Gompers and the AFL's executive council counseled against a sympathy strike. The strike remained strong in many western railroad centers, but in Chicago it was all but over. It took until August 2 for strikers in the West and the ARU to concede defeat.

A bitter Debs never forgave Gompers for failing to back the strike. After serving a six-month sentence in the Woodstock jail for contempt of court, Debs returned to the labor movement as a hero. Believing that economic action was insufficient to challenge corporate domination of the lives of its employees, Debs soon turned to independent politics. He became the most forceful spokesman for the new Socialist Party of America and between 1900 and 1920 served five times as its presidential candidate.

The Essays in Historiographical Context

Despite the strike's centrality to the crisis of the 1890s it remains neglected as an object of historical study. Historians have looked at the strike in different ways. Those writing in the progressive–New Deal tradition portrayed it as a rebellion of rational and liberty-loving workers against the suffocating paternalism of Pullman's planned community. For progressives the strike represented the failure of the laissez-faire model of industrial capitalism, with its willingness to sacrifice workers' basic rights and welfare to the dictates of the unregulated market. Progressives championed institutional intervention in the market in the form of unions and an activist state.[15] By the 1950s and 1960s a new generation of historians portrayed late nineteenth-century episodes of working-class unrest, such as the Pullman boycott, as marginal to core themes in American history. Some emphasized a procapitalist consensus they believed Americans of all classes shared. Others stressed a continuing process of social and economic modernization.[16] Beginning in the 1960s and 1970s historians working in the burgeoning field of "new" labor history pushed the boundaries of scholarship beyond the institutionalism that the progressives championed as an alternative to the market, and they compellingly challenged the older social science assumption that conflict was the exception to the rule in modern American society. Much of the new labor history has been social and cultural in nature, embedding the lives and organizations of workers in artisan traditions, in class and ethnic communities, and, more recently, in relations of race and gender.[17] Despite its accomplishments the new labor history has not produced a study of the Pullman strike comparable in scope to the 1942 monograph by the progressive historian Almont Lindsey. Moreover, the general failure of labor historians—with some notable exceptions—to address the complex relations between workers and the political system has led them to neglect investigating the Pullman strike in the context of the crisis of the 1890s.

The essays in this collection emphasize several themes central to recent developments in labor and political history. They examine continuities and changes in the bases of labor organization and strikes stretching back from Pullman and the ARU to the Knights of Labor and forward to the shopmen's strike of 1922. They suggest how gender identities shaped contemporary views of the strike and how new photographic technology was used to construct and contest the meaning of the strike. Contrary to influential recent studies by historians of labor and the law, an essay in this collection views the role of the federal judiciary as qualified and ambivalent rather than as uniformly antilabor. Many of the essays challenge the notion that the course of the labor movement in this period was determined by the state independent of social and economic pressures.[18]

To the contrary, the social crisis precipitated by the events of 1894 and afterward powerfully influenced labor legislation and the course of politics. Finally, as these essays demonstrate, the strike was a political event that became an arena in which the meaning and future of producerism were contested. Out of the maelstrom of controversy surrounding the Pullman strike new currents of liberal reform gained impetus, seeking at once to revitalize democracy and promote the corporate reconstruction of American society.

In the first essay of the volume, "Dress Rehearsal for Pullman: The Knights of Labor and the 1890 New York Central Strike," Robert E. Weir offers an extended narrative account of the Knights-led New York Central strike in 1890 that bore "an uncanny resemblance" to the subsequent Pullman strike. The Knight's Grand Master Workman Terence V. Powderly, like Debs four years later, actively discouraged the strike but was forced by a rebellious rank and file to lend his support and authority to the walkout. Once it was undertaken, the strike was hobbled by persistent conflict with the railroad brotherhoods. Moreover, both organizations failed to enlist broader federations of workers in sympathetic strike actions that would have afforded critical support. Ironically, it was Debs himself who influenced the Supreme Council of the United Order of Railroad Employees to reject a sympathy strike in 1890, just as Gompers would later do in 1894. Both strikes faced a formidable array of opponents that included a hostile judiciary as well as the combined opposition from railroad capital. Ultimately, the New York Central strike tolled the death knell of the Knights of Labor, just as Pullman did for the ARU.

Susan E. Hirsch in "The Search for Unity among Railroad Workers: The Pullman Strike in Perspective" has also utilized comparison to illuminate the Pullman strike. But, unlike Weir, she looks ahead from 1894 to the 1922 shop craftworkers' strike and compares labor relations in Chicago with those in Wilmington, Delaware. Hirsch shows that Pullman strikers drew significant support from the community, both within Pullman and in nearby Chicago. But where such local solidarity did not exist, as at the Wilmington carshops and many eastern railroad centers, effective strike action did not materialize. By 1922 community support was less important to the success of strikes. Nationalizing forces, notably the intervention of the federal government beginning with the Erdman Act and intensifying during World War I, created new conditions for solidarity that transcended local class cultures and fueled the shopmen's strike. Yet, just as in 1894, weakened by the lack of solidarity from other segments of organized labor, the strikers succumbed to a federal injunction. Hirsch's conclusions return students of Pullman to a pervasive theme in this collection: the paramount importance of government and politics in any examination of the labor movement.

In "A Modern Lear and His Daughters: Gender in the Model Town of Pullman" Janice L. Reiff explores the town of Pullman as gendered territory. Reiff shows that the older progressive view that Pullman's paternalism undermined the independence—what was then termed "the manhood"—of his employees did not go far enough. A different kind of paternalism—men of all classes over women and children—also existed but was never criticized by progressive reformers. Indeed, as Reiff points out, contemporary American manhood required the subordination of women and children and created among workers and reformers a profound ambivalence toward life in Pullman. On the one hand, Pullman's shopmen chafed at the company's low wages that prevented them from supporting their wives at home; on the other hand, many approved of the way Pullman's paternalism in the town reinforced a Victorian family lifestyle. Reiff shows that the boundary between these two forms of paternalism was often porous, especially when the company intervened in family life over the heads of male heads of household.

Once the strike was proclaimed, Pullman seemed to have abandoned both kinds of paternalism. He not only did not care for his workers but also appeared to have abandoned the women and children of his town to destitution. Public opinion swung to the side of the strikers. Eventually, however, the Pullman women's active role in the strike belied their public image as helpless victims. After assaulting strikebreakers, they were tagged as "amazons," thereby forfeiting public sympathy. Meanwhile, Pullman's attempt to succor needy families and strikers' actions in keeping these families from crossing picket lines also undermined the formerly strong public support the strike had received. Reiff's demonstration of the power of gendered discourse and the grip of the family wage in Pullman makes it clear that gender must occupy a central place in any reinterpretation of the Pullman strike.

Larry Peterson's essay, "Photography and the Pullman Strike: Remolding Perceptions of Labor Conflict by New Visual Communication," shows the Pullman strike was the culmination of an extended, profound crisis in the representation of the labor question. According to Peterson the pictorial record of the strike reveals a "crisis of representation" that derived from labor's new power and, coincidentally, precipitous advances in visual technology and artistry. In the 1880s and 1890s images of labor and capital had been influenced by styles of visual representation developed in new print media illustrations and popular stereopticon photographs. These stylized, often classical constructions arose from a process of deliberate selection and choice. The 1890s witnessed rapid technological changes that afforded greater spontaneity and opened new possibilities for creating images that embodied underlying patterns of class conflict. The flood of images from the strike, while still largely avoiding the actual moments of conflagration, reveals a medium capable of providing labor and its grievances new visibility.

The progressive settlement house reformer Jane Addams became one of the most fascinating and significant figures connected with the Pullman strike. In the early stages of the strike Addams sought to mediate. Victoria Brown in "Advocate for Democracy: Jane Addams and the Pullman Strike" shows how Addams tried to "carve out her own unique stance toward the Pullman strike in particular and the 'labor question' in general." Unlike previous historians who have viewed Addams as a timid and temporizing member of the middle class, Brown portrays Addams as a woman who developed a mature philosophical and political position grounded in, but transcending, her experience as a woman. Addams's distinctive contribution came in her article "A Modern Lear," which compared George Pullman with Shakespeare's King Lear and likened embattled labor to his daughter Cordelia. Addams argued that employers' refusal to recognize their employees' autonomy led to tragedy for all. Her goal was not for the rebels to win but for the larger interest of the industrial family to prevail.

Legal historians debate whether society or the law itself was the primary agent in structuring the rules by which business was regulated and the interests of workers and their employers adjudicated in the nineteenth century. Melvyn Dubofsky in his essay entitled "The Federal Judiciary, Free Labor, and Equal Rights" argues that the current fashion that sees an autonomous legal culture as determinative—a discourse that "creates" social reality—fails to account for the extent to which the law and the courts "echoed beliefs and values that resonated through broader spheres of popular culture." He offers an alternative, "mixed" narrative of labor and the law in the late nineteenth century that accords partial autonomy to the law and simultaneously sees it reflecting a broader cultural tension between individual and group interests. Victorian legal principles upheld a stark individualism that left little space for the collective action of workers. Those principles were nurtured by post–Civil War free labor ideas, popular social Darwinism, and a tradition of "civic republicanism" that enjoyed wide currency. The Victorian commitment to individualism and the free market was challenged by an alternative set of principles woven into the practice of trade unions, articulated by academic social scientists, and made palpable by the "rising intensity of class conflict." A new legal discourse emerged that rejected the unfettered rule of the market and justified group rights and collective action by labor as well as capital. Out of the turmoil of Pullman and the labor conflicts of the 1890s a new legal discourse appeared that accorded collective bargaining some legitimacy, set new standards of fairness for employment, and rationalized a more interventionist role for the state in the relations between railroad labor and capital. This new discourse was evident in the final report of the U.S. Strike Commission, in Richard Olney's rethinking of the proper relations between labor and capital, in the Erdman Act, and in the reports of the U.S. Industrial Commission.

The idea that Pullman should be understood in the context of the emergence of a "new liberalism" is developed by both Shelton Stromquist and Richard Schneirov. In "The Crisis of 1894 and the Legacies of Producerism" Stromquist sees a series of developments, not least the Pullman strike, which promoted and then shattered an impressive producers' alliance based on the industrial unionism of railroad men, coal miners, and workers in other industrial sectors of the economy. The failure of the AFL to endorse the call for a general strike in support of the Pullman boycott and the federation's reaction to the producerist agenda in the debate over its political program suggest the extent to which developments surrounding the strike altered the political landscape. New reform alliances claiming a share of the producerist legacy surfaced to challenge the republican patrimony of the ARU and its collectivist supporters. Conservative trade unionists rode the crest of the crisis uneasily, neither disavowing their own producerism nor affirming the radicals' program. At crucial moments—the Briggs House conference, the Congress on Industrial Conciliation, and the AFL convention itself—the trade unionists put forward an alternative agenda and cultivated new allies. Among those whose support they sought was a diverse coalition of social reformers, mesmerized by a vision of social harmony, and reform-minded business leaders and professionals who promoted the federation of civic interests. This new liberal politics, which "used a discourse of social harmony to marginalize class-based ideologies," nonetheless found pragmatic support among trade unionists anxious to weather the storms of economic depression. Its most zealous advocates, however, were a new generation of progressive reformers whose contributions lay largely in the future.

That future is the topic of Richard Schneirov's essay, "Labor and the New Liberalism in the Wake of the Pullman Strike." Schneirov shows how Chicago was a laboratory where progressive reformers engaged in organizational and political experimentation. In doing so he challenges the emerging narrative adopted by many labor historians who view the defeat of the Pullman strike and the labor-Populist alliance as tragically foreclosing a more emancipatory set of possibilities in twentieth-century America. Schneirov argues that a new liberal political movement emerged partly in response to the newfound strength of craft-industrial organizations relying on the trade agreement and union label boycott. The new liberalism, contends Schneirov, was not fundamentally antilabor or antidemocratic. Rather, it was "a synthetic and inclusive movement and mode of thought that drew in significant ways on the democratic upsurge of the period and recognized the presence of organized labor and socialism." Schneirov focuses on the rise of the Civic Federation of Chicago and its offshoot, the Municipal Voters' League, to argue that a liberal reform politics enjoyed considerable cross-class support, including important segments of the labor movement. The prospects that this movement awakened among reformers served to stimulate the launching of the National Civic Federation, which after 1899 drew together corporate leaders, trade unionists, and reformers in furtherance of a new liberal agenda in the Progressive Era.

In the epilogue, "The Pullman Boycott and the Making of Modern America," David Montgomery points out that the Pullman confrontation "framed issues involving the most desirable relationship between organized society and what is called the 'free market' that haunt our current discussion of the Pullman boycott, not like ghosts of Christmas past but like ghosts of Christmas yet to come." Drawing on Karl Polanyi's classic study, Montgomery argues that corporate and government regulation of market activity was society's way of protecting itself from the ravages of the self-regulating market.[19] In our time, as the market is unleashed from regulatory control, we are compelled to ask, as Debs did a hundred years ago, who will champion society's interests vis-à-vis the market. Montgomery's point was given added poignancy by the fact that bitter, ongoing struggles, whether of Staley workers in Decatur, Illinois, Bridgestone/ Firestone rubber workers in Des Moines and Decatur, or Caterpillar workers in Peoria, were never far from the minds of conference participants.

While the legacies of the Pullman strike continue to be contested, these essays testify to the pivotal importance of this strike and its aftermath for understanding the course of working-class history and American history. They also suggest the continuing vigor of the new labor history, even as it ages, and its engagement with questions that illuminate in new and unexpected ways one of the most important events in labor's past.

Notes

1. Treatments of the 1890s as a period of crisis and adjustment are ubiquitous. See, for instance, Samuel P. Hays, *The Response to Industrialism, 1885–1914* (Chicago: University of Chicago Press, 1957), 192; Harold U. Faulkner, *Politics, Reform, and Expansion, 1890–1900* (New York: Harper, 1959), chap. 1; Robert Wiebe, *The Search for Order, 1877–1920* (New York: Hill and Wang, 1967), chaps. 3 and 4; Robert Wiebe, *Self-Rule: A Cultural History of American Democracy* (Chicago: University of Chicago Press, 1995), 113–16, 122–31; Walter La Feber, *The New Empire: An Interpretation of American Expansion, 1860–1898* (Ithaca, N.Y.: Cornell University Press, 1963), chap. 2; Ray Ginger, *The Age of Excess: The United States from 1877 to 1914*, 2d ed. (New York: Macmillan, 1975), chap. 8; Walter Dean Burnham, *Critical Elections and the Mainsprings of American Politics* (New York: Oxford University Press, 1970), chap. 4; Morton Keller, *Affairs of State: Public Life in Late Nineteenth Century America* (Cambridge, Mass.: Belknap of Harvard University Press, 1977), chap. 15; Martin J. Sklar, *The Corporate Reconstruction of American Capitalism, 1890–1906: The Market, the Law, and Politics* (New York: Cambridge University Press, 1988), chaps. 1 and 2; Martin J. Sklar, *The United States as a Developing Country: Studies in U.S. History in the Progressive Era and the 1920s* (New York: Cambridge University Press, 1992), chap. 2; David Montgomery, *The Fall of the House of Labor: The Workplace, the State, and American Labor Activism, 1865–1925* (New York: Cambridge University Press, 1987), 43–57, 171–78; James Livingston, *Origins of the Federal Reserve System: Money, Class, and Corporate Capitalism, 1890–1913* (Ithaca, N.Y.: Cornell University Press, 1986), chap. 2.

2. Wiebe, *Search for Order;* Alan Trachtenberg, *The Incorporation of America: Culture and Society in the Gilded Age* (New York: Hill and Wang, 1982). For recent surveys of social and political change in the Gilded Age, see Charles W. Calhoun, ed., *The Gilded Age: Essays on the Origins of Modern America* (Wilmington, Del.: SR Books, 1996); Walter Licht, *Industrializing America: The Nineteenth Century* (Baltimore: Johns Hopkins University Press, 1995); Mark Wahlgren Summers, *The Gilded Age or the Hazard of New Functions* (Upper Saddle River, N.J.: Prentice-Hall, 1997).

3. Robert G. Barrows, "Urbanizing America," in *Gilded Age,* ed. Calhoun, 92; *Chicago Tribune,* May 7, 1890; Ira Berlin and Herbert G. Gutman, "Class Compo-

sition and the Development of the American Working Class, 1840–1890: Immigrants and Their Children as Wage Earners," in *Power and Culture: Herbert G. Gutman and the American Working Class*, ed. Ira Berlin (New York: Pantheon Books, 1987).

4. Matthew Josephson, *The Politicos* (New York: Harcourt, Brace, 1938); Paul Kleppner, *The Third Electoral System, 1853–1892: Parties, Voters, and Political Cultures* (Chapel Hill: University of North Carolina Press, 1979); John C. Teaford, *The Unheralded Triumph: City Government in America, 1870–1900* (Baltimore: Johns Hopkins University Press, 1984); William R. Brock, *Investigation and Responsibility: Public Responsibility in the United States, 1865–1900* (Cambridge: Cambridge University Press, 1984); Stephen Skowronek, *Building a New American State: The Expansion of National Administrative Capacities, 1877–1920* (New York: Cambridge University Press, 1982). For surveys, see Vincent P. De Santis, "The Political Life of the Gilded Age: A Review of the Recent Literature," *History Teacher* 9 (November 1975): 73–106; Charles W. Calhoun, "The Political Culture: Public Life and the Conduct of Politics," in *Gilded Age*, ed. Calhoun, 185–213; and R. Hal Williams, "The Politics of the Gilded Age," in *American Political History: Essays on the State of the Discipline*, ed. John F. Marszalek and Wilson D. Miscamble (Notre Dame, Ind.: University of Notre Dame Press, 1997), 108–42.

5. Nathan Fine, *Labor and Farmer Parties in the United States, 1828–1928* (New York: Rand School of Social Science, 1928); Leon Fink, *Workingmen's Democracy: The Knights of Labor and American Politics* (Urbana: University of Illinois Press, 1983); Worth Robert Miller, "Farmers and Third Party Politics," in *Gilded Age*, ed. Calhoun, 235–60; Richard Oestreicher, "Urban Working-Class Political Behavior and Theories of American Electoral Politics, 1870–1940," *Journal of American History* 74 (March 1988): 1257–86; Richard Schneirov, *Labor and Urban Politics: Class Conflict and the Origins of Modern Liberalism in Chicago, 1864–97* (Urbana: University of Illinois Press, 1998).

6. For detailed political accounts of this period, see H. Wayne Morgan, *From Hayes to McKinley: National Party Politics, 1877–1896* (Syracuse, N.Y.: Syracuse University Press, 1969); R. Hal Williams, *Years of Decision: American Politics in the 1890s* (New York: Wiley, 1978); Lawrence Goodwyn, *The Populist Moment: A Short History of the Agrarian Revolt in America* (New York: Oxford University Press, 1978); and Summers, *Gilded Age or the Hazard of New Functions*.

7. Fink, *Workingmen's Democracy*, esp. 184–95, 221; Shelton Stromquist, *A Generation of Boomers: The Pattern of Railroad Labor Conflict in Nineteenth-Century America* (Urbana: University of Illinois Press, 1987), chaps. 3, 5, and 6; Schneirov, *Labor and Urban Politics*, chaps. 8 and 12; Daniel R. Ernst, *Lawyers against Labor: From Individual Rights to Corporate Liberalism* (Urbana: University of Illinois Press, 1995); James Livingston, "The Social Analysis of Economic History: Conjectures on Late Nineteenth-Century American Development," *American Historical Review* 82 (February 1987): 69–95; John R. Bowman, "When Workers Organize Capital-

ists: The Case of the Bituminous Coal Industry," *Politics and Society* 14, no. 1 (1985): 289–327.

8. Stromquist, *Generation of Boomers*, chap. 2.

9. Burnham, *Critical Elections and the Mainsprings of American Politics;* Walter Dean Burnham, "The System of 1896: An Analysis," in *The Evolution of American Electoral Systems,* by Paul Kleppner, Walter Dean Burnham, Ronald P. Formisano, Samuel P. Hays, Richard Jensen, and William G. Shade (Westport, Conn.: Greenwood, 1981), 170–83; Paul Kleppner, *Who Voted? The Dynamics of Electoral Turnout, 1870–1980* (New York, Praeger 1982); Paul Kleppner, *Continuity and Change in Electoral Politics, 1893–1928* (Westport, Conn.: Greenwood, 1987); Chester McArthur Destler, *American Radicalism, 1865–1901: Essays and Documents* (New London: Connecticut College, 1946); Michael McGerr, *The Decline of Popular Politics: The American North, 1865–1928* (New York: Oxford University Press, 1986); Arthur S. Link and Richard L. McCormick, *Progressivism* (Arlington Heights, Ill.: Harlan Davidson, 1983); Skowronek, *Building a New American State;* Mary O. Furner, "The Republican Tradition and the New Liberalism: Social Investigation, State Building, and Social Learning in the Gilded Age," in *The State and Social Investigation in Britain and the United States,* ed. Michael J. Lacey and Mary O. Furner (Cambridge: Cambridge University Press, 1993).

10. Sklar, *Corporate Reconstruction of American Capitalism;* Sklar, *The United States as a Developing Country,* chaps. 1, 2, and 7; Alfred D. Chandler Jr., *The Visible Hand: The Managerial Revolution in American Business* (Cambridge, Mass.: Harvard University Press, 1977); James Weinstein, *The Corporate Ideal in the Liberal State, 1900–1918* (Boston: Beacon, 1968); Glenn Porter, *The Rise of Big Business, 1860–1920,* 2d ed. (Arlington Heights, Ill.: Harlan Davidson, 1992), 91 (quote); Livingston, *Origins of the Federal Reserve System.*

11. Melvyn Dubofsky, *The State and Labor in Modern America* (Chapel Hill: University of North Carolina Press, 1994); Mary O. Furner, "Knowing Capitalism: Public Investigation and the Labor Question in the Long Progressive Era," in *The State and Economic Knowledge: The American and British Experiences,* ed. Mary O. Furner and Barry Supple (New York: Cambridge University Press, 1992); Montgomery, *Fall of the House of Labor;* Bruno Ramirez, *When Workers Fight: The Politics of Industrial Relations in the Progressive Era, 1898–1916* (Westport, Conn.: Greenwood, 1978); Sanford M. Jacoby, *Employing Bureaucracy: Managers, Unions, and the Transformation of Work in American Industry, 1900–1945* (New York: Columbia University Press, 1985).

12. The following summary account can be supplemented by Almont Lindsey, *The Pullman Strike: The Story of a Unique Experiment and of a Great Labor Upheaval* (Chicago: University of Chicago Press, 1942); Harry Barnard, *Eagle Forgotten: The Life of John Peter Altgeld* (Secaucus, N.J.: Lyle Stuart, 1938); Stanley Buder, *Pullman: An Experiment in Industrial Order and Community Planning, 1880–1930* (New York: Oxford University Press, 1967); Nick Salvatore, *Eugene V. Debs: Citizen and Social-*

ist (Urbana: University of Illinois Press, 1982); Stromquist, *Generation of Boomers;* and Carl Smith, *Urban Disorder and the Shape of Belief: The Great Chicago Fire, the Haymarket Bomb, and the Model Town of Pullman* (Chicago: University of Chicago Press, 1995).

13. Quoted in Smith, *Urban Disorder and the Shape of Belief,* 234.

14. Quoted in Lindsey, *Pullman Strike,* 318–19.

15. Charles A. Beard and Mary R. Beard, *The Rise of American Civilization,* vol. 2 (New York: Macmillan, 1927), 235–38; Perlman, *History of Trade Unionism in the United States;* Lindsey, *Pullman Strike;* Sidney Fine, *Laissez-Faire and the General-Welfare State: A Study of Conflict in American Thought, 1865–1901* (Ann Arbor: University of Michigan Press, 1956); Donald McMurray, *The Great Burlington Strike of 1888: A Case History of Industrial Relations* (Cambridge, Mass.: Harvard University Press, 1956).

16. Major consensus historians include Louis Hartz, *The Liberal Tradition in America: An Interpretation of American Political Thought since the Revolution* (New York: Harcourt, Brace and World, 1955); and Richard Hofstadter, *The Age of Reform: From Bryan to FDR* (New York: Vintage Books, 1955); modernization is the major theme in Wiebe, *Search for Order;* and Hays, *Response to Industrialism.*

17. For surveys of the new labor history, see J. Carroll Moody and Alice Kessler-Harris, eds., *Perspectives on American Labor History: The Problems of Synthesis* (De Kalb, Ill.: Northern Illinois University Press, 1989); Melvyn Dubofsky, *Industrialism and the American Workers, 1865–1921,* 2d ed. (Arlington Heights, Ill.: Harlan Davidson, 1985); Leon Fink, "American Labor History," in *The New American History,* ed. Eric Foner, rev. ed. (Philadelphia: Temple University Press, 1997), 333–52. For recent discussions of race and gender, see David R. Roediger, *Towards the Abolition of Whiteness: Essays on Race, Politics, and Working Class History* (New York: Verso, 1994); and Ava Baron, ed., *Work Engendered: Toward a New History of American Labor* (Ithaca, N.Y.: Cornell University Press, 1991).

18. William Forbath, *Law and the Shaping of the American Labor Movement* (Cambridge, Mass.: Harvard University Press, 1991); Victoria Hattam, *Labor Visions and State Power: The Origins of Business Unionism in the United States* (Princeton, N.J.: Princeton University Press, 1993); Christopher L. Tomlins and Andrew J. King, eds., *Labor Law in America: Historical and Critical Essays* (Baltimore: Johns Hopkins University Press, 1992). Compare Karen Orren, *Belated Feudalism: Labor, the Law, and Liberal Development in the United States* (New York: Cambridge University Press, 1991).

19. Karl Polanyi, *The Great Transformation: The Political and Economic Origins of Our Time* (New York: Farrar and Rinehart, 1944).

1

Dress Rehearsal for Pullman: The Knights of Labor and the 1890 New York Central Strike

Robert E. Weir

JUST BEFORE 7:00 P.M. on Friday, August 9, 1890, a train from Chicago disembarked at New York City's Grand Central Station. Moments later the ciphered message "Webster's Dictionary" flashed along telegraph lines to every station along the Hudson River and Harlem lines of the New York Central Railroad. Suddenly, movement of trains in and out of Grand Central halted, and annoyed commuters sought explanations for the delays. At about 8:00 P.M. a New York Central official announced that no more trains would leave the station that night, leaving passengers to stampede for ticket refunds and scurry for scarce hotel space.

Thus opened the New York Central strike of 1890. It began in response to long-smoldering resentments between management and the labor organization that controlled many of the New York Central's shopmen, freight handlers, switchmen, and laborers: the Noble and Holy Order of the Knights of Labor (KOL). Once underway, both management and labor predicted a swift end to the strike, with both sides forecasting victory (though the KOL entered the fray reluctantly and was less confident in private than its bold public proclamations). What neither side foresaw was the far-reaching consequences of the struggle. By the time the strikers limped to defeat in mid-September the KOL's base in the industrial Midwest and Northeast reeled from a blow from which it would not recover. Further, patterns were established that doomed the KOL's successor along northern lines, the American Railway Union (ARU). The New York Central strike proved to be a dress rehearsal for the Pullman debacle four years later, with several of the key actors appearing on both stages.

Pullman, of course, stands as one of the most dramatic and well-told labor wars in the history of American capital-labor relations. What is often unappreciated is the context that spawned the ARU. As Shelton Strom-quist, Philip Foner, Walter Licht, and others have shown, few Gilded Age concerns suffered from labor strife as contentious and continuous as the railroads.[1] The Knights of Labor emerged, waxed, and waned with rail-road strikes. It grew in numbers and power after the railroad strikes of 1877; climbed to its apex after the Gould strike of 1885; declined after botched strikes in 1887 and 1888; and lost hope for revival after the failed New York Central strike of 1890.

Historians have been quick to note the prevalence of miners, shoe-workers, and textile operatives in the KOL, but they have been slower to acknowledge how its fortunes were linked to railroads. The Knights had fewer than 9,000 members when it gathered for its first convention in January 1878, six months after the great labor uprising of 1877. Scranton, Pennsylvania, was a center of troubles on the Delaware, Lackawanna and Western line, and Terence V. Powderly—the city's mayor and soon to be the KOL's general master workman—blasted corporate abuses on the line and in company-owned mines. The Knights held their convention in Reading, Pennsylvania, the site of several violent clashes among Pennsyl-vania Railroad strikers.[2] The KOL was not officially involved in the 1877 strikes, but many of its machinists, blacksmiths, miners, and millwrights left their posts.[3] Of the thirty-two delegates to the first convention, three were locomotive engineers, and another half dozen were machinists and boilermakers. The presence of engineers within KOL ranks proved espe-cially controversial, since several joined after they were expelled from the Brotherhood of Locomotive Engineers (BLE) for violating their "obliga-tions" by striking.[4]

As an organization, the KOL benefited from the 1877 troubles. It grew threefold within two-and-a-half years. The efforts of such skilled organiz-ers as Joseph Buchanan expanded the KOL west of the Mississippi River and made it a national organization in more than pretense. By the early 1880s thousands of Union Pacific Railroad workers were dues-paying Knights.[5] It was, however, the KOL's 1885 victory over Jay Gould's South-western Railway conglomerate that catapulted it to national fame and power. On the eve of the strike the KOL had about 111,000 members; by mid-1886 it had more than 729,000 "official" members and perhaps a third again that number who met without an official charter.

As the Knights of Labor expanded its influence in the railroad indus-try, it drew the ire of not only employers hell-bent on breaking the organization but also railroad brotherhoods and trade unions. The brotherhoods and trade unions were determined to protect their jurisdictional turf and were not yet ready to consider a federation in which power would be shared among organizations. The most troublesome was the Brotherhood of Locomotive Engineers, headed by the quarrelsome Peter M. Arthur, a cautious and proud man who fit the profile of a "labor aristocrat."[6] Under his tutelage, the BLE operated more like a medieval guild than a labor union.

By the late 1880s the BLE represented over 80 percent of the nation's locomotive engineers, and its members enjoyed high wages and cordial relations with many employers. Organized under the motto "Sobriety, Truth, Justice and Morality," the BLE was loathe to call strikes and notorious for the narrowness of its craft vision. The BLE seldom supported nonengineers, workers whom Arthur contemptuously dismissed as the "lower grades of labor."[7] Still angry about the KOL's acceptance of striking engineers in 1877, Arthur and the BLE refused to support the KOL in its 1885 struggle against Jay Gould's Southwestern Railway conglomerate. Arthur recoiled in horror when more engineers quit the BLE for the Knights in the wake of victory. When the Knights struck Gould again in 1886, the BLE helped Gould break the strike, a fact that Powderly publicly denounced.

Powderly's remarks proved to be the opening salvo of a series of publicly waged battles between the KOL and the BLE that culminated in 1890. The BLE sabotaged the Knights again during the 1887 Reading strike, and some Knights retaliated by scabbing during the BLE's lost Brooklyn Elevated Railway strike that same year.[8] When the BLE struck the Chicago, Burlington and Quincy line in 1888, a handful of Knights displaced in the Reading troubles gleefully took the places of BLE men. To his credit, Powderly issued an official call to support the BLE, but Arthur personally blamed Powderly for each scab.[9] Arthur bided his time and plotted vengeance against the Knights. His refusal to see capital as antagonistic or to entertain the idea that engineers and other railroad workers had common interests remained an ideological touchstone that denied needed support to both the Knights of Labor in 1890 and the Pullman strikers four years later.

Like the Pullman strike, the labor action against the New York Central began dramatically, offered tantalizing moments when victory seemed possible, and then fizzled. If the situation inside Grand Central Station on August 9 was confused, outside chaos reigned. The Chicago Limited was

due to arrive at 7:30 P.M., and its engineer waited in a tunnel for the signal to enter the station. It never came, and within an hour the tunnel was
choked with trains backed up behind the Chicago Limited. When weary
Chicago travelers—including New York Central superintendent C. M.
Bissell—finally made it to Grand Central Station, they left their luggage
behind because there was no one to unload it. In the freight yards more
than a thousand cars stood idle, while two hundred boats awaited unload-
ing at New York Central warehouses along the Hudson River between
Fifty-ninth and Seventy-ninth streets. When no freight handlers appeared,
the next day found New Yorkers short some 6,000 bags of coffee, 100,000
quarts of milk, their daily mail, and several thousand barrels of flour and
sugar.[10]

Rumors flew, and reporters sought scoops. H. William Webb, the New
York Central's third vice president, promised all would soon return to
normal and declared the entire matter a conspiracy by some 850–900 dis-
gruntled Knights of Labor. But it soon became clear to reporters that the
best informants were the men walking the lines with cheap copies of
Webster's Dictionary tucked under their arm. In truth there were 3,000 men
out, and as many as 19,000 rail workers eventually left their jobs. For several weeks it looked as though the Knights might actually win, and the
strike continued to disrupt New York Central operations until September 17, 1890.[11]

❖ ❖ ❖

It was no small foe the Knights of Labor tackled in 1890. The New York
Central was established in 1853, when Erastus Corning and Russell Sage
consolidated ten bankrupt lines in hopes of forming a rival to the Pennsylvania Railroad. Linking lines gave the New York Central access to Boston, New York City, and the Midwest. Rapid growth occurred after 1867,
when majority control of New York Central stock passed to Cornelius
Vanderbilt, who already owned lines connecting Albany and Buffalo.
Vanderbilt sought lines farther west, a task he accomplished by buying
several lines to Chicago in 1869. Upon his death in 1877 Vanderbilt be-
queathed some $94 million worth of railroad property and securities to
his son William.

The younger Vanderbilt promptly expanded his father's empire. By the
time of the 1890 strike the New York Central consisted of six major trunk
lines connecting New York City to most major cities and ports in the
Northeast and Midwest. One branch was the Nickel Plate road that ran

through Terre Haute, Indiana, where young Eugene Debs was a fireman. Other lines gave the New York Central access to such important metropoles as Buffalo and Syracuse, New York; Cleveland, Columbus, Cincinnati, and Toledo, Ohio; Detroit, Michigan; Indianapolis, Indiana; and St. Louis, Missouri. There were few important industrial or port cities not serviced by the New York Central.

Powerful individuals were associated with the New York Central. In addition to its principal owner, William Vanderbilt, the New York Central's board included Chauncey Depew, widely touted as a possible Republican presidential candidate for 1892; H. William Webb, a Vermont Central Railway magnate; and Richard Olney, the future U.S. attorney general who was soon to be infamous for issuing injunctions against the American Railway Union during the Pullman strike.[12]

Economic and political clout did not generosity make. William Vanderbilt inherited his father's ruthlessness as well as his railroads. He was infamous among workers for his statement "The public be damned. I am working for my stockholders" and was fond of repeating that remark. Vanderbilt dispelled any doubts about his cold-hearted business sense when he justified 1890 wage cuts by claiming that "the workmen now earn the equivalent of a barrel of flour each day." At the time his personal net worth was over $200 million.[13] Further, the New York Central was better-equipped to deter potential strikes than many competitors because of its highly centralized operations that included employee screening, personnel record-keeping, company welfare plans, seniority systems designed to reduce turnover, and the "Brown system," a detailed blacklist of rail workers suspected of being troublesome.[14] Employee control was so thorough that others—including the General Managers' Association after 1893—emulated its practices.

Arrayed against the highly structured railroad was a bewildering collection of employee organizations, such as the Brotherhood of Locomotive Firemen, the Brotherhood of Railroad Trainmen, and the Switchmen's Mutual Aid Association. As their designations indicate, many were proto-unions that functioned more like craft clubs than labor advocacy groups. In 1889 several brotherhoods formed the Supreme Council of the United Orders of Railway Employees, ostensibly to coordinate actions. That proved a lofty goal that the brotherhoods endorsed in principle but seldom in practice. It was handicapped from the start by the Brotherhood of Locomotive Engineers' refusal to consider council membership. The BLE further undermined unity through its cordial relations with employers, especially the New York Central. Even in the fiery days of 1877 the BLE had honored agreements with the New York Central and had refused to strike.[15]

The core of the council consisted of the firemen, trainmen, and switchmen, many of whom held dual membership in the Knights of Labor. As the Knights of Labor added shopmen and brakemen to its ranks, it began to look like the first real challenge to management hegemony along the New York Central. The KOL likely exaggerated its strength, but New York Central officials gave every evidence of taking it seriously. By 1890 they came to the conclusion that the KOL had to be broken and that no compromise was possible.

❖ ❖ ❖

KOL leaders were cognizant of the New York Central's power and its own weakness. The Knights had butted heads with William Vanderbilt once before and had fared poorly; in 1882 a freight handlers' strike along the New Jersey Central was crushed when Vanderbilt imported Italian scabs. Nonetheless, fevers ran high for a strike among Knights in Albany, New York, where the New York Central operated huge shops and switching yards. Terence Powderly advised Edward J. Lee, master workman of Albany District Assembly 246, to "go cautiously . . . [and] secure yourselves in your footholds before stepping into unknown depths. . . . Remember that you are coping with one of the greatest corporations in America, and that it can bring to its aid, in a struggle, millions of dollars where organized labor cannot bring in as many cents."[16] When Lee pressed him about when the KOL should take action, Powderly opined that either the presidential campaign season of 1892 or the summer of 1893—when the New York Central could anticipate thousands of customers bound for the Columbian Exposition—would put the Knights in a better bargaining position.

Powderly's personal distaste for strikes was buttressed by the sagging fortunes of the Knights of Labor. By mid-1890 the KOL had about 150,000 members, no more than one-fifth of its membership just four years earlier. As the KOL lost members and money, it could ill afford hasty acts. Still, though historians often write off the KOL after 1888, there is evidence that leaders were coming to grips with membership erosion and were taking steps to remedy it. There was certainly serious shrinkage in the twenty-four counties affected by the New York Central strike; in 1888 there were 859 KOL locals but only 495 one year later. Suggestively, though, the

KOL founded 95 new assemblies in those areas in 1890, most of them before the strike. Both the numbers and official correspondence suggest that the KOL was in the midst of a revitalization program at the time of the strike. Nor was the organization as impotent as it might appear from shrinking membership roles. The KOL still sported vibrant locals, its activities were reported in the press, Powderly's views were solicited by journalists and politicians, and it maintained a paid Capitol Hill lobbyist to push the KOL's legislative agenda. Though there was a falloff from the halcyon days of 1886, Knights continued to get elected to local offices at a time when there was serious debate in the organization about third party affiliations.[17]

What the KOL needed—and did not get—was time to regroup. When Edward Lee advised Powderly that men were being fired and that half of his district wanted to strike, Powderly told him that members would be better off seeking work elsewhere than trusting in a strike to restore their jobs.[18] The New York Central, however, was determined to force the issue if Powderly was not. In late July the New York Central fired twenty men with an average of nearly twelve years experience for "unsatisfactory work." All were Knights of Labor, including Lee, a twenty-year employee of the New York Central who had never before been disciplined.[19] The strike began shortly after Lee's dismissal, and Powderly moved quickly by sending John J. Holland of the KOL's general executive board to arbitrate.

It was soon apparent, however, that the New York Central intended to break the Knights at all costs. Since Chauncey Depew was in Europe, New York Central negotiations were left in the hands of H. William Webb, who insisted on the company's right to hire and fire at will. One day into the strike he ordered Superintendent C. M. Bissell to issue a notice: "It is the intention of this company to fight the present strike to the end. All employees who remain loyal to the company will receive protection. Those who do not work to-morrow [Saturday] will be considered as having left service and their places will be filled as soon as possible."[20] Webb promptly dispatched Pinkerton guards along New York Central lines and began accepting applications for replacements.

For the next several weeks Webb issued press releases claiming the strike was broken.[21] But the farther one ventured from New York City, the more tenuous the New York Central's grip was. Albany was nearly shut down, and Webb had to hire extra Pinkertons when the city's police superintendent refused to guard New York Central property. The *Albany Evening Journal* applauded the superintendent's decision and accused the

New York Central of importing "bruisers and thugs . . . from the slums of New York." The next evening's paper charged that Webb issued orders to the Pinkertons "to shoot down strikers" in Albany and "charge the mob" in Syracuse.[22] Across New York state Webb found seething discontent over the New York Central's monopolistic stranglehold. When he appealed for aid from probusiness governor David Hill, he was told curtly that it was not the state's business "to operate the railroad [or] to interfere in a labor controversy." Nor would city officials in Syracuse cooperate with New York Central requests, and even conservative newspapers were loathe to support the railroad.[23] Any remaining company goodwill disappeared when Pinkerton thugs precipitated the troubles predicted by the *Albany Evening Journal.* In a turnabout from usual labor disputes local authorities often praised the orderliness of strikers and arrested Pinkertons for disorderly conduct, assault, and attempted murder.[24] In Buffalo the police commissioner threatened to withdraw protection of New York Central property if one more Pinkerton entered the city. City officials across the Empire State were just as likely to lambaste Webb, the New York Central, and the hiring of Pinkertons as to disapprove of the Knights of Labor.[25]

By the second week of August the strike spread to Buffalo, Dayton, Cleveland, and Indianapolis, and such papers as the *Boston Transcript, Cleveland Plain Dealer, New York Times,* and *New York Tribune* printed denunciations of company policy and the Pinkertons.[26] Soon the strike spread to Chicago, and even the General Managers' Association—which represented several New York Central branch lines—worried that Webb and the New York Central were creating a negative business climate. Wall Street business leaders who originally championed the railroad began to express hopes for a negotiated settlement. Robert Grannis, vice president of the Mutual Insurance Company, remarked, "The extension of the strike would . . . affect business very seriously." Gardiner Sherman, president of the Seventh National Bank, added that though he supported New York Central management, "I believe every effort ought to be made to arrive at a settlement, so as to not clog the wheels of commerce." The *New York World* charged that Webb was running empty trains to give the illusion that the strike was broken.[27]

Webb ignored the pressure, but his comments exacerbated negative sentiment concerning the New York Central. He told one reporter that the company was prepared to "spend two million dollars to squelch this strike if it is necessary." When asked about rumors of an impending sympathy strike of firemen and freight handlers on all New York Central lines, he vowed to replace the firemen and close the freight yards. Lest there be any doubt of his resolve, he added that "the New York Central will go out of business rather than recede from its position."[28] Public opinion shifted so sharply to the Knights that the New York legislature opened hearings to investigate company abuses and Pinkerton violence. Despite sharp railroad attorneys who tried to browbeat witnesses, the hearings were a public relations nightmare for the railroad. One witness denounced Webb as "a man who never did one stroke of work to secure the wealth he now abuses. It came to him by inheritance, not having worked for any part of it; he does not fully appreciate it, and regards it as something to be used by himself alone."[29]

By contrast Powderly appeared the voice of reason, and he continually pledged to call off the strike if the New York Central agreed to arbitration. Sinking revenue and public pressure forced Webb to meet with Powderly on August 21. There was little doubt that the New York Central had been stung financially. Businesses in Springfield, Massachusetts, reported delays of over a week in receiving western freight moving on New York Central lines. Perhaps more troublesome was a rumor that the Armour Corporation intended a $1 million lawsuit against the New York Central to recoup losses on undelivered contracted shipments. Webb, however, refused to negotiate on hiring and firing practices. When the KOL executive board member John Devlin asked him bluntly if it was his intention to ignore the public and New York Central employees, Webb "took refuge in silence."[30]

It was obvious to friend and foe alike that the key to the KOL's success lay in its ability to expand the strike to all New York Central operations. One Knight noted that its very existence "in Eastern States" depended on its victory over the New York Central: "if the strike is extended and lost, good-by to the organization in this part of the country."[31] At this stage victory depended on the support of railroad brotherhoods, especially those affiliated with the Supreme Council. The KOL executive board members John Hayes, A. W. Wright, and J. J. Holland met with Frank P. Sargent of the Brotherhood of the Locomotive Firemen, George W. Howard of the Order of Railway Conductors, S. E. Wilkinson of the Brotherhood of Railroad Trainmen, and Frank Sweeney of the Switchmen's Mutual Aid Association.

The KOL was heartened when Sargent declared that the locomotive firemen would support the strike and when switchmen in Buffalo walked out. But Powderly still had to contend with his nemesis, Peter M. Arthur of the Brotherhood of Locomotive Engineers. The BLE did little to disguise its glee at seeing the KOL in a fix. One New York City engineer told the *Tribune*, "We are going to pay back the Knights of Labor in their own coin. They went back on us when we were in trouble, and now we intend to get square."[32]

Powderly tried to shame the BLE into aiding the Knights by addressing an open letter to Arthur in the press, but Arthur refused to be outmaneuvered by a man he detested. He told the press that he would be glad to respond to any letter addressed to him "officially" but that he would not presume to speak for members without consulting them. He maintained that the "Brotherhood will take no official cognizance of the Central trouble unless complaints come from our own members."[33]

Still, had the Knights been able to convince the Supreme Council to support the strike, the engineers would have found it difficult to remain aloof. It was not to be. Sargent's early enthusiasm notwithstanding, talks went badly after such underlings as John Hall and John Downey of the Switchmen's Mutual Aid Association and Eugene Debs and John Hannah of the Brotherhood of Locomotive Firemen expressed doubts that their orders should be involved.[34] Debs, like Arthur, limited his concerns to his organization. Speaking as secretary-treasurer of the firemen, Debs quoted constitutional provisos and argued that the Supreme Council had no authority to authorize a strike; only individual brotherhoods could do so. Rank-and-file members agreed. One fireman remarked that "if there is a strike called . . . I shall not go out. And you will find a great many more of my own mind."[35]

Debs remarks revealed the Supreme Council to be a toothless tiger. Frank Sargent proved unable to speak even for the firemen's leadership, let alone its rank and file, and none of the other brotherhoods provided solid support for the Knights. In the end the Supreme Council was not much different from scores of other Gilded Age labor congresses that delivered stirring rhetoric but few concrete actions. The Supreme Council ultimately issued a strongly worded resolution that gave approval to the KOL strike and Powderly's handling of it. It also condemned Webb, the Pinkertons, and other railroad officials, but it refused to call out its members. As the *Boston Evening Transcript* properly put it, the Supreme Council "had only sympathy to offer."[36]

The Supreme Council's withdrawal stunned the KOL, though it continued to put forth a bold public face. Privately Powderly told Albany District 246 that members had struck against his counsel, and he begged them to not "curse the order" should they fail.[37] The KOL had three remaining hopes, all of them faint: arbitration, a change of heart by the engineers, or a general strike. Arbitration quickly evaporated when Webb curtly told Florence Donavan of the New York State Board of Mediation and Arbitration that "there is nothing to arbitrate" and that the New York Central would not submit to any board decision. Webb no doubt realized that the Supreme Council's decision not to join the strike gave the New York Central the upper hand, especially given the number of scab applications the New York Central processed. By then he also once again enjoyed wide support in the business community that more than compensated for the cold shoulder the New York Central received from local political officials. Arbitrators eventually met, and they announced their decision in favor of the Knights in early September, but the KOL realized even before the decision that there was no way to enforce the findings.[38]

Still, the Supreme Council's withdrawal gave hope that the engineers might have a change in heart, especially since Arthur disliked the other railway brotherhoods even more than he disliked the KOL. That hope proved equally vain when on August 28 Arthur attacked Powderly through his own open letter and insisted that the engineers would "attend strictly to their own business." He also resurrected charges of KOL scabbing during the Chicago, Burlington and Quincy strike.[39]

This left only what one paper called "the desperate act" of a general strike. An additional thousand KOL flagmen, track laborers, and switchmen left their posts, an effort that accomplished little more than their dismissals. Delaware and Hudson yardmen refused to handle freight, and scores of men on the Nickel Plate left their posts. There were even reports from Chicago that some firemen had joined the strike out of solidarity for the Knights and disgust for the Supreme Council's tepid endorsement of the KOL. KOL leaders hoped to force a settlement by tying up port freight from Boston and New York that was routed through Albany. If the KOL could hold out long enough, perhaps it could win new allies.[40] It was a pointless gesture that ended in dismal failure. By the end of August most newspapers declared the strike a loss and relegated its final days to the back pages, while the rest of the labor movement left the Knights twisting in the wind. American Federation of Labor president Samuel Gompers made no attempt to disguise his lack of sympathy; he saw both the Knights and the Supreme Council as dual unions. There was nary a mention of the New York Central strike during the AFL's December convention, though Gompers did invite the Order of Railway Trackmen to join the AFL. Many of these men once held dual membership in the Knights.[41] The *National Labor Tribune* dropped its support and accused Powderly of mismanaging an "impulsive" strike. Tom Barry, an ex-Knight, unleashed the vile charge that Powderly took a bribe from the railroads during the 1888 Burlington strike. For his part, Eugene Debs told the Associated Press that the Supreme Council never considered giving full support for such an ill-conceived strike.[42]

Monday, September 1, 1890, was Labor Day, and the news out of Albany boded badly for the Knights. A passenger train bound for Montreal had been derailed late the preceding evening and striking Knights were being blamed for the sabotage, despite their protest that it was the work of Pinkerton agent provocateurs.[43] The strike lingered a few more pathetic weeks, marked by acts of minor violence and the arrest of four Knights for the August 31 derailing. There was little left to do except villainize the victors. Webb was denounced as a "perjurer" and Arthur as a coward. The Knights turned full guns on Chauncey Depew, cast aspersions on his manhood, and called him a "mere figure-head," who sat back while others did his dirty work.[44]

The KOL's demonization of its enemies proved to be its most successful tactic in the long run. Republican party stalwarts questioned Depew's European vacation during the strike and were troubled by his delegation of authority. Depew's political reputation was tarnished by the strike, and he was never again considered seriously as presidential timbre. Likewise, 1890 was the only year H. Walter Webb served as a vice president for the New York Central. And labor leaders who agreed with Powderly on virtually nothing else shared his opinions on P. M. Arthur.

The KOL called off the strike on September 17. The executive board issued an upbeat memo claiming moral victory, financial damage to the New York Central, and the coming of legislation to curb railroad abuses.[45] Some predictions—including anti-Pinkerton laws and government regulations of railroads—came to pass, but few Knights of Labor remained to witness them. The two most noticeable results of the New York Central strike lay in the destruction of the KOL's northern industrial base and the way in which strategies used against the Knights were replicated four years later against Pullman strikers. The first result set the stage for the second.

In late September three Knights confessed to derailing the Montreal express, and Webb reiterated his opinion that "the Knights of Labor must go." The loss of the New York Central strike and the withering press condemnation that ensued destroyed the KOL's revitalization plans for the Northeast and Midwest. In the counties affected by the strike 175 locals collapsed by the end of 1890; another 110 disappeared before the close of 1891. By the end of 1893 only 111 locals continued to operate in a region that five years earlier had supported 859. Of those still operating, 72 (approximately 65 percent) operated in the greater New York City area. The KOL nearly disappeared in Albany, Buffalo, Syracuse, Boston, Chicago, Cleveland, and St. Louis; it vanished altogether in Columbus, Ohio; Detroit; Indianapolis; and Terre Haute, Indiana. The KOL was a shell of its former self even in New York City, where 36 locals operated in 1893, down from 127 at the time of the New York Central strike. By the end of 1893 the KOL's remaining strength was located in rural areas. (See tables 1–3.)[46]

The destruction of the KOL in the Northeast and Midwest left a vacuum for those railroad workers not members of brotherhoods. The damage was

Table 1. Local Assemblies, Selected Years

Counties	1884	1888	1889		1890	
			LAs	Foundings	LAs	Foundings
Albany, N.Y.	9	48	25	0	32	7
Dutchess, N.Y.	1	5	2	0	3	1
Erie, N.Y.	16	14	9	0	7	4
Monroe, N.Y.	20	20	19	0	18	7
Montgomery, N.Y.	0	6	3	0	2	1
New York (except City)	33	102	71	0	67	9
New York City	68	204	117	2	127	24
Onandaga, N.Y.	8	9	8	2	6	3
Oneida, N.Y.	24	9	7	1	6	4
Rensslaer, N.Y.	11	11	9	2	4	1
Ulster, N.Y.	0	15	9	0	9	2
Westchester, N.Y.	1	7	7	0	7	3
Essex, N.J.	14	23	11	0	10	2
Gloucester, N.J.	10	29	13	0	15	5
Passaic, N.J.	1	11	5	2	3	0
Union, N.J.	2	12	7	0	5	0
Marion, Ind.	4	12	6	0	2	0
Cook, Ill.	43	105	54	0	52	8
Suffolk, Mass.	7	45	24	3	18	4
Wayne, Mich.	18	29	15	1	7	1
St. Louis, Mo.	18	47	34	0	20	2
Cuyahoga, Ohio	22	32	12	2	11	5
Franklin, Ohio	4	11	7	0	4	1
Hamilton, Ohio	16	53	21	0	14	1

Source: Based on data presented in Jonathan Garlock, *Guide to the Local Assemblies of the Knights of Labor* (Westport, Conn.: Greenwood, 1982).

Table 2. Local Assembly Collapses, 1890–93

Counties	1890s		1891 Collapse	1892 Collapse	1893: Extant Pre-1890 LAs
	LAs	Collapse			
Albany, N.Y.	32	22	4	3	3
Dutchess, N.Y.	3	2	2	0	0
Erie, N.Y.	7	4	2	0	1
Monroe, N.Y.	18	5	4	1	8
Montgomery, N.Y.	2	1	0	0	0
New York (except City)	67	21	14	3	26
New York City	127	11	64	8	36
Onandaga, N.Y.	6	5	0	0	1
Oneida, N.Y.	6	5	1	0	0
Ulster, N.Y.	10	4	2	1	3
Westchester, N.Y.	7	5	1	0	1
Essex, N.J.	10	5	1	1	3
Gloucester, N.J.	16	12	2	0	3
Passaic, N.J.	3	1	0	0	1
Union, N.J.	5	2	1	0	2
Marion, Ind.	4	2	1	1	0
Cook, Ill.	52	37	2	2	4
Suffolk, Mass.	18	6	3	0	3
Wayne, Mich.	7	4	1	2	0
St. Louis, Mo.	20	8	2	0	8
Cuyahoga, Ohio	11	3	1	2	5
Franklin, Ohio	4	1	2	1	0
Hamilton, Ohio	14	6	2	2	2

Source: Based on data presented in Jonathan Garlock, *Guide to the Local Assemblies of the Knights of Labor* (Westport, Conn.: Greenwood, 1982).

Table 3. Aggregate Data

Date	Total
Local assemblies	
1884	350
1888	859
1889	495
1890	449
End of 1893	111
Local assembly foundings	
1889	15
1890	95
Local assembly collapses	
1890	175
1891	110
1892	27
1893	21

Source: Based on data presented in Jonathan Garlock, *Guide to the Local Assemblies of the Knights of Labor* (Westport, Conn.: Greenwood, 1982).

not contained to the affected regions. As Shelton Stromquist demonstrates, other rail workers soon abandoned the Knights of Labor for the American Railway Union, especially those in the West who were disenchanted by the loss of the second Gould strike and angry over longtime champion Joseph Buchanan's expulsion from the Knights.[47] Terence Powderly himself was a casualty. His handling of the New York Central strike was one of the factors cited by those who relieved him of master workman duties in 1893.

Powderly actually bore little blame for the New York Central debacle. For once his reluctance to take action was warranted. He warned every Knight involved that the KOL was not strong enough to defeat the New York Central. Once the strike broke out, though, Powderly's conduct was admirable, his support steadfast, and his tactics reasonable.

❖ ❖ ❖

If there was a villain in the tragedy, it was Peter M. Arthur, not Terence V. Powderly. Arthur's narrow craft identity, personal rancor toward Powderly, and petty pursuit of "revenge" doomed the Knights. He added toadyism to class betrayal by inviting Chauncey Depew to address a BLE convention held weeks after the strike collapsed. Even cautious labor leaders were sickened when Depew called the BLE the "best labor organization in the United States" and insisted the nation owed the engineers a "debt of gratitude for the courage, fidelity and intelligence with which they stood by their posts and performed their duties during the recent troubles on the New York Central." Depew even thanked the BLE for safeguarding "the public and the corporation against the demands of intemperate violence."[48]

It was one thing to withhold support for the KOL and criticize its decisions, as most of the railroad brotherhoods had done, but it was quite another to embrace a man like Depew. Arthur's accommodationism proved too much for the other brotherhoods to stomach, and they began to search for alternatives. The American Railway Union was founded in 1893, the very year Powderly was dismissed by the KOL, and its guiding ideals often mirrored those of the Knights. The ARU's declaration of principles advocated temperance, called for mandatory arbitration of disputes, and echoed Powderly's call for government ownership of railroads. Veiled critiques of exclusivity signaled that the ARU saw itself as champion of all railroad workers, not labor aristocrats. Further, the ARU's organizational structure and membership composition resembled those of the

KOL during its heyday. In some cases, declining KOL locals and western district assemblies were folded directly into the ARU, even though a few areas probably practiced racial tolerance in defiance of the ARU's ban on black members.[49]

Eugene Debs did little to honor himself during the New York Central strike. Still reeling from perceived KOL betrayal in 1888, Debs shaped attitudes that led the Supreme Council to reject a sympathy strike or financial aid to the KOL. By 1893, however, Debs had begun to rethink his earlier decisions. He made his peace with the KOL well enough to tolerate dual unionism; numerous dues-paying Knights entered the ARU. In the end Debs was converted to the KOL's wider vision of class interest and the rudimentary forms of industrial unionism it pioneered among railroad workers, especially along western lines.

Debs learned much from the Knights, but he failed to understand the full lesson from 1890. Although there were important differences between the two strikes, the New York Central strike was a veritable dress rehearsal for the Pullman strike, with Debs cast in the Powderly role.[50] Much like the KOL after its strike against Jay Gould in 1885, the ARU experienced an infusion of new members after an unexpected partial victory over the Great Northern in early 1894. But much like those Knights, new ARU members had more enthusiasm than tactical wisdom. Like Powderly in 1890, Debs found himself the head of a weak organization, whose members clamored for retaliation against George Pullman's wage cuts, and he did everything in his power to persuade members not to strike. When Pullman workers first approached the ARU, Debs withheld ARU support for the strike and warned of the "danger in extremes."[51]

Again like Powderly, Debs proved unable to stem the rising tide from below and became a reluctant strike leader. Once thrust into that role, Debs was more than Powderly's equal in waging what he knew to be a losing battle. The pattern of the Pullman strike's demise bears an uncanny resemblance to what happened in the New York Central strike four years earlier. The Supreme Council disintegrated after 1891, thereby shattering any semblance of federation and forcing Debs to appeal to each railroad brotherhood individually. As in 1890, several passed resolutions of support, but most stayed aloof. A few, such as the Order of Railway Conductors and the Brotherhood of Railroad Trainmen, openly declared contempt for Debs and the ARU.

Once again, Samuel Gompers and the American Federation of Labor abandoned a labor organization. Gompers summarily rejected Debs's call for a general strike and dismissed his evocation of the KOL's "an injury to one [is] the concern of all."[52] Once again P. M. Arthur insisted that his engineers play no part in the strike, threatened expulsion for any who did, and declared his members could freely take the place of strikers.[53]

Ironically, the Knights of Labor was among the few labor organizations to respect the ARU sympathy strike. In a leap of solidarity denied it four years earlier, the Knights of Labor supported the ARU enthusiastically and urged its members to honor the boycott. Scores of Knights actually took out ARU membership in solidarity during the troubles. By 1894, of course, the support of the weakened KOL did not mean as much as the support of the Supreme Council would have meant to the KOL in 1890. The KOL's pioneering effort at industrial organization was a good idea in 1890, and it remained so in 1894. But neither Powderly nor Debs persuaded fellow rail workers of the soundness of the concept.

Railroad workers failed to appreciate the importance of a united front and concerted action, but business leaders did. The General Managers' Association remained solid and stolid during the Pullman boycott. In 1890 New York Central officials demonstrated that patience was the best stance of powerful corporations with deep pockets. There is no doubt that the company lost a lot of money during the strike, but it could afford to do so longer than its workers could go without paychecks. At several junctures Webb and the New York Central were under pressure from the public, local government, and members of the business community to negotiate a settlement, but it refused to buckle. Webb knew he had the support from the only group that mattered—stockholders.

In 1894 George Pullman took a similar "the public be damned" attitude. Like Webb four years earlier, Pullman stuck to his position, while successfully avoiding all attempts at arbitration. His mouthpiece, Thomas Wickes, issued a terse statement, "We have nothing to arbitrate," which echoed Webbs's 1890 declaration.[54] Pullman had the support of a General Managers' Association willing to employ agents provocateurs and lobby for federal and legal efforts to crush the ARU. The KOL estimated that the New York Central lost as much as $20 million to defeat the Knights; business losses may have been four times as much as a result of Pullman.[55]

Faced with an appalling lack of labor solidarity and an even more powerful foe, Debs and the ARU had even less chance in 1894 than the Knights had in 1890. The ARU fell prey to the same combined forces that defeated the Knights: a lack of mandatory arbitration laws, a press that grew more hostile as the strike wore on, unsympathetic courts, private mercenary forces, agents provocateurs, and the combined might of organized capital. Add the state militia, federal troops, an antilabor attorney general, and the liberal use of court injunctions, and one appreciates the Sisyphean task facing Eugene Debs. Like Powderly in 1890, he knew he probably could not win, but he could not convince the rank and file to accept what it could not change.

Debs even faced many of the same characters who undid the KOL. Both Chauncey Depew and William Vanderbilt received personal tours of Pullman from founder George Pullman in 1893, and Vanderbilt was a shareholder and member of the board of directors. Richard Olney—by then attorney general of the United States—played a pivotal role in crushing the strike. Stock dividends apparently mattered more than conflict of interest.

In 1890 the Knights of Labor could not convince its natural allies that "an injury to one is the concern of all." Over the next four years Debs also failed to impart that lesson to enough converts. Such failing made corpses of both the Knights of Labor and the American Railway Union. The lesson was clear enough to one of the wits who penned cartoons for the magazine *Puck*. In a graphic that appeared in July 1894 the goddess of "Law and Order" stands at the edge of a pit marked "Dumping Ground for Kings of Misrule." She has John P. Altgeld by the scruff of the neck and an airborne Eugene Debs has just been dropped. Awaiting him when he hits are four other fallen kings. It is clear from Debs's drop trajectory that he will be deposited face-to-face with King Powderly.[56] Had such a scene ever occurred, the two men could have commiserated over distressingly similar tales.

Notes

The author thanks Susan Hirsch, Bruce Laurie, Nick Salvatore, and Shelton Stromquist for their helpful remarks.

1. Shelton Stromquist, *A Generation of Boomers: The Pattern of Railroad Conflict in Nineteenth-Century America* (Urbana: University of Illinois Press, 1987); Philip Foner, *The Great Labor Uprising of 1877* (New York: Monad, 1977); Philip Foner, *History of the Labor Movement in the United States*, vol. 2 (New York: International, 1955); Walter Licht, *Working for the Railroad: The Organization of Work in the Nineteenth Century* (Princeton, N.J.: Princeton University Press, 1983); Norman Ware, *The Labor Movement in the United States, 1860–1895: A Study in Democracy* (Gloucester, Mass.: Peter Smith, 1959).

2. Terence V. Powderly, *Thirty Years of Labor, 1859–1889* (New York: Augustus M. Kelly, 1967), 99–130.

3. Harry J. Carman, Henry David, and Paul Guthrie, eds., *The Path I Trod: The Autobiography of Terence V. Powderly* (New York: AMS, 1968), 203.

4. Stromquist, *Generation of Boomers*, 50.

5. For more on the relationship between the Knights of Labor and Union Pacific workers, see Stromquist, *Generation of Boomers*. See also Joseph R. Buchanan, *The Story of a Labor Agitator* (Freeport, N.Y.: Books for Libraries, 1971).

6. The use of the term *labor aristocrat* in American labor historiography owes much to the pioneering work of Robert Gray, *The Labour Aristocracy in Victorian Edinburgh* (Oxford: Oxford University Press, 1976).

7. Quoted in Carman, David, and Guthrie, *Path I Trod*, 164.

8. *John Swinton's Paper*, July 31, 1887.

9. Carman, David, and Guthrie, *Path I Trod*, 167–68.

10. Most urban papers in the Northeast and Midwest give variants of the same Associated Press story for the strike's opening. For typical features, see *Albany Evening Journal*, August 9, 1890; and *New York Tribune*, August 9, 1890.

11. *Albany Evening Journal*, August 9, 1890; *Cleveland Plain Dealer*, August 10, 1890; *Journal of the Knights of Labor*, August 9, 1890; *New York Times*, August 9–10, 1890; *New York Tribune*, August 9, 1890.

12. For more on the history and consolidation of the New York Central, see Stewart Holbrook, *The Story of American Railroads* (New York: Crown, 1947); Edward Hungerford, *Men and Iron: The History of the New York Central* (New York: Thomas Y. Crowell, 1938); Matthew Josephson, *The Robber Barons: The Great American Capitalists, 1861–1901* (New York: Harvest, 1962); and Frank Walker Stevens, *The Beginnings of the New York Central Railroad: A History* (New York: G. P. Putnam's Sons, 1926).

13. Josephson, *Robber Barons*, 186–87, notes that William Vanderbilt's original comment "The public be damned" was often taken out of context. It was uttered before the Hepburn Committee of the New York State legislature in 1879. At the time, Vanderbilt was addressing allegations of his collusion with oil refiners and milk distributors. Once reported, however, Vanderbilt embraced the remark as a personal affect, which he uttered periodically for dramatic effect.

The remark about worker wages is quoted from a letter from Terence Powderly to Edward Lee, April 17, 1890, in *Papers of Terence V. Powderly*, microfilm edition, University of Massachusetts, Amherst. Hereafter cited as *PP*.

14. For more on management strategies in the railroad industry, see Stromquist, *Generation of Boomers*. See also Licht, *Working for the Railroad*.

15. Foner, *Great Labor Uprising of 1877;* Licht, *Working for the Railroad;* Stromquist, *Generation of Boomers;* George Estes, *Railway Employees United: A Study of Railroad Brotherhoods* (Portland, Oreg.: Shadow, 1931).

16. Powderly to Edward Lee, February 3, 1890, in "Report of the General Master Workman," *Proceedings of the Knights of Labor General Assembly, 1890,* in *PP.*

17. For a list of locales with operating Knights' assemblies, see Jonathan Garlock, *Guide to the Local Assemblies of the Knights of Labor* (Westport, Conn.: Greenwood, 1982). For the vitality of the Knights into the 1890s, see Ware, *Labor Movement in the United States;* and Robert Weir, "Beyond the Veil: The Culture of the Knights of Labor" (Ph.D. diss., University of Massachusetts, 1990). For the Knights' political activities, see Leon Fink, *Workingmen's Democracy: The Knights of Labor and American Politics* (Urbana: University of Illinois Press, 1983).

18. Powderly to Lee, April 17, 1890; Lee to Powderly, July 30, 1890; Powderly to Lee, August 2, 1890, in *PP.*

19. *Journal of the Knights of Labor,* August 14, 1890. In addition, there were long-standing grievances over overtime pay, job classification, wage differentials, and a promised daily wage that never materialized.

20. Quoted in *New York Tribune,* August 10, 1890.

21. *Albany Evening Journal, New York Times, New York Tribune,* August 10–17, 1890.

22. *Albany Evening Journal,* August 11–12, 1890, August 12, 1890 (first quote), August 13, 1890 (second quote). For other grievances between the New York Central and its workers in the greater Albany area, see *Journal of the Knights of Labor,* August 14, 1890. See also the *National Labor Tribune,* August 16, 1890.

23. *Albany Evening Journal,* August 12, 1890.

24. Ibid., August 14–18, 1890; *New York Tribune,* August 18, 1890.

25. *Journal of the Knights of Labor,* August 21, 1890.

26. *Boston Evening Transcript,* August 19, 1890; *Cleveland Plain Dealer,* August 11–15, 1890; *New York Times,* August 11–19, 1890; *New York Tribune,* August 19, 1890.

27. *New York Tribune,* August 22, 1890 (Grannis and Shermon quotes); *New York World,* n.d., quoted in *Journal of the Knights of Labor,* August 21, 1890. For a study in the growing concerns of the business community, contrast remarks in the *New York Times,* August 12, 1890, with those made to the *New York Times,* August 22, 1890. See also *Albany Evening Journal,* August 19, 1890; and *New York Tribune,* August 19–22, 1890.

For the record, the General Managers' Association (GMA), founded in 1886, was still in existence at the time of the New York Central strike. Readers of Almont Lindsey, *Pullman Strike: The Story of a Unique Experiment and of a Great Labor Upheaval* (Chicago: University of Chicago Press, 1942), often come away with the impression that the GMA lay dormant from 1888 to 1892. Such was not the case. Although it was hardly the powerful organization Debs faced, the 1890 group was an important gauge of the sentiments of Chicago-based rail magnates.

28. Quoted in *Boston Evening Transcript,* August 19, 1890.

29. *New York Tribune,* August 21, 22, and 23 (quote), 1890.

30. Ibid., August 16, 21, 22, and 23 (quote), 1890.

31. Ibid., August 19, 20 (quotes), and 21, 1890; *New York Times,* August 19, 1890.

32. *New York Tribune,* August 22, 1890.

33. Ibid., August 22–23, 1890; *New York Times,* August 22 and 23 (quote), 1890.

34. Hall was a grand organizer in the Switchmen's Mutual Aid Association, and Downey was the vice grand master. Debs was general secretary-treasurer for the Brotherhood of the Locomotive Firemen, and Hannah was the vice grand master.

35. Quoted in *New York Tribune,* August 23, 1890.

36. Ibid., August 24 and 26, 1890; *New York Times,* August 26, 1890; *Boston Evening Transcript,* August 26, 1890.

37. *Journal of the Knights of Labor,* August 28, 1890 (quote); *New York Tribune,* August 26, 1890.

38. *New York Times,* August 23 (quote) and 24, 1890; *New York Tribune,* August 24–27, 1890; *Journal of the Knights of Labor,* September 4, 1890.

39. Quoted in *Boston Evening Transcript,* August 28, 1890.

40. *Albany Evening Journal,* August 27, 1890; *New York Tribune,* August 27, 1890 (quote).

41. Nick Salvatore, ed., *Seventy Years of Life and Labor: An Autobiography by Samuel Gompers* (Ithaca, N.Y.: ILR, 1984), 118–26. See also *Report of Proceedings of the American Federation of Labor,* 10th Annual Report, Detroit, December 8–13, 1890.

42. *National Labor Tribune,* August 30, 1890; *New York Tribune,* August 28, 1890.

43. *Albany Evening Journal,* September 1, 1890.

44. *Journal of the Knights of Labor,* September 11, 1890.

45. The official circular calling off the strike and denouncing the New York Central is located in *PP.* It was reprinted in the *Journal of the Knights of Labor,* September 18, 1890. For more on Chauncey Depew, see Robert Marcus, *Grand Old Party: Political Structure in the Gilded Age, 1880–1896* (New York: Oxford University Press, 1971); *Dictionary of American Biography,* vol. 5 (New York: Charles Scribner's Sons, 1930).

46. *New York Times,* September 22–23, 1890, and October 3, 1890 (quote); *Independent,* October 2, 1890. All countings of Knights of Labor local assemblies come from a painstaking stroke count using Jonathan Garlock's data as my base. For the most thorough listing of KOL assemblies in existence, see Garlock, *Guide to the Local Assemblies of the Knights of Labor.*

47. Stromquist, *Generation of Boomers.*

48. Quoted in *Address before the 27th Annual Convention of the Brotherhood of Locomotive Engineers at Pittsburg, Oct. 16, 1890* (New York: E. C. Lockwood, 1890). See also *Locomotive Engineers' Monthly Journal,* September–November 1890.

49. See Stromquist, *Generation of Boomers,* 78–84, for ways in which Debs's ARU paralleled the Knights of Labor. Several assemblies of Union Pacific shopmen and trackmen had black members, and there is no indication that these men were expelled.

50. Technically, the ARU was embroiled in a boycott, not a strike, and it faced an even more awesome array of foes than those that defeated the Knights. In ad-

dition to an intransigent corporation and a supportive business community Debs and the ARU faced the power of the courts, a revived General Managers' Association, and federal militia with considerably more skill and prestige than the Pinkerton thugs in the New York Central's employ. Nonetheless, striking similarities between the New York Central strike and Pullman remain.

51. Nick Salvatore, *Eugene V. Debs: Citizen and Socialist* (Urbana: University of Illinois Press, 1982), 128, 129 (quote).

52. Ibid., 136; Lindsey, *Pullman Strike*, 264–65.

53. Lindsey, *Pullman Strike*, 264–65.

54. Quoted in ibid, 129.

55. *Journal of the Knights of Labor,* September 25, 1890; Lindsey, *Pullman Strike,* 335–36.

56. *Puck,* July 1894.

2

The Search for Unity among Railroad Workers: The Pullman Strike in Perspective

Susan E. Hirsch

THE ENDURING IMAGE OF the Pullman strike and boycott is a promising national movement of workers struck down by big business and the federal government. By the 1890s workers needed to unify nationally to achieve victories over major employers, although they debated whether craftwide or industrywide organizing was most effective. A sense of common cause among railroad workers developed across the country by the 1890s because railroad ownership had concentrated in a small number of firms that were imposing nationwide patterns of wages, benefits, and work rules. The American Railway Union (ARU) and the Pullman strike and boycott of 1894 were the products of this new form of working-class solidarity. As industrial unions became common in this century, the ARU seemed to represent the first, albeit unsuccessful, step on the road to the future.[1]

Yet the reality behind the image was more complex. The ideal of unity represented by the ARU was not realized in 1894 because competing allegiances pulled railroad workers in different directions. Racial prejudice was always a potent source of division, and the ARU, like the railroad craft unions, excluded black workers. Furthermore, the union had few members in the eastern United States where unemployment was high. Many eastern railroad workers also refused to forsake their craft unions for the ARU. Unity was even absent among Pullman workers. Pullman repair-shop workers in Wilmington, Delaware, did not support the Pullman workers in Chicago but instead stayed on the job repairing cars shipped in from the West.

The lack of solidarity among Pullman workers was rooted in the very different experiences and perspectives of workers in these cities. In

Wilmington workers were incorporated into a local culture dominated by a business class that was hostile to unions. Labor movements developed in the nineteenth century in communities like Chicago, where workers had created an autonomous space for themselves in which a working-class ethos legitimized labor organization. In this respect the Pullman strike was similar to other nineteenth-century strikes that foundered on the problem of creating solidarity beyond the local community when the community was the primary source of militancy and support.

Although craft exclusivity and racial prejudice would continue to hamper industrywide organizing among railroad workers, in the twentieth century workers in such places as Wilmington often ignored local disapproval and joined national movements. During World War I Wilmington shop workers joined unions along with other Pullman workers. They were as faithful to the three-month railroad shopmen's strike in 1922 as Chicago workers were, although Wilmington remained an antiunion town. New sources of solidarity had replaced allegiance to the local community.

From this perspective the Pullman strike was a transitional strike, evidencing both the nineteenth-century reliance on the supportiveness of local communities and the trend toward industrywide allegiance. The history of Pullman workers reveals both the growing importance of common experiences on the shop floor and the role of the federal government in displacing the attachment to local viewpoints and understandings among railroad workers.

In *A Generation of Boomers* Shelton Stromquist explored how the ARU developed from worker insurgency that was rooted in both craft and community but expanded beyond them.[2] The ARU's organizational form developed from railroad workers' previous attempts in the Knights of Labor and craft unions to form system federations: in each rail system the locals of the various crafts would create a federation to present unified demands to management. This method respected craft lines but fostered the strength of an industrial union. Stromquist also showed how the ARU's development was based in specific communities in the Midwest and West: the "boomers" transported their craft union traditions as they moved to new towns farther west and nurtured prounion working-class communities where none had existed.

Similarly, the Pullman strike originated in both the specific shop-floor grievances of Chicago's Pullman workers and the militancy of their community.[3] By the 1870s Chicago workers had a well-earned reputation for labor activism and radical politics. George Pullman built the Pullman Car

Works and his model town of Pullman several miles south of the populated area of the city to insulate his employees from these influences. Distance did not solve Pullman's labor problems, however. Living close together in the model town or its surrounding neighborhoods of Roseland and Kensington, Pullman workers had the propinquity to form a cohesive community. Working for one big company meant they shared a common experience of subordination to management. Moreover, they were not isolated from the union and political movements of the larger city, since leaders of these groups were frequent speakers in the halls near the model town.

Solidarity among Pullman workers had not developed from a common heritage but was created in the industrial city. Most Pullman workers in Chicago were migrants from very different places. According to an 1892 census 28 percent of Pullman wage earners were native-born Americans, and the rest, the vast majority, were immigrants from virtually every European nation. The largest groups of immigrants came from northern and western Europe; 23 percent of the workers were Scandinavian, 13 percent were German, 12 percent were Dutch, and 13 percent were British or Canadian.[4] Although some workers had union backgrounds or came from communities of class-conscious workers, others did not. By the 1890s, however, a tradition of union activism had been created among these diverse workers because of their common experiences on the shop floor, the encouragement of the wider Chicago labor movement, and their creation of social spaces autonomous from Pullman's planned community.

Workers began to develop autonomous spaces as they moved outside the model town. Many workers objected to Pullman's refusal to sell them homes and thus settled in nearby Roseland and Kensington. High rents in Pullman sent others to these "suburbs," too. These neighborhoods also became the locus of working-class culture for those who lived in Pullman. From churches to saloons, the institutions Pullman's workers created and sustained were outside the model town and reflected their diverse cultural origins. Pullman families, for instance, supported both Roman Catholic and Protestant churches, which had separate congregations for English-speakers, Germans, and Swedes. Ethnic clubs, from the British-American Association of Chicago to the German turnverein, met frequently in local halls. When workers used the facilities Pullman provided, they did so selectively. Even Pullman's much touted athletic program seemed to appeal primarily to English-speakers, since German and Swedish names were conspicuously underrepresented on team rosters.[5] In making choices and creating institutions that Pullman did not control, workers made a space in which they could come together.

What brought workers together was a Pullman management style that exacerbated workers' sense of being exploited. Pullman, like many others, still searched for an effective management structure for the company's far-flung operations. The Pullman Car Works, despite its great size, relied on a traditional shop system in which a superintendent gave individual foremen goals to meet but left them free to choose their own methods to fulfill those goals at the lowest cost. Foremen could hire, fire, set wages, and discipline as they saw fit; they did not have to follow seniority in layoffs and recalls. Some foremen were fair, but others played favorites, demanded kickbacks, and cursed and hit workers. This variation in treatment rankled workers. Foremen often failed to coordinate their efforts, and the resulting inefficiencies in production hurt piece-rate workers, who might lose hours waiting for work.[6]

Other aspects of Pullman's management system deepened the workers' sense of injustice. George Pullman was building his company by underbidding other firms for large contracts. The only way to make a profit from these contracts—and Pullman insisted that everything, including the model town, produce a profit—was by cutting labor costs. Foremen and managers who did not produce the desired results were quickly fired, and turnover among management became a hallmark of the Pullman Car Works. George Pullman insisted that wage rates be changed with every new contract for railroad cars to reflect greater or lesser difficulty in any particular job. Whether a foreman set the new rates fairly or not, frequent changes created numerous occasions for workers to wonder if they were being shortchanged. Suspicion marked the relations between workers and management.[7]

Pullman workers in Chicago began organizing to resist this management regime almost as soon as the plant opened. They were concerned not only about their wages and unfair foremen but also about maintaining craft skills and craftworkers' customary control of the labor process as the company transformed its production methods. By 1885 car builders, cabinetmakers, carvers, wood machine hands, blacksmiths, hammersmiths, and freight-car builders had all joined craft unions and staged strikes or threatened to do so. Because foremen fired organizers, the unions often held secret meetings. The halls of Roseland and Kensington provided the safe spaces workers needed for organizing.[8]

Solidarity among Pullman workers grew more slowly than militancy, however. If all crafts were not simultaneously affected by a wage cut, for instance, unity was hard to achieve. Union meetings had to have speeches in German and Swedish as well as English, but workers of different nationalities might still reject joint action. In 1885 one union official complained that Swedes did not respond to organizing appeals and would accept any wages. This attitude was common among men who were more migrants than immigrants, regardless of their birthplace. They sought to make as much money as quickly as possible to return to their homelands in better financial positions or to support family members left behind. So many Pullman workers were such migrants that in 1892 there were three adult men for every adult woman in the town of Pullman. More married men commuted to the Pullman Car Works from the outlying areas, but single migrants had been a significant proportion of Pullman's labor force since the opening of the works. A local doctor, John McLean, suggested that many Pullman workers still were attached to their homelands and very ambivalent about the United States and Pullman. They liked the higher wages at Pullman, he believed, but questioned the quality of life that provided so little leisure.[9]

Despite their differences, Pullman workers found common ground by early 1886 from repeated wage cuts, long hours, and tyrannical supervision. The Knights of Labor, which sent Joseph Buchanan from Denver to organize Pullman workers, was key to creating a general movement. As other railroad workers in the Midwest and West flocked to the Knights, about 1,800 workers at the Pullman Car Works joined, too. The Knights attracted the most members, but Pullman workers were reaching out to and being courted by all elements of the Chicago labor movement. Those who joined craft unions coordinated their actions with craftsworkers elsewhere in Chicago. At union halls in Roseland and Kensington, the anarchists Albert Parsons and Michael Schwab spoke to large crowds that cheered all denunciations of the Pullman Company, although few commentators thought the anarchists had many followers among Pullman workers.[10]

In May 1886, when the Knights called a general strike for the eight-hour day, the entire work force at the Pullman Car Works walked out in solidarity with thousands of others in Chicago. The strikers belonged to different organizations, but they united to create the Law and Order League to ensure that no violence or disorder spoiled their image as respectable members of the community. Pullman's Knights distanced themselves from the anarchists after the Haymarket bombing and praised the police. Despite the peaceful nature of the 1886 strike, George Pullman rejected the workers' demands for higher pay and shorter hours and set a precedent for how the company would deal with strikes in the future. He locked out the workers for two weeks and then reopened under armed guard. In what would also set a precedent for the future, many, if not most, of the striking workers returned to the shop on the company's terms. Many, however, continued to belong to unions, including the Knights of Labor, which led Pullman's Labor Day Parade the following September.[11]

Despite the defeat of the eight-hour movement, Pullman workers did not abandon their struggle with the company. Issues of craftworkers' customary control of the work process increasingly came to the fore. Carvers struck in 1887 when part of their work was given to cabinetmakers and again the next year when they were given a foreman not of their own choosing. Throughout the early 1890s the Pullman Company experimented with new methods of mass production in its lumber and freight-car building departments, and workers again responded with strikes. As it sought to replace craft control of the work process with managerial control, the company hired more foremen and superintendents who were not craftsmen. This exacerbated the old issues of setting fair wages and mismanagement.[12]

The company's response to the depression of 1893—wage cuts averaging about one-third—once more galvanized workers to joint action. This time they flocked into the American Railway Union. The militancy of Pullman's Chicago workers created the Pullman strike, and the year-old ARU was less the instigator of the insurgency than the vehicle by which workers organized themselves.[13] The Pullman workers struck despite contrary advice from ARU leaders based on the standards they held in common. As the strike leader Thomas Heathcoate explained, "We do not expect the company to concede our demands. We do not know what the outcome will be, and in fact we do not care much. We do know that we are working for less wages than will maintain ourselves and families in the necessaries of life, and on that one proposition we absolutely refuse to work any longer."[14]

During the first month of the strike there was an outpouring of support for Pullman workers from the entire city of Chicago; not only other union members but also members of the middle and business classes contributed to the strike relief fund and sought to pressure the company to negotiate. The strength of the working class and its perspective in Chicago meant many people were willing to see the strikers as having just griev-

ances and as sober, responsible citizens. Bertha Palmer, the leader of
Chicago's social elite, believed that the company had been "grasping or
oppressive in their measures." She was vice president of the newly formed
Civic Federation of Chicago and supported its effort to arbitrate the strike.
Like many others, she was very angry with Pullman for refusing to participate. The strikers themselves effectively wielded community imagery
to build local support and to reconcile potential ethnic divisions in their
midst, emanating this time from Dutch workers.[15] The Dutch had not
organized with other workers in their crafts; they formed a separate local of the ARU after the lockout began. According to an ARU leader wages
had fallen so low that their ties to their homeland now reinforced union
thinking: "All unite in saying that since the last reduction they could make
more and live better in their own country."[16]

The ARU supplemented worker militancy and community support by
sanctioning the strike and using its organizational resources to help the
strikers withstand the company's lockout. ARU leaders solicited relief
funds from railroad workers nationwide, secured third-party arbiters, and
organized Pullman repair-shop workers in Saint Louis, Missouri, and
Ludlow, Kentucky. Rank-and-file militancy among western railroad workers continued to drive the strike, however. From the first Pullman workers expected that a national boycott might be necessary to force the Pullman Company to negotiate. Only three days after the strike began Thomas
Heathcoate reported that workers in Saint Paul, Minnesota, were refusing
to handle Pullman cars—that is, they were beginning a boycott.[17] When
Pullman workers sought more support at the ARU's annual convention,
union members were ready to register not only their solidarity with Pullman workers but also their dissatisfaction with their own employers. They,
too, had experienced drastic wage cuts on top of long-standing grievances.
Despite warnings from the leadership that this was not an opportune
moment, the ARU membership voted a boycott of Pullman cars.

The boycott was effective throughout the Midwest and West; workers
refused to handle Pullman cars, and repair shopmen on many railroads
walked out. Workers struck at Pullman's Saint Louis and Ludlow shops
and at the Illinois Central's large Burnside Repair Shop near the Pullman
Car Works.[18] The type of unity that Stromquist depicts among railroad
workers in the western boom towns sustained the strike even in larger
cities. In Saint Louis daily meetings at the Central Turner Hall rallied the
five hundred Pullman workers and another thousand from the railroads.
In Ludlow Pullman workers struck in conjunction with yard workers from

the Cincinnati Southern Railroad. Thomas Wickes, vice president of the Pullman Company, averred that the company felt compelled to close the Ludlow shop when the local police did nothing to protect Pullman property and strikebreakers the company hired.[19]

The high level of community support in Chicago made it difficult for the Illinois Central and other railroads that tried to recruit strikebreakers. One newspaper reported, "Many men who have never belonged to labor unions in their lives have voluntarily given up their positions to join the ranks of the strikers, after having gone to work to fill the vacancies created by the action of the strikers. . . ."[20] ARU members everywhere used the claims of worker and community solidarity to create such cohesion. Rallies and assistance to strikers were the positive face of working-class community cohesion. But the negative sanctions of sabotaging railroad property and intimidating strikebreakers also were critical to maintaining community solidarity. Although Pullman's Chicago workers usually are portrayed as blameless in the violence of the later stages of the strike because none of it took place in the town of Pullman, there is good evidence of their participation in acts of sabotage and intimidation of strikebreakers and in the mobs that burned railcars.[21]

Not all railroad workers shared a sense of solidarity, however. By establishing the ARU as a white persons' union (for it did admit women), white railroad workers immediately alienated black railroad workers, some of whom were recruited as strikebreakers. Most detrimental to the ability of Pullman strikers to pressure the company, the ARU alienated Pullman's two thousand black porters. If the black porters had been striking too, Pullman service might have been crippled even without the boycott. The company had reinforced racism by hiring only white men as car builders or repair-shop workers and only black men as porters. It also allowed only a few African Americans to live in the town of Pullman. The Pullman strikers never questioned the racial exclusivity of their strike, their jobs, or their community. ARU members in general saw no irony in complaining about black strikebreakers.[22] Most of the strikebreakers, however, were white easterners, unemployed railroad workers who had never been drawn into the western-based movement.

Workers at Pullman's only eastern repair shop, in Wilmington, Delaware, also ignored calls for companywide and industrywide unity. The ARU sent organizers to Wilmington, and they held a mass meeting on May 27 with about two hundred in attendance. The first speaker, L. W. Rogers, a director of the ARU, detailed the problems of Pullman workers in a tone that suggested the distance and lack of communication between Wilmington and Chicago workers. Although Rogers appealed to the primarily native-born American workers by framing the strike in the familiar rhetoric of the American revolutionary struggle—the plutocrats were equivalent to royalty, the unionists to the patriots, and the nonunionists to Tories (Loyalists)—neither this appeal nor that of H. B. Martin of the Knights of Labor was effective in convincing workers to join the ARU or the strike.[23]

Only about fifty or sixty of the almost seven hundred Pullman workers in Wilmington joined the ARU. Most Pullman workers were frightened of losing their jobs, and none left the shop. The Pullman Company was reported to have sent "spotters" to all mass meetings, and it hired extra watchmen for the shop. Pullman workers in Wilmington shared much with their counterparts in Chicago; they had had their wages cut and complained of incompetent and unfair supervision.[24] This was not enough, however, to overcome their fear. As one shop worker charged, "If the men said that they were satisfied they lied, and if so they were afraid of being discharged. They had not the manhood to say that they were dissatisfied."[25]

More was involved than the threat of unemployment, however. Pullman workers in Wilmington lacked the support needed to sustain them through a strike, because they had not developed an autonomous oppositional culture that would legitimize such action. Those local railroad workers who were organized belonged to such craft unions as the Brotherhood of Locomotive Engineers and the Order of Railway Conductors, and many of them scoffed at the ARU. One conductor was quoted as remarking, "The railroad men here aren't such ——— fools as the railroad men out West. We are in the orders for the insurance we get out of them and we would not quit work if the organizations ordered us to strike."[26]

More generally, Wilmington's working class was not strongly self-conscious or well-organized and thus could not provide the kind of support Chicago's could. According to the historian Carol Hoffecker, Wilmington's manufacturing workers had never had a successful union or radical tradition and were cowed or accommodationist by turns. Pay levels in Wilmington were consequently lower than those in nearby Philadelphia or Baltimore. Discontent among skilled workers surfaced sporadically, but no strong craft organizations or large-scale strike activity resulted. The Knights of Labor claimed a large membership in the city in early 1886 but quickly lost a strike in the leather industry—the only major strike in Wilmington in the nineteenth century.[27]

George Pullman moved his repair shop to Wilmington from Elmira, New York, in September 1886 to take advantage of the low-wage, non-union conditions. Two hundred and fifty Elmira workers relocated to Wilmington, only to find their wages cut from $2.50 to $2.00 a day. Some returned north rather than accept these rates; others struck and appealed to the Knights of Labor in Philadelphia for aid. They obtained a compromise rate of $2.25 per day. Nonetheless, in 1894 they resisted the appeals of the Knights to support the Pullman strike.[28]

Wilmington's workers lacked solidarity with one another and with workers elsewhere because they were incorporated into a local culture shaped by its manufacturers. Wilmington was an industrial city in which manufacturers rather than merchants or professionals dominated public discourse. As individual entrepreneurs, they believed their fitness to rule was unbounded. Labor was to look to capital for leadership; unions were a threat to the economic order that rewarded the deserving. Most Wilmington companies had local owners who ruled in a paternal manner. A son of the business class described labor-management relations in almost feudal terms: the managers saw "the men" as collectively troublesome, but they liked and trusted them as individuals. Although employers would fire any worker attempting to unionize, they also pushed for municipal government improvements during the depression of the 1890s to give work to jobless men.[29] Few Wilmington workers even tried to contest this paternal regime.

The cultural dominance of resident manufacturers rested on Wilmington's size and demography. Wilmington, which had a population of 76,000 in 1900, was small enough to have a unified elite leading a highly stratified social order. The small group of successful manufacturers dominated not only the local economy but also Wilmington's governmental and social organizations. In larger cities scale alone allowed for the development of semiautonomous communities, and the multiplicity of local elites further reinforced the possibility for competing perspectives. In Chicago, moreover, workers were less likely to accept the cultural authority of manufacturers because most of the workers were immigrants. They were divided from American-born employers by language and culture as well as by class. Most Wilmington workers were native-born white Americans who shared a common language and history with the manufacturers. Immigrants never constituted a large portion of the Wilmington population; 67 percent of working-age men were native-born whites, while 13 percent were native-born blacks.[30]

Racial prejudice also furthered Wilmington's paternal regime among white men. Skilled jobs, such as railcar building and repair, were reserved for white men, especially the native-born; black men were primarily casual laborers without opportunities for economic advancement. The Pullman shop force reflected this hierarchy: 80 percent of a sample of Pullman's Wilmington shop workers who were hired before the 1894 strike were native-born white Americans; none was black.[31] Further, in Wilmington, as in much of the South, the appeal of white supremacy could be used to override or dampen the class struggle. Wilmington's white residents had legally segregated the public schools, and most public accommodations were segregated by custom. Race baiting figured in every election, and many black residents were disenfranchised by poll taxes.[32]

The Pullman strike and boycott were undercut by racial prejudice, craft exclusiveness, regional variations in ARU membership, and the lack of community support in some cities, such as Wilmington. These factors hampered the ARU in its struggle with the railroads and ensured the union's defeat when the federal government put its weight behind the corporations. In the face of federal troops and a sweeping injunction not even the most militant local communities could sustain the strike and boycott. Pullman workers in Chicago refused to end their strike in mid-July when the boycott collapsed, but they were isolated and almost destitute. A month later approximately two thousand strikers returned to work on Pullman's terms.

The factors that undercut the strike and boycott in 1894 did not remain equally detrimental to union organizing and strike solidarity. By the 1920s railroad workers had thriving national unions, and in strike situations they looked beyond their local communities for support and legitimation. The 1922 strike of 400,000 railroad shopmen was not undercut by eastern workers or dependent on the strength of local working-class communities. Shopmen in all parts of the country, including virtually all 12,000 Pullman repair shop and yard workers, stayed out for three long months.[33] Pullman's Wilmington workers, many of whom were long-term employees and some of whom had been the nonstrikers of 1894, were as faithful to the strike as others were. The Wilmington organization was even acting as a parent local and organizing two small groups of Pullman workers at train yards in Baltimore and Philadelphia.[34]

As in 1894, however, railroad workers were not completely unified. In 1922 the racial situation was more complex than it had been thirty years earlier. Some of the shopcraft unions now admitted black workers, if only in segregated locals, while other black workers formed American Federation of Labor (AFL) federal labor unions. Because of the pervasive racism of AFL unions, companies could still recruit black strikebreakers if they chose to, but at the same time other black workers were on strike.[35] Further, the 1922 strike, unlike the 1894 strike, did not shut down the railroads, even in the West, because operating railroad workers refused to strike in sympathy with shopmen.[36] Now cooperation between on-train and off-train railroad workers was absent.

Except for the changing racial situation, the new configuration of nationwide unity among shop workers, coupled with a division between on-train and off-train workers, arose primarily because of a new factor in railroad labor relations—the federal government. Although President Grover Cleveland had used federal courts and troops to crush the ARU, his probusiness position was controversial. Many Americans feared unbridled class warfare and wanted the state to mediate conflict. The transformation of the federal government's role began in the fall of 1894, when Cleveland appointed a commission to investigate the causes of the Pullman strike and make recommendations for avoiding such disruptions in the future.

The U.S. Strike Commission's report criticized both Pullman's intransigence and the actions of the railroad companies, and, like the Civic Federation of Chicago, it looked to arbitration to eliminate such instances of class warfare in the future.[37] In 1898 Congress responded with the Erdman Act, which created machinery for voluntary mediation of railroad labor disputes and recognized the right of on-train railroad workers to unionize. With this support the brotherhoods of operating workers—engineers, conductors, firemen, and trainmen—joined together to form system federations and welcomed government mediation as an alternative to strikes. From this point on operating and repair-shop workers never again cooperated in strikes. While unions of operating workers grew, shop workers, who had not been granted legal sanction to unionize, struggled. In 1911 the shopcraft unions formed system federations on the Illinois Central and the Harriman-controlled railroads, but the companies successfully broke them.[38]

The federal government's response to the demands of mobilization during World War I was the critical factor in spreading the system federation movement to all shop workers and in creating national solidarity among them. When the government nationalized the railroads and established the United States Railroad Administration (USRA), the USRA insisted that railroads recognize and bargain with unions. By outlawing piece rates and instituting the eight-hour day and union work rules, the USRA recognized shop workers' long-standing demands. Moreover, the USRA mandated a single "mechanic's rate" for all craftworkers in repair shops, which emphasized the equality among them and unified the trades further.[39] Railroad shop workers flocked into the AFL shopcraft unions and their system federations; Pullman repair-shop and yard workers formed their system federation, #122, in 1919.

Under government control the unions obtained the shop workers' long-term allegiance because unions were necessary for the implementation of government policy. The USRA did not replace managers at the individual railroads but only set policy. Looking forward to a future without government control, many managers refused to implement directives. Pullman workers, for instance, benefited from the newly mandated policies only when they had unions to file grievances with the government.[40]

If a system federation fought for those policies for all workers, it could overcome even the racism that had divided black and white workers. Large numbers of black car-cleaners, the bulk of Pullman's yard force, overlooked the racism of the white-dominated AFL unions and formed AFL federal labor unions or joined segregated locals of the Brotherhood of Railway Carmen when that union dropped its total bar on black members in 1921.[41] System Federation #122 filed hundreds of grievances to force Pullman managers to implement the new policies for every shop and for every worker—white or black, male or female. Workers' attachment to the system federation dated from this period when it delivered union-defined craft jobs as well as wages and hours better than any Pullman workers had known.[42]

Government policy opened up, however, a new divide between Pullman's manufacturing and repair-shop workers. The Pullman Company had separated its repair shop in Chicago from the Pullman Car Works in 1900, and now it fought government takeover of the plant on the grounds that manufacturing and railroad operations were distinct. Pullman manufacturing workers wanted to be included under government management, but the USRA rejected their pleas.[43] Joint action between Pullman manufacturing workers and nearby railroad workers had not ended in 1900. Workers at the Pullman Car Works, Pullman's Calumet Repair Shop, and the Illinois Central's Burnside Repair Shop had formed locals of the AFL shopcraft unions in the first years of the century, and they had cooperated to achieve one notable success—the nine-hour day. But in 1904 the Pullman Company broke its workers' unions, and Pullman workers did not join with Burnside craftworkers in the system federation movement in 1911. Only the government takeover provided Pullman shop workers, but not manufacturing workers, with a new opportunity to organize.[44]

At this juncture the labor activism of Pullman manufacturing workers and shop workers took separate paths. During the war manufacturing workers were divided; some belonged to no union, while others were attracted to the Industrial Workers of the World, the Brotherhood of Railway Carmen, or the organizing drive in the steel industry. At the Pullman Car Works the company could continue to hamper unionization efforts by all means, fair or foul, and it was in the forefront of the movement to develop Employee Representation Plans (company unions).[45] A few blocks from the Pullman Car Works, at Pullman's Calumet Repair Shop, workers were members of an AFL system federation and allied with shop workers across the country. When the 1922 strike began, most employees of the Pullman Car Works did not strike in sympathy with neighbors from Burnside or fellow Pullman workers from the Calumet Repair Shop. Manufacturing workers had none of the benefits of the union period to make them believe that the railroad unions were worth fighting for.

For Pullman shop workers, like other railroad shopmen, allegiance to national institutions now was stronger than allegiance to neighbors, when their jobs were at issue. Pullman's Wilmington shop workers were the best example of that transition. They had few new grievances that might have made them more militant during World War I than they had been in the 1890s. Management had introduced no major changes in shop-floor practice, and only the war-induced labor shortage created an increase in the proportion of less skilled helpers.[46] The social activities of the shop, like the shop choir led by the foreman of the upholstery department, still brought supervisors and employees together.[47] In 1922 Pullman's Wilmington workers were still mainly native-born, often local-born, white Americans (75 percent). A few black men (3 percent of the work force) now worked in unskilled jobs at the shop, as they did at other Wilmington plants. If they shared a similar heritage with the 1894 shop force and had few new grievances, the 1922 shop force had had a wholly new experience of working for several years under union contracts. That experience made them, along with other railroad shop workers in Wilmington, solid supporters of the system federations.

In 1922 Wilmington's shop workers maintained their strike in the absence of community support.[48] Wilmington remained an antiunion town, and the railroad shopmen's strike was the only major strike there in the first three decades of the twentieth century. The city's population had grown slowly to 110,000, but the balance of native-born whites, native-born blacks, and immigrants had not altered. Neither had the social hierarchy that bound them. Further, Wilmington was becoming a white-collar city as the Du Pont Company established its headquarters and research facility there. What happened in twentieth-century Wilmington was, according to Carol Hoffecker, what Du Pont wanted, and the Du Pont Company was one of the most successful American corporations in its antiunion strategies.[49] Industry was declining, and many of the local manufacturing firms that did not go out of business became branches of national corporations. As workers' ties to local elites were broken, the old paternalism disappeared. Outside direction, however, did not create more proworker feeling in the middle class. When workers organized, they were quickly crushed, and local police joined private detectives in intimidating peaceful strikers. Although Wilmington experienced a brief boom in manufacturing during World War I, it left no legacy of successful worker organizations except among railroad workers.[50] Government regulation of labor relations in the railroad industry allowed the shopcraft unions to survive even in antiunion Wilmington.

In Chicago and Wilmington Pullman shop workers conducted their strike activities similarly. They cooperated with other railroad shop workers and obtained some rhetorical support from other unions but no sympathy strikes. Wilmington's Central Labor Union, for instance, compiled a list of "friendly merchants," so that members might help by rewarding the friends of labor. Shop workers kept their spirits up with daily meetings and mass picketing. In the early days of the strike Pullman workers at Wilmington forced a few men who crossed their picket line to join the strike by heckling them and covering their homes with large yellow signs saying "SCAB." As the strike progressed, violence escalated nationwide. Beatings of strikebreakers and sabotage of railroad property became common, even in places like Wilmington that had not seen such activity in 1894. For Wilmington shop workers these activities were sanctioned by shopmen nationwide, not the wider Wilmington community.[51]

The shopmen's strike was broken as the Pullman strike had been, primarily by a federal government injunction against the unions. Not all of the system federations suffered the fate of the ARU, however. In September 1922 some railroads settled with their workers, agreeing to take back strikers with their seniority intact, albeit with the pay cut that had triggered the strike. Such hard-line companies as Pullman and the Pennsylvania Railroad refused to negotiate. In October the Pullman Company began to reopen its shops, using large numbers of new black workers as the other hard-liners were doing. When faced with the loss of their jobs, many Pullman strikers returned to work.[52] As in 1894, Pullman workers fought hard, but many also valued their jobs and returned on the company's terms rather than lose them.

Situating the Pullman strike in the context of railroad workers' organizing from the 1880s to the 1920s reveals the changing sources of workers' solidarity. Local traditions would always be important for union organization: the strongest leadership and the first steps in union organizing came from the most class-conscious communities—in the Pullman case, Chicago. The Calumet Repair Shop workers led every organizing drive by Pullman shopmen, and they received encouragement from the many union members and radicals in Chicago's working class. Encouragement no longer meant community-based strikes, however, because workers now looked first to their ties with others in their industries. Increasingly, workers at the Pullman Car Works saw themselves as part of the steel industry, not the railroad industry, and their links to Pullman and Burnside shop workers weakened. Nonetheless, even in cities like Wilmington that had no militant working-class communities or successful unions, nationalizing forces, such as the federal government, could encourage workers to identify with national unions in their industry and give them the courage to reject local influences.

The defeat of most system federations in 1922 did not lead railroad shop workers to turn away from the national unions. The experience of working under union contracts during World War I became the standard against which Pullman and other railroad shop workers gauged their lot. Within a year of defeating its employees and rebuilding its shop forces, the Pullman Company felt compelled to establish a national contract with the company union it had foisted on the shop workers. Although this contract diverged from union ones on work rules, it mandated union wage rates and recognized seniority as the basis for layoffs and recalls. The company never reverted to paying piece rates in its repair shops, although it continued to do so in the Pullman Car Works, and it raised hourly rates whenever the AFL shop craft unions secured higher wages from other railroads. Pullman shopmen accepted this "compromise," but they would strike over any attempt to diverge further from union standards.[53] During the New Deal, when the federal government once more granted workers' right to organize, Pullman and railroad shop workers jettisoned their company unions and joined their AFL system federations again.

Notes

1. Almont Lindsey, *The Pullman Strike: The Story of a Unique Experiment and of a Great Labor Upheaval* (Chicago: University of Chicago Press, 1942), chronicles the strike on a national canvas. Shelton Stromquist, *A Generation of Boomers: The Pattern of Railroad Labor Conflict in Nineteenth-Century America* (Urbana: University of Illinois Press, 1987), chap. 1, analyzes the development of an impulse toward industrial unions among railroad workers. The role of the ARU and the Pullman strike and boycott in the contest between craft and industrial unions is a staple of histories of the American labor movement. Bruce Laurie, *Artisans into Workers: Labor in the Nineteenth Century* (New York: Noonday, 1989), chap. 6, presents an excellent analysis of that contest and the role of the ARU.

2. Stromquist, *Generation of Boomers,* combines the two central threads of the new labor history—the role of working-class culture in the development of working-class consciousness and the role of shop-floor struggle in craft union practice and culture. Earlier works take a different approach. Lindsey's *Pullman Strike* focuses primarily on institutions, emphasizing the actions of union leadership, employer associations, and various branches of government.

3. Stanley Buder, *Pullman: An Experiment in Industrial Order and Community Planning, 1880–1930* (New York: Oxford University Press, 1967), situates the origins of the strike in the tensions of the planned community but not in the development of an autonomous working-class culture.

4. Mrs. Duane Doty, *The Town of Pullman: Its Growth with Brief Accounts of Its Industries* (Pullman, Ill.: T. P. Struhsacker, 1893), 35.

5. "In the Southern Suburbs," *Chicago Herald,* May 13, 1886; "Pullman Britishers Awake," *Chicago Tribune,* October 7, 1887; Doty, *Town of Pullman,* 46; Wilma J. Pesavento and Lisa C. Raymond, "'Men Must Play; Men Will Play': Occupations of Pullman Athletes, 1880 to 1900," *Journal of Sport History* 12 (Winter 1985): 242.

6. "The Trouble at Pullman," *Chicago Daily News,* October 2, 1885; "Complaints from Pullman," *Chicago Herald,* January 25, 1886; "Claims of the Carvers," *Chicago Herald,* January 9, 1988; Richard Edwards, *Contested Terrain: The Transformation of the Workplace in the Twentieth Century* (New York: Basic Books, 1979), 18–21, 116, 143–44.

7. "Annual Shake Up at Pullman," *Chicago Herald,* June 5, 1883; "Poor Pay at Pullman," *Chicago Herald,* October 2, 1885; "At Pullman," *Chicago Tribune,* October 3, 1885; "Pullman," *Chicago Times,* August 6, 1886; "Men and Moneybags," *Chicago Herald,* August 14, 1886; "Pullman," *Chicago Tribune,* March 29, 1887; "News from the Suburban Towns," *Chicago Tribune,* November 16, 1887; William H. Carwardine, *The Pullman Strike,* 4th ed. (Chicago: Charles H. Kerr, 1971), 91.

8. "A Strike at Pullman," *Chicago Daily News*, September 30, 1885; "Threatening Trouble," *Chicago Inter-Ocean*, September 30, 1885; "Poor Pay at Pullman," *Chicago Herald*, October 2, 1885; "The Trouble at Pullman," *Chicago Daily News*, October 2, 1885; "Struck Work," *Chicago Inter-Ocean*, October 2, 1885; "At Pullman," *Chicago Tribune*, October 3, 1885; "Strikes Are Increasing," *Chicago Herald*, February 23, 1886.

9. "Threatening Trouble," *Chicago Inter-Ocean*, September 30, 1885; "A Strike at Pullman," *Chicago Daily News*, September 30, 1885; Buder, *Pullman*, 81, 89; Doty, *Town of Pullman*, 33.

10. "The Situation at Pullman," *Chicago Times*, October 1, 1885; "The Pullman Workmen," *Chicago Tribune*, October 1, 1885; "Struck Work," *Chicago Inter-Ocean*, October 2, 1885; "At Pullman," *Chicago Tribune*, October 3, 1885; "Strikes Are Increasing," *Chicago Herald*, February 23, 1886; "Eight-Hour Movement at Pullman," *Chicago Tribune*, April 16, 1886.

11. "Great Strike at the Pullman Car Works," *Chicago Tribune*, May 5, 1886; "Demonstration at Pullman," *Chicago Herald*, May 9, 1886; "All Quiet at Pullman, Of Course," *Chicago Herald*, May 10, 1886; "Keeping Up Steam," *Chicago Times*, May 10, 1886; "Hyde Park," *Chicago Daily Graphic*, May 11, 1886; "Holiday Parade at Pullman," *Chicago Herald*, September 7, 1886; Buder, *Pullman*, 140; Lindsey, *Pullman Strike*, 28–29.

12. "A Pullman Strike," *Chicago Evening Journal*, July 22, 1887; "Hard Times at Pullman," *Chicago Herald*, August 2, 1887; "Pullman Makes a Concession," *Chicago Herald*, September 2, 1887; "Odd Strike at Pullman," *Chicago Tribune*, January 1, 1888; "Claims of the Carvers," *Chicago Herald*, January 9, 1888; "They Leave Pullman," *Chicago Herald*, January 24, 1888; Buder, *Pullman*, 142, 150; Doty, *Town of Pullman*, 73–74; United States Strike Commission, *Report on the Chicago Strike of June–July, 1894* (Washington, D. C.: Government Printing Office, 1895), 90, 421, 423, 441.

13. United States Strike Commission, *Report*, 6, 442.

14. Quoted in "For a Living Wage," *Chicago Times*, May 13, 1894.

15. Quoted in Susan Hirsch and Robert Goler, *A City Comes of Age: Chicago in the 1890s* (Chicago: Chicago Historical Society, 1990), 80; Janice L. Reiff, "Community Credit, Basket Brigades and the Mayor's Office: The Local Politics of the Pullman Strike" (Paper delivered at the 1994 annual meeting of the Organization of American Historians, Atlanta, Ga., April 17, 1994).

16. Quoted in United States Strike Commission, *Report*, 91.

17. "Pullman Men Out," *Chicago Times*, May 12, 1894; "Aid from St. Paul," *Chicago Times*, May 14, 1894; "They Cheer the Speaker," *Chicago Daily News*, May 14, 1894.

18. "K. of L. Offers Its Aid," *Chicago Daily News*, June 27, 1894; "The Railroad Strike," *Labor* (Saint Louis), July 7, 1894; Harry Jebsen Jr., "The Role of Blue Is-

land in the Pullman Strike of 1894," *Journal of the Illinois State Historical Society* 67, no. 3 (1974): 275–93; Lindsey, *Pullman Strike,* chap. 11.

19. Lindsey, *Pullman Strike,* 268–69; United States Strike Commission, *Report,* 589.

20. "Took Down the Gates," *Chicago Daily News,* June 29, 1894.

21. "Kensington Mob Has Arms," *Chicago Daily News,* July 6, 1894; United States Strike Commission, *Report,* 338.

22. "Colored Men Take Places," *Chicago Daily News,* June 29, 1894; Eugene Debs, *The Negro Workers* (New York: Emancipation Publishing, 1923), 8; Philip S. Foner, *Organized Labor and the Black Worker, 1619–1981* (New York: International, 1981), 104–5.

23. "Massmeeting of Laborers," *Every Evening* (Wilmington, Del.), May 28, 1894.

24. "Massmeeting of Laborers," *Every Evening,* May 29, 1894; Carol E. Hoffecker, *Wilmington, Delaware: Portrait of an Industrial City, 1830–1910* (Charlottesville: University of Virginia Press, 1974), 22–28; Lindsey, *Pullman Strike,* 268–69; United States Strike Commission, *Report,* 554, 570–72, 589.

25. Quoted in "Pullman Workman," *Every Evening,* July 10, 1894.

26. "No Prospect of Any Strike Here," *Every Evening,* July 9, 1894.

27. Hoffecker, *Wilmington,* 115–36. The Wilmington *Every Evening and Commercial* covered labor issues extensively during 1886. Throughout April and May articles detailed the Knights' attempts to organize leather workers, construction workers, and machinists.

28. "Pullman's Men on a Short Strike," dateline Wilmington, no title, September 6, 1886, Pullman Scrapbooks, Town I, Pullman Company Archives, Newberry Library, Chicago; Hoffecker, *Wilmington,* 119–38.

29. Quoted in Henry Seidel Canby, *The Age of Confidence* (New York: Farrar and Rinehart, 1934), 25; Hoffecker, *Wilmington,* 59, 123.

30. Throughout the nineteenth century the largest group of immigrants was Irish. The few eastern and southern Europeans who were coming to Wilmington found work primarily in the leather industry. United States Census Office, *Report on the Population of the United States at the Eleventh Census, 1890: Population* (Washington, D. C.: Government Printing Office, 1895–97), table 188, 740.

31. Statistics on Pullman shop workers are derived from samples of Calumet (Chicago), Wilmington, and Richmond, California, shop workers employed by Pullman between 1906 and 1965. The profile of Wilmington shop workers employed before the strike is of workers who still were employed in 1906, and they are not necessarily a representative sample of the early work force. The lack of change in the demographic profile of the Wilmington shop workers between 1906 and 1922, however, suggests that the statistics are reasonably accurate. For a discussion of the samples, see Susan Hirsch and Janice Reiff, "Job Segregation and the Replication of Local Social Hierarchies," in *Essays from the Lowell Conference*

on Industrial History, 1982 and 1983, ed. Robert Weible (North Andover, Mass.: Museum of American Textile History, 1985), 276–94.

32. Hoffecker, *Wilmington,* 117–18; Carol Hoffecker, *Delaware: A Bicentennial History* (New York: W. W. Norton, 1977), 108–9, 185–86, 189.

33. Colin J. Davis, "Bitter Conflict: The 1922 Railroad Shopmen's Strike," *Labor History* 33 (Fall 1992): 433–55, gives the best modern overview of the strike.

34. Fifty-six percent of Wilmington shop workers at the time of the 1922 strike were hired before 1912; 11 percent had been in the shop during the 1894 strike, including George Herdman, secretary-treasurer of the 1922 strike committee. From the *Every Evening:* "Pullman Workers Went on Strike at Local Plant Today," July 10, 1922; "Little Change in Strike at Pullman," July 11, 1922; "Pullman Strikers Are Marking Time," July 19, 1922; "Pullman Strike May Soon Be Settled," September 29, 1922; Second Weekly Report from John F. Nelson, general chairman, Pullman System Federation #122, to J. F. McGrath, vice president, AFL Railway Employes Department, March 31, 1922, AFL Railway Employes Department, Records, 1917–70, Kheel Center, Martin P. Catherwood Library, Cornell University (hereafter AFLRED).

35. "Colored Men at the B. & O. R.R. Shops Here," *Daily Calumet* (Chicago) July 8, 1922; Letter from B. M. Jewell, president, AFL Railway Employes Department, to J. F. Nelson, general chairman, Pullman System Federation #122, July 26, 1922, AFLRED.

36. Margaret Gadsby, "Strike of the Railroad Shopmen," *Monthly Labor Review* 15 (December 1922): 1–21. Davis, "Bitter Conflict," discusses the lack of support from the unions of clerks, signalmen, switchmen, and maintenance-of-way workers.

37. United States Strike Commission, *Report,* xlvi–liv.

38. The five shopcraft unions represented machinists, carmen, sheet metal workers, boilermakers, and blacksmiths. They were joined later by the electricians. Robert E. L. Knight, *Industrial Relations in the San Francisco Bay Area, 1900–1918* (Berkeley: University of California Press, 1960), 152–54, 252–53; David Montgomery, *The Fall of the House of Labor: The Workplace, the State, and Labor Activism, 1865–1925* (New York: Cambridge University Press, 1987), 246–48; Selig Perlman and Philip Taft, *History of Labor in the United States, 1896–1932* (New York: Macmillan, 1935), 368–73.

39. Walker D. Hines, *War History of American Railroads* (New Haven, Conn.: Yale University Press, 1928), 162–68, 177–78. The shopcraft unions maintained a single mechanic's rate until the 1960s.

40. Letter from John Scott, acting president, AFL Railway Employes Department, to Frank McManamy, assistant director, Division of Operation, United States Railroad Administration (hereafter USRA), September 16, 1919; Letter from John B. Payne, director general of the railroad, in records of employee #2000, Calumet Shop; Confidential Memorandum from F. L. Simmons, assistant federal

auditor, to C. S. Pflager, mechanical superintendent, November 18, 1919, all in Pullman Company Archives, Newberry Library. The records of the USRA document hundreds of complaints that were filed as Pullman managers refused to implement new policies, but only at those sites where workers protested. Division of Labor, Railway Board of Adjustment #2, USRA, RG 14, National Archives (hereafter USRANA).

41. Letter from B. M. Jewell, president, AFL Railway Employes Department, to J. F. Nelson, general chairman, Pullman System Federation #122, July 26, 1922, AFLRED; Letter from J. F. Nelson to B. M. Jewel, October 19, 1922, AFLRED.

42. After the company was returned to private hands, management violated its contracts so flagrantly that over 90 percent of Pullman shop and yard workers voted to strike in 1921. "Pullman Shop Crafts Fight for National Agreement Conditions," *New Majority* (Chicago), June 18, 1921.

43. Letters from Charles A. Fisher, Pullman Car Works, to Secretary of the Treasury William McAdoo, October 10, 1918, and November 5, 1918, Subject Classified General File 1918–22, E-38-3, USRANA.

44. "Car Builders Go on Strike," *Chicago American,* September 7, 1901; "Pullman Car Builders on Strike," *Chicago American,* August 3, 1902; "Strikers Win at Pullman," *Chicago American,* August 15, 1902; "Pullman Trades Ask Sunday Off," *Chicago Tribune,* December 16, 1902; "Pullman Car Men Gain Great Victory," *Chicago American,* February 1, 1903; "Pullman Laundry Girls Strike," *Chicago Tribune,* April 24, 1903; "Big Strikes Impend," *Chicago Evening Post,* February 26, 1904; "Big Shops Start, Ignoring Unions," *Chicago Tribune,* September 26, 1904.

45. "One Big Union in and around Chicago," *Industrial Solidarity,* April 8, 1916; "Pullman Workers Get Sample of 'Company Union' Tactics," *New Majority,* March 5, 1921; David Montgomery, "Nationalism, American Patriotism, and Class Consciousness among Immigrant Workers in the United States in the Epoch of World War I," in *"Struggle a Hard Battle": Essays on Working-Class Immigrants,* ed. Dirk Hoerder (De Kalb: Northern Illinois University Press, 1986), 343–44; Larry Peterson, "The Intellectual World of the IWW: An American Worker's Library in the First Half of the Twentieth Century," *History Workshop* 22 (Autumn 1986): 158–59. Pullman manufacturing workers were able to unionize only during World War II when the National Labor Board oversaw a union election.

46. These conclusions rely on an analysis of Wilmington shop payrolls for 1906, 1911, 1917, and 1921, Pullman Company Archives, Newberry Library.

47. *Pullman Car Works Standard* 1 (March 1917): 11.

48. Colin J. Davis, "The 1922 Railroad Shopmen's Strike in the Southeast: A Study of Success and Failure," in *Organized Labor in the Twentieth-Century South,* ed. Robert H. Zieger (Knoxville: University of Tennessee Press, 1991), shows that while community support and women's auxiliaries helped strikers hold out, the degree of intransigence of the companies and the effectiveness of the structure of each railroad's system federation determined the success or failure of the strike

on any particular line. Since Wilmington workers held out for three months, we might surmise that the Pullman System Federation was a well-organized one.

49. The 1920 census reported that two-thirds of men of working age were native-born white Americans, and 11 percent were native-born blacks. The largest groups of immigrants were now Italians and Poles, rather than Irish, but their numbers were still modest by the standards of more northerly cities. United States Bureau of the Census, *Fourteenth Census of the United States, 1920: Population* (Washington, D. C.: Government Printing Office, 1922), 173; Carol Hoffecker, *Corporate Capital: Wilmington in the Twentieth Century* (Philadelphia: Temple University Press, 1983), 5–39, 94; Hoffecker, *Wilmington,* 138–39; Charles N. Lanier Jr., "Labor in Delaware," in *Delaware: A History of the First State,* vol. 2, ed. Henry Clay Reed (New York: Lewis Historical Publishing, 1947), 551–68.

50. On the unsuccessful attempt to organize in the leather industry, see Yda Schreuder, "The Impact of Labor Segmentation on the Ethnic Division of Labor and the Immigrant Residential Community: Polish Leather Workers in Wilmington, Delaware in the Early Twentieth Century," *Journal of Historical Geography* 16 (October 1990): 402–24.

51. From the *Every Evening:* "To Notify All Men at Pullman to Quit," July 13, 1922; "Pullman Strikers Say They Are Gaining," July 14, 1922; "Accused of Annoying Railroad Workers," July 15, 1922; "Little Change in Pullman Situation," July 17, 1922; "Central Union Pledges Support to Striking Shopmen," July 19, 1922; "G. M. Gilkey Is Attacked by Mob, Dragged from Car," July 28, 1922; "Striking Shopmen Say They Will Win Fight," August 2, 1922; "James B. Stevenson Brutally Assaulted," August 5, 1922; "P.R.R. Fourteenth St. Bridge Dynamited at 2:35 This Morning," August 31, 1922. The Chicago *Daily Calumet* contained almost daily articles with such titles as "Rioting in Burnside, One Man Badly Beaten," July 26, 1922; "Two Men Shot in Burnside Strike Riots," July 29, 1922; and "Burnside Shopman Slain by Sluggers on Way to Work," August 3, 1922. For a similar picture of activities in that railroad town, see Jim Flynn, "The 1922 Strike of Railroad Shopcraft Workers in Aurora, Illinois" (Unpublished paper in author's possession, April 18, 1983).

52. Eventually, 42 percent of Wilmington strikers returned to the shop; 70 percent of Calumet strikers did; and 65 percent of Richmond strikers went back to work.

53. Memo from F. L. Simmons to L. S. Hungerford, June 29, 1923, in file "Rates of Pay Ordered by USRR Labor Board in Decision 1036"; Memorandum of F. L. Simmons, March 30, 1934, in file "Wage Reductions," both in Pullman Company Archives, Newberry Library.

3

A Modern Lear and His Daughters:
Gender in the Model Town of Pullman

Janice L. Reiff

AS THE PULLMAN STRIKE struggled toward its painful conclusion in the late summer of 1894, Jane Addams penned a critique of the experiment at Pullman, Illinois, that had just ended so dramatically. Rejecting current explanations that blamed either George Pullman or his ungrateful workers, she sought a more satisfactory understanding of the events to explain the failure of the model town that she had once viewed favorably, make sense of the social cleavage that had torn Chicago apart, and offer lessons for the future that would prevent another strike like Pullman ever happening again.[1] Acknowledging the critical importance of the recent events for Chicago and urban America, she found her insights in the struggle between Shakespeare's Lear and his daughters that led to the destruction of his kingdom. In this literary analogy she "modified and softened" her own judgments of individuals and events and provided an accessible framework for understanding what had happened to the audiences with whom she shared her critique, the Chicago Woman's Club and the Twentieth Century Club of Boston.[2]

The first and most developed part of her analysis compared George Pullman with Lear. At the heart of that comparison lay her belief that Pullman, like a king, held too much power and had lost sight of how to use it. Just as Lear had expected his daughters to accept his decisions gratefully and on his terms, Pullman could not acknowledge that his workers were adults, capable of assessing their needs and their rights. When the social and economic crisis of 1893 struck the town, he still expected those who lived there to accept the situation as he wanted it—despite falling wages, rising unemployment, and growing hunger. Like Lear, when the workers demanded new solutions in May of 1894, he could only resent their disloyalty. Just as with Lear and Cordelia, when the break came, there could be no reconciliation because George Pullman could never understand how his narrow commitment to a certain profit made such a reconciliation impossible.

This aspect of Addams's analysis was easy for her audience to understand and appreciate. Previous commentators had described Pullman's model town on Chicago's far south side as paternalistic. Almost ten years earlier the economist Richard T. Ely had condemned the town as un-American because of its paternalism.[3] He described how George Pullman himself had established all the boundaries for residents in Pullman. Pullman let them know how he thought they should vote. His rental policies meant that Pullman families could not own their own homes. Workers seemed afraid to say what they thought because they feared retaliation. Ely's logic was simple. If Pullman's rules and methods did not give his residents full rights in how they lived their lives, the town was undemocratic and therefore un-American. Such an environment could not be good, no matter how much one praised its cleanliness, its housing, and its educational opportunities, because it undermined the very notion of American manhood and the rights associated with it. In the years following Ely's critique examples of Pullman's abuses of workers' rights grew more abundant—as did the list of rights denied. Eventually the list came to include not only the right to vote without interference and the right to home ownership but also the right to join a union, to drink beer whenever and wherever they pleased, and to sit on their stoops in shirtsleeves. As the list expanded, so did the rhetoric of antipaternalism. From the mid-1880s it was not unusual for labor activists to call Pullman workers slaves.[4] Clearly by the beginning of the strike Pullman—the man, the company, and the town—epitomized for many the worst of the system that denied the manhood of industrial workers. So general was this consensus that the American Railway Union president Eugene V. Debs, the U.S. Strike Commission, Chicago's working classes, many of its elites, the *Chicago Tribune*, and, eventually, even members of the General Managers' Association could all agree on at least parts of it.[5]

If George Pullman's responsibility for the strike at Pullman and the chaos it inflicted on the city was easy for Addams to outline, the second aspect of her analysis was not. Here she emphasized that Pullman and those who worked and lived in his factory and town shared the blame. Just as Lear and his children had lost sight of their shared interests, all the characters in the Pullman tragedy had lost sight of the common good. In this analysis workers had benefited from their wages at the Pullman Car Works, and residents had enjoyed the amenities the town provided, but the strikers' sweeping rejection of all things Pullman had risked any future likelihood that employers, and even philanthropists, would ever again assume a more hospitable social and physical environment as one of their responsibilities. At the same time, George Pullman's refusal to accept the workers' need and right to organize collectively—even though they had proven themselves capable and responsible participants in the industrial process—had lessened the likelihood that employers would voluntarily incorporate workers' insights or acknowledge their unions. In this combination lay the Shakespearian tragedy of the Pullman strike. Because neither side would acknowledge the achievements of the other or appreciate its contribution, the divisions became angrier and deeper and spread throughout the country. If Lear's kingdom could burn, so might industrial America. Instead of working together for a shared future, both sides had been hurt by fighting over a rapidly changing past.

This second element of her analysis was much more difficult for her audience to appreciate. Especially in the months immediately following the strike, the idea of a common good or shared interest seemed inconceivable to those who had experienced or seen the hunger, destruction, injustice, and violence that resulted from it. Even journals that had previously welcomed her essays balked at the controversial message of "A Modern Lear."[6] Not until 1912 would it be published, and then in the *Survey* as a companion piece to Graham Taylor's study of Pullman as a Chicago industrial neighborhood. In the heyday of progressivism her call resonated with a far broader audience than it did in the embattled 1890s.

Yet, a century later, it remains difficult for historians to reconsider Pullman, the town, and the strike, through Addams's second lens.[7] The story of Pullman the paternalist continues to work well in the various narratives of nineteenth-century America. It illustrates the bitter conflict between labor and capital, a kind of morality tale where oppressed workers reassert their manhood in the face of monumental efforts to deny it. Few scholars have seen reason to attempt to see Pullman in any other light. Nonetheless, this essay presents a new, gendered way of looking at the town and the 1894 strike. It looks at the issue of paternalism not as the relationship between George Pullman and his workers but in terms of a broader set of social relations and responsibilities within the model town that had implications far beyond Chicago's south side. Taking an explicit

cue from Addams's focus on the family and an implicit hint from the fact
that Lear's children were, after all, daughters, this essay meets her challenge by looking less at the workers and more at those who were dependent on them. With that perspective it is possible to use what was common and shared to find new ways of considering the model town, the
strike, and the implications of both for twentieth-century struggles to
solve the problems of industrial society.

A Gendered Vision of Pullman

The critical first step toward realizing this gendered understanding
of Pullman lies, as Addams argued, in finding what was shared by Pullman workers, Pullman management, and Chicagoans in general. I would
argue that what was common was a widely held conviction that men
should work; that women, children, and other dependents should be cared
for; and that the family was the critical center of the social order. This
assumption was physically built into the model town by Pullman and his
architects. It attracted men and families to Pullman as a place to work and
a place to live. It was the basis for the praise heaped on the town of Pullman by planners, labor advocates, settlement house workers, and even
employees in the Pullman Car Works. It was also central to the notion of
male rights and manliness in that his work made the home and the wom-
anly ideal within it possible.[8]

The shared nature of this belief was apparent in what was and was not
written about Pullman. In the years leading up to the 1894 strike, investigators who looked at the lives of women and children in Pullman declared
them to be more desirable than comparable lives in virtually any other
location they studied. Compared with such working-class areas as Five
Points, Hull-House, Back of the Yards, and Homestead, Pullman seemed
to provide its families with a life that other working-class Americans and
immigrants could only dream.[9] In particular Pullman provided married
women protection from the city. Typical was the 1884 report of a team of
state labor commissioners headed by Carroll Wright: "In fact the women
were in love with the place; its purity of air, cleanliness of houses and
streets, and lessened household burdens, are advantages over their former
residences which brought out the heartiest expressions of approval. . . .
Pullman has really wrought a greater change for the women than for any
other class of its dwellers." Equally typical were the biting critiques of the
model town written before the strike that became strangely silent or

grudgingly positive when they came to the topic of women and children. Even Ely's indictment contained positive testimony about the town and its women.[10] A system that allowed a man to take care of those dependent on him inside the home was something to be desired, even if Pullman's paternalism was seen as wrong outside the home.

Yet if virtual unanimity reigned on the goal of providing adequately for women and children, how to achieve it and who should be responsible for it were consistently negotiated inside Pullman and strained by conditions outside. For George Pullman his visionary planning, his greater paternalism as it were, lay at the heart of this success. His architectural and social plans for the town aimed at a community built on strong families defined along the lines of George Pullman's rigidly gendered world.[11] By building homes close to the car works and providing no cafeteria, Pullman could encourage men to eat lunch at home with their wives and children. Taverns were prohibited to encourage men to spend their evenings at home and their money in the interests of their families.[12] Few jobs for women of any age were designed for the car works or the town. Instead, women were to foster an atmosphere in the homes that echoed the moral and physical environment of the town. Within those homes wives and children would be protected from the vicissitudes of the industrial world that their husbands faced daily at the Pullman Car Works. Inside the home men would find the comfort and solace they needed from the women who lived there. Even such an outspoken opponent of Pullman as the Reverend William Carwardine could describe that relationship in the following glowing terms: "Blessed are those women, found in every sphere of life, who, like angels of lights, accompany the sorrowful sons of men, to illumine the darkness of their ways, to sweeten the sorrows of life's cup of bitterness, to share the burden too heavy to be borne alone, and to sing the cheering song of hope in the night of desponding gloom."[13]

While most Pullman workers ascribed to this ideal, few were willing to credit George Pullman or his visions for the degree to which the ideal was achieved. The physical attributes of the town were not the cause of this "improved" status of their wives and children; rather, the town was just the site for it—a town/neighborhood that allowed their families to take advantage of the opportunities that were due them as the dependents of American workers. Credit should more appropriately be given to the workers themselves for their hard work that permitted their families to take advantage of the amenities the town offered. Children and wives did not have to work outside the home, and few had to bring work into the home to make ends meet because Pullman workers could and did provide for their families. Indeed, their wages and their decision to work at and live in Pullman made it possible not only to provide but to provide a healthful, safe, and pleasant environment for their families that also offered options for the future—home ownership outside Pullman, educational opportunities for children, and additional money for savings or to send to relatives elsewhere.

It was precisely because this most fundamental tenet of American manhood—providing for one's family—was achievable for so many Pullman workers that a profound ambivalence permeated their attitudes toward life in Pullman. Few would argue that Pullman was the ideal employer or landlord. Many would have preferred not to have to walk the four blocks to one of the twenty-six taverns in Kensington to have a beer. All would have liked lower rents, steadier work, and some insurance against injury and old age. Without a doubt all wished that company spies, paid and voluntary, were not present to report on questionable activities. Many parents of unemployed teenaged daughters pushed for more women's jobs for them to assume. Catholics and Lutherans were probably dissatisfied that they had to walk to the unsettled area across the railroad tracks from Pullman to services instead of being able to remain in town. Virtually all would have liked Pullman better had they not always feared the heavy hand of George Pullman's will, which on many occasions they had seen translated into actions they feared and hated.

Yet for those who chose to work and live in Pullman these were inconveniences and annoyances that could be tolerated in exchange for the wages and the kind of lifestyle and opportunity for families that Pullman also provided. While men struggled over notions of independence and success in the constraining atmosphere of Pullman, their wives seemed to have achieved at least some aspects of the home-based ideal that the workers, reformers, and Pullman all considered appropriate for women. In helping their wives to enjoy aspects of those evolving definitions of womanhood and their families to develop possibilities for the future, the married Pullman workers reasserted their manhood that the system seemed otherwise to undermine.[14]

For that reason they lived and worked in Pullman. Some families came to Pullman for what it offered and represented as well as for the available jobs.[15] Those who found that the negatives outweighed the positives left; those who read the scales differently stayed. The balance was, however, contested because Pullman and his residents saw the reasons for this "success" so differently. It was also a precarious balance because its success was highly dependent on adequate wages and because the limits of the two paternalisms—that of George Pullman and that of the male workers within their homes—were never clear. This was especially the case when people or situations did not fit agreed-upon categories. Whenever that fragile balance shifted, concerns about women and gender roles became both visible and volatile.

At the heart of this gendered reading of Pullman lay several recurring themes. The first revolved around the nature of control within and the boundaries around the household. The second turned on the issue of who provided for households when accidents or economic circumstances prohibited the household from providing the protection its members deserved. The third involved the implications of work for those Pullman women who worked outside the home. All three issues emerged in the years leading up to the strike and boiled to the surface during it. In fact they explain much of the widespread public support Chicagoans gave the Pullman strikers in the long, hungry summer of 1894.

This first issue addressed the physical and functional boundaries around the paternalisms. Certainly this was a critical element in the ongoing debate over the company's refusal to sell workers their homes in Pullman and its powerful influence on the use of public space. On those issues, opinion was very divided. When the struggle had to do with controlling time and resources within the household, however, almost all commentators came down on the side of the male provider and his family. Pullman residents were so confident of that response that they shared violations of it with the Chicago newspapers.[16] As one women complained to a reporter in 1886, "One fine morning a number of men . . . will knock at your door and tell you that they have come to whitewash your house. They will not bother you with questions, . . . but they just go in and do it . . . all charges for repairs . . . will be DEDUCTED FROM YOUR WAGES next pay day. You would have liked to wait another week . . . because you wanted to buy a pair of shoes for your boy. The company can't care about that!"[17] Pullman trespassed not only on the family's space but also on its wage, both of which the dominant ideology would have made the responsibility of the male worker.

Another example illustrates even more clearly the contention over authority in the household and gender roles. In this instance a molder described the scene he found when he returned home after work. There he found his wife in tears. "She told me that the agent had called, and had found a little heap of offal in a corner of the kitchen. My wife had been sick that day and had not been able to do her housework as thoroughly as usual. The inspector then began talking roughly and threatened that they would have us put out of the house."[18] Although the unspoken implication behind his remarks was that no company official should be in his house, his subsequent explanation emphasized that the company agent was a man and that a man should not be intervening in his household, that such visits would be better made by a woman. The Pullman Company heeded his message and largely abandoned such visits. Instead, the Pullman Women's Union, composed of the wives of Pullman's more well-to-do citizens and the town's professional women, informally took over those tasks.[19] These women served as a kind of welcome wagon to new residents to Pullman, especially targeting immigrant women they felt needed assistance in learning to cope with both the Pullman and the American systems. Some residents found their services unnecessary and invasive, but others, particularly families who had exhausted all their financial resources, actively sought out their help. The Women's Union thus began to distribute money and services to the needy Pullman families who were always present but rarely acknowledged.[20]

The presence of needy families and the constant fear that an accident or layoff might plunge any family into the same condition provided the circumstances for the second conflicted area within this general consensus. Who was responsible for those not protected by steady work or a steady worker? That question was always open because the ultimate responsibility inside Pullman was always unclear. The resonance of the question beyond Pullman made it a powerful magnet for outside attention as well.

The experience of the widow Bucklin illustrates the constant negotiation over the appropriate answer. On May 7, 1883, the *Chicago Herald* published a letter to the people of Chicago from J.T., a "poor mechanic" unable to get out of Pullman and afraid to give his real name. In it he called the people of Chicago's "kind attention to a sad and painful case of landlordism in Pullman . . . a family by the name of Bucklin." About a year earlier Captain Bucklin and his two sons had drowned in a boating accident on Lake Calumet, leaving his wife and six daughters with no visible means of support. A collection was taken inside Pullman, and the Pullman Company allocated Mrs. Bucklin one of the large homes on Florence Avenue to use as a boardinghouse to support herself and her daughters. After three rent-free months the company began assessing its usual fees.

For whatever unspecified reasons, Mrs. Bucklin was unable to make a go of the boardinghouse, and she fell severely behind in her rent, causing the Pullman Company to ask her to leave. As J.T. continued the story:

> They got ten days' notice to get out, and before it expired they sent men from Pullman's works and pitched out her furniture in the yard, because the other tenant wanted to get in on the order issued. . . . Poor Mrs. Bucklin and her daughters cried bitterly, and she fainted away, and I heard the Baptist clergyman was there and wept also. What I ask of you is to send one of your reporters to the people that know about the outrage, and ask them what they think about Mr. Pullman and his methods, and also to Mrs. Bucklin. It is a sad and shameful case, and wants your kind attention. . . .[21]

Reporters from the Chicago papers rushed to Pullman to chronicle the family's plight. In every instance they presented it in terms of which J.T. would heartily approve—the heartless Pullman Company was picking on a defenseless widow and her daughters, and, as proprietor of the model town, it should stop the cruelty and then solve the problem. Fear of public condemnation for abandoning Mrs. Bucklin led the company to pay to move her to a new boardinghouse in Grand Crossing and make her initial rent payments there.

This strategic use of public opinion, combined with an appeal to a sense of corporate obligation when usual protections faltered, worked in several other instances to force the Pullman Company into similar generous actions. More often, however, the company was willing to suspend its commitment to the strictly gendered ideal that had been built into the model town. One of its first capitulations was already apparent in the Bucklin story. The house she was given for boarders was, in fact, one of the showpiece managers' homes on Florence Boulevard. Not only did that violate the social hierarchy built into the model town, it also transgressed the initial social commitment to flats designed for single families. Boarding was never an idea anyone eagerly embraced, yet it was a practice both workers and management could accept inside the broader framework. By the economic downturn of the mid-1880s the company had accepted boarding as a partial solution for several problems facing the model town. It provided supplemental income to households hit by layoffs and pay cuts, the same households where union activity was often the strongest. Boarding created additional housing for a work force that was already more numerous than the available housing either in Pullman or in neighboring Roseland and Kensington. Moreover, it kept many single male employees within the controlled Pullman environment and away from the more questionable activities that gave Kensington the nickname of Bumtown.

Pullman families embraced boarding first as a means of meeting economic crisis and later, when prosperity returned, as a way of enabling a better future. The three dollars a week earned for each person who ate with them and five dollars a week for each person who both lived and ate with them let families go beyond meeting basic expenses and provided the down payments for many homes in Roseland.[22] By 1892 almost half of the Pullman homes hosted at least one boarder—and almost a fourth of the Pullman work force lived in their own homes outside Pullman. Boarding also allowed the town's married women to stay inside their homes and provided jobs for many of its single women.[23]

Both of these options seemed preferable to the other schemes the Pullman Company advanced to provide jobs for women and children. Although the *Tribune* claimed that manufactories that hired women and children had always been a part of Pullman's long-range planning, this strategy first appeared publicly in 1883. That year George Pullman hired a former executive in a thread company with a view toward bringing a knitting works to Pullman. The balloon the company floated involved as many as two thousand jobs, specifically designed for those women and children who had not previously worked in factory jobs, at least in Pullman. Although such a factory had the potential to increase household incomes substantially, there was little enthusiasm for the idea. At best, Pullmanites shared the sentiments of the *Chicago Daily News* when it described the employment of women and children in such a factory as something "which is profitable to both the employers and the employees, and is not unhealthy, however uncongenial it may be to the latter."[24] This uncongeniality discouraged all attempts at building such a factory until 1888, when a knitting factory was finally built on the edge of the city. Designed to provide two hundred jobs, it never attracted that many workers and failed before the Pullman strike.[25]

The Pullman Car Works was more successful in attracting women workers. The upholstery department had provided jobs for some fifty women since the beginning, and a handful of women worked as more highly paid embossers in the paint department. When the Pullman laundry finally opened in 1892, another hundred women joined the ranks of Pullman workers. These jobs, less desirable because of the wages and working conditions, became the Pullman jobs of last resort.[26] Included in the ranks of the laundresses were higher proportions of daughters supporting widowed mothers and other women upon whom the entire burden of family support fell.

As is clear, many, arguably even most, Pullman women worked. Yet the broader significance of that work provided the third ongoing discussion about the role of women in the model town. Ostensibly, families inside the town and the Pullman management agreed that honest work, whether working in a knitting factory or paint department or taking boarders into their homes, was a worthy and appropriate task for women, even if it was not the ideal. In a rare instance when the *Tribune* spoke equally well for both labor and management, it described these working women as "industrious, intelligent, and exemplary in their lives and deportment" and contended that "from their ranks hundreds of the future wives and mothers of Pullman will be drawn."[27] Yet this point apparently needed to be made constantly, both inside and outside Pullman.

Any attempt to question the reputations of these working women met strong opposition. For example, the ubiquity of boarders was often scrutinized for its potentially immoral impact on women and families.[28] Perhaps as a result, boardinghouse keepers were regularly described in the most moral of terms. Indeed, Mrs. Bucklin and her daughters continued to appear in the Pullman social news long after they departed to their boardinghouse in Grand Crossing, and their devout and cultured natures were regularly highlighted. The reputation of women who worked in the car works was even more fiercely guarded. When the newly organized Calumet Pleasure Club let it be publicly known that the young women who worked there were not welcome at its dances, "A Citizen" immediately fired off a letter to the editor of the *Chicago Herald:* "If such is the case I would like to ask the club to show me where it can find a more select and respectable lot of young ladies than there are in Pullman. . . . in order to be successful they [the club's members] denounce the young ladies who earn an honest living and receive more salary than these would be swells."[29]

Gendered Ideals in the 1894 Strike

All of these issues came together on the eve of the Pullman strike in the person of Jennie Curtis, the seamstress who was credited by many with winning the American Railway Union's support for the strikers. Curtis's story is well known to anyone familiar with the traditional strike narratives.[30] When her father died, he left the family in debt to the Pullman

Company for back rent and with no resources or reserves. As a result, she had to work for the company to support the family, and both the current and back rents fell squarely on her shoulders. As economic conditions worsened in the year before the strike, the Curtis family situation, like that of many others, became increasingly precarious. When the ARU began organizing in the car works, Curtis took a lead in organizing women workers. Throughout the strike's early phase she played an important role, yet in every instance her participation was defined within Pullman's carefully gendered world. No event better symbolized this than her widely publicized dance with Chicago Mayor John P. Hopkins at the first benefit for the Pullman strikers. A former employee and resident of Pullman, Hopkins chose Curtis as his partner to honor her dual identity as striker and woman.[31]

Those identities, along with that of being a fatherless child, also played a prominent role in her presentation to the convention of the ARU.[32] One of the key injustices she described was having to pay off her father's debts. In doing so she drew attention to injustices of a paternalistic system that did not provide for those who were innocent victims of unfortunate circumstance. Another injustice was one she shared with her male counterparts. Having been thrust into the role of provider, she could not support her family when there were cutbacks in wages and hours. A third illustrated a unique, gendered twist. She complained about her forelady who did not treat her or her coworkers with the respect due them as future wives and mothers.

If Curtis's speech provided the final push necessary to convince the ARU delegates, despite Eugene V. Debs's hesitancy, that they should boycott Pullman cars, it did so in large part because it played on the idealized gender themes that had already won the general public's support for the strikers' cause.[33] Pullman workers understood from the beginning of the strike that their support had to come not only from labor but also from a much wider public, including people like Addams, if they were to win. The themes that Curtis used so effectively with the railwaymen therefore assumed great importance. The victimization of women and children, couched in terms of George Pullman's paternalism that prohibited the smooth functioning of the male wage earners' ability to provide, became a key theme in winning the public's hearts and minds.

The story of that suffering was easy to construct because it so closely reflected the reality of the Pullman families in the months leading up to the Pullman strike. As the general economy worsened in 1893 and orders for railroad cars fell at Pullman, the company laid off workers and cut wages.[34] Workers who could find better jobs elsewhere left, leaving empty flats that Pullman encouraged those still working to occupy. More immediately crucial, however, they left hundreds of vacant boarding rooms and beds, each of which had earlier contributed to family coffers. The discriminatory policies on cuts within the works further undermined certain workers. Seamstresses' wages, for example, fell from a bimonthly average of $16.87 to $8.28, while average wages for the rest of the work force fell from $25.53 to $16.85.[35]

At the same time, household expenses increased as the bitter winter of 1893–94 raised the cost of heating and spread sickness. The results were devastating for Pullman residents. Mechanisms to help individuals and families through economic crisis crumbled and collapsed. The Pullman Women's Union minutes for 1893–94 document an ever-lengthening list of needy families in debt to grocers, butchers, doctors, and coal dealers. Having exhausted the support of extended family members and religious and ethnic benevolent associations, hungry Pullman families turned to the Women's Union for help.[36] In neighboring Roseland the families of Pullman workers who had bought their way out of the town sought help from the Roseland Women's Union. When the resources of that organization failed, it turned to the Pullman Women's Union, emphasizing the needy's connections to Pullman. Because the need outstripped the available funding, the request was denied.

By May of 1894 the situation had grown so desperate that Pullman workers turned at last to George Pullman. For many the meeting was the inevitable confrontation between employer and employees with a clearly defined set of workplace demands for higher wages, more hours, and the abolition of arbitrary work rules. But for others the meeting involved a logic consistent with that used by J.T. a decade earlier to describe the Bucklin eviction. George Pullman and the Pullman Company had an obligation to provide for those who could not provide for themselves. When Vice President T. H. Wickes and then George Pullman refused to shoulder that obligation, the Pullman Strike Committee fixed responsibility for the economic crisis in Pullman on George Pullman, not on the general economic conditions that afflicted millions of other workers in Chicago and across the country. George Pullman, his model town, and his employment policies caused women and children in Pullman to suffer. If he deserved credit for creating the environment that made their lives better, then he also deserved the blame when their lives were worse. If the labor of the male workers provided for their families, then the man who took away that labor or at least appropriate pay for it was equally to blame.

That bilevel analysis provided an effective framework for strikers to publicize their cause. By the end of the first week of the Pullman strike even the *Tribune*, a longtime opponent of strikes, described the situation in Pullman as follows:

> Starvation is threatening many families in Pullman. The people are largely Americans who have been used to earning and enjoying the comforts of life, and they are proud. They are extremely reluctant to give their names, and many of them are enduring the pangs of hunger rather than let their condition be known. . . . It must not be understood that want has been known in Pullman only since the strike began . . . But still it is a fact that many a sober, intelligent man, an expert mechanic, for a man must be an expert to work in the Pullman shops, has fallen at his work for want of sufficient food.

The story recounted the plight of various Pullman families. In one three-room apartment the reporter found a Pullman worker, his sick and hungry wife, and his three children. The wife claimed that her family had gone without food and that her husband had fainted at work from hunger. "I do not want to live this way any longer," she said. "I sometimes think I will take the children and jump into the lake."[37] Stories identifying starving families appeared regularly in the Chicago newspapers and often in national publications. Almost all the stories blamed the hunger on Pullman policies.[38] Men who could not earn enough to support their families could not be guilty. They were superior workman—as George Pullman had boasted for fourteen years. They played by the rules as society and Pullman described them, did not drink or spend their money foolishly, and sent their children to school, not into the factory. Their wives led exemplary lives, creating the home environment that every reformer prescribed. If there was hunger, the fault was Pullman's.

This rhetoric shaped how the strike was managed as well. For example, maintaining an air of propriety was critical. Violence might break out elsewhere in Chicago or the United States but *not* in Pullman. It would have sullied the image that was necessary to maintain support and to keep relief supplies coming. That intersection of image and reality also affected the distribution of relief. The Pullman Strike Committee decided early that aid went only to ARU members with dependents. Single men, whether union or not, were refused aid. This strategy responded to those most desperately in need and provided a powerful basis for appeal to potential donors. As time passed, a preference for the families of strikers living inside Pullman rather than outside Pullman also emerged, reflecting the idea that it was Pullman's landlord status that made this strike different from others.[39]

Partly because of these strategies, food and other critical supplies poured in from all kinds of unexpected sources. Chicago, Cook County, and the state of Illinois were all contributing to the Pullman strikers at the same time President Grover Cleveland was smashing the ARU. Mayor Hopkins, once a favored employee of Pullman but now a bitter enemy, spearheaded the city's drive for aid and assistance.[40] The Cook County Board provided both county relief and personal contributions.[41] Governor John Peter Altgeld visited the homes of starving Pullman families, stopping to talk with the infirm and the mothers of hungry children. News artists captured those images—of a poor blind widow and a mother with her hungry child—for the local papers.[42] Local ethnic and daily newspapers from the *Swedish Tribune* to the *Chicago Tribune* established strike funds to help ward off starvation in strikers' families. Despite riots along the stockyard rail lines the Swift Company sent a carload of meat for the hungry women and children of Pullman.[43] Combined with donations from workers and unions from across the country, these helped to keep minimal food available.

Clearly, both male and female strikers had captured the moral high ground by emphasizing that they were fighting for their rights to protect the women and children dependent on them. The point was not lost on George Pullman that any attempts to end the strike would have to deny the strikers their singular claim to this position. Pullman shrewdly began to use these gendered roles to his advantage. When the decision was made to reopen the car works, the company invited the laundresses to return first. Strategically it was a masterful move. Those returning were daughters of Dutch workers from Roseland, whose families had suffered from selective relief policies, and young Pullman women supporting widowed mothers and siblings, who had begun the strike with fewer resources than their male counterparts had.[44] In both cases some income was critical for maintaining the family. They returned, as one Pullman laundress said, not as scabs: "I am working to earn bread for myself and my mother." To the still-striking workers and their families, they were scabs and deserved to be treated as such. But to the general public, they were also women deserving of special treatment, a distinction that the company could play to its advantage. As the local police accompanied the Hollanders down the hill from Roseland, "several hundred women, wives and sisters of the strikers" met them at Pullman's western edge, threw mud at them, and "reviled the girls."[45]

One can only guess what the public response would have been to this confrontation had the strikebreakers been male. Now those same individuals and groups who had supported the Pullman strike because of the responsible workers and their vulnerable families threatened to turn away. The *Tribune* headlined its report on the story with "They Cry for Gore: Amazons Menace the Holland Laundry Girls at Pullman." It labeled one particularly aggressive defender an "old hag of a woman," and even the more "comely looking acted as if they had gone mad."[46] Women were no longer victims in Pullman; they were also victimizers. Starving women deserved support and sympathy; confrontational women denying starving women and families deserved nothing. Pullman strikers certainly did not see the incident in the same light. Pullman women had been integrally involved with the strike from the beginning, seeking the hungriest to give them food, organizing dances and other money-making activities to replenish strike funds, looking for jobs outside Pullman to support their families, chasing scabs to keep the car works closed, and struggling to keep their families intact. Pullman women—wives, mothers, daughters, and striking employees—were heroines, acting to help the strikers achieve their goal of what was best for all.

Yet as the strike moved into its third month, the issue of what was best for all became increasingly contested. Single men who remained in Pullman had not had relief in months. Families in Roseland and Kensington, half of the Pullman strikers, had seen their portion of supplies diminish as relief shipments came marked for the "neediest families in Pullman." Gradually these workers began to return to the car works, and those living in Pullman started to follow. As a Pullman resident asked plaintively, "What's a poor fellow like me to do?"[47] For some 40 percent of the prestrike force the solution was to return to work.[48] Continuing to strike had become the option that kept them from improving their families' condition. Returning to work meant not only a job but also five dollars from the company to meet immediate needs and the promise of additional credit at local stores that, after months of deferring payment, had denied strikers any more assistance.[49] Moreover, after having been publicly excoriated for threatening evictions, the company now forgave back rent, relieving renters of one of their largest debts and strikers of one of their most powerful charges against the company. Visiting reporters wrote of families whose fathers had returned to work and streets where children with full stomachs now played happily. For these heads of families, some 40 percent of the prestrike work force, the strike of 1894 had ended, and the negotiations over what it meant to be a provider began again.

For those who continued to hold out the results were devastating. With work again available, contributions to strike relief lessened dramatically. Without relief, these families experienced what the Chicago press recounted in terms of hunger and tears. Tears streamed down the "sunburned cheeks of a tall yellow-haired Swede" as he peered through the window of an empty relief headquarters because his wife and his babies were starving and he could not help them. Women wept bitterly in the gallery of the Kensington Turner Hall while organizers described how many former ARU members had returned to their jobs and reviewed the desperate conditions of the families of workers still on strike. By the fourth week in August the strike was over. The Salvation Army assumed control of relief, opening it up to those without ARU cards, the unmarried, and residents of all the affected communities. Trains brought women carrying food baskets from Chicago to relieve the hunger in Pullman. The *Tribune* made this task even easier by publishing a list of Pullman's neediest families, complete with names, circumstances, and addresses.[50]

To many Chicagoans, even those who blamed labor and the ARU for the chaos and violence of the boycott, the neediest families still seemed the victims of George Pullman. Those blacklisted had to find work elsewhere, a task made more difficult by Pullman's vindictiveness.[51] Those who wanted their jobs back but were not rehired were also seen as victims of Pullman's unwillingness to bend. They, too, had to look elsewhere or hope that they could return to their Pullman jobs when economic conditions improved. In the meantime their families went hungry because the Pullman system had promised much but under pressure had taken away even more.

Conclusion

The 1894 strike revived and expanded the questions about urban, industrial society that the Pullman experiment had originally promised to answer. If men were to work and provide for their dependents, who was responsible for those dependents when conditions kept male workers from working and providing? If employers could not be trusted to see and seek the common good when it conflicted with their own perceived best intentions, who or what might be expected to make the structural changes and provide the protections that seemed necessary to avoid the class warfare that shocked Chicago and the nation during the summer of 1894? What were the limits of social planning?

These were the questions with which Addams struggled as she wrote "A Modern Lear." She did not have the answers, but what she suggested by using Lear and his daughters was the common ground of a highly gendered view of society that would shape reform in the United States in the decades following the Pullman strike. Understanding what was common and what was contested about that view of society allows us to see the Pullman strike as a window not only into the nineteenth-century debate over citizen workers but also into the very gendered social imagination of the twentieth century.[52]

It is not surprising then that "A Modern Lear" did not appear until eighteen years later, when a new set of answers had been offered for the questions raised by the Pullman strike. Nor is it surprising that many of those answers rested on gendered solutions to urban America's problems. If Pullman had shown how easily society could be torn apart, Lear's daughters demonstrated how all sides might attempt to hold it together.

Notes

An earlier version of this essay appeared in the *Journal of Urban History* 23 (March 1997): 316–40. Copyright © 1997 by Sage Publications. Reprinted by permission of Sage Publications.

1. Jane Addams, *Twenty Years at Hull-House* (New York: Macmillan, 1910), 214, suggests that nothing in her experience prepared her for the class bitterness she saw that summer.

2. Jane Addams, "A Modern Lear," in Graham Romeyn Taylor, *Satellite Cities* (New York: D. Appleton, 1915), 68–90.

3. Richard T. Ely, "Pullman: A Social Study," *Harper's Monthly* 70 (February 1885): 452–66.

4. New York Sun, October 10, 1885, and *Chicago Times*, September 4, 1886, Pullman Scrapbooks, series A, Pullman Company Archives, Newberry Library, Chicago (hereafter PANL). My forthcoming book discusses how successful Pullman was in exerting his will.

5. For Debs, citizenship, and manhood, see Nick Salvatore, *Eugene V. Debs: Citizen and Socialist* (Urbana: University of Illinois Press, 1982); United States Strike Commission, *Report on the Chicago Strike of June–July, 1894* (Washington, D.C.: Government Printing Office, 1895).

6. Carl Smith, *Urban Disorder and the Shape of Belief: The Great Chicago Fire, the Haymarket Bomb and the Model Town of Pullman* (Chicago: University of Chicago Press, 1995), 255–58, describes this effort fully.

7. In addition to Pullman studies cited elsewhere in the notes, for this tradition, see Almont Lindsey, *The Pullman Strike: The Story of a Unique Experiment and of a Great Labor Upheaval* (Chicago: University of Chicago Press, 1942), the classic text on the strike itself; Richard Sennett, *Authority* (New York: Knopf, 1980), 62–67, for the grimmest picture of Pullman; Gerald Zahavi, *Workers, Managers, and Welfare Capitalism* (Urbana: University of Illinois Press, 1988), 3, for Pullman and the town as "small, gray, lifeless communities, created and dominated by visions of wealth, power or misguided patriarchy"; and James Brady Smithson, "The Incorporation of Community: An Analysis of the Model Town of Pullman, Illinois, as a Social Experiment" (Ph.D. thesis, Cornell University, 1988), for Pullman as an experiment in community. Stanley Buder, *Pullman: An Experiment in Industrial Order and Community Planning, 1880–1930* (New York: Oxford University Press, 1967), goes into the teens and twenties but with less emphasis or detail than on the model town. Only Douglas P. Hoover, "Women in Nineteenth Century Pullman" (M.A. thesis, University of Arizona, 1988), specifically considers women.

8. Eileen Boris, *Home to Work* (Cambridge: Cambridge University Press, 1994), 21–48, and Alice Kessler-Harris, *A Women's Wage* (Lexington: University of Kentucky Press, 1990), discuss this assumption.

9. Addams, *Twenty Years at Hull-House*. Although one must use evidence from a later date cautiously, the portrait of the Rudzikas women in Upton Sinclair's novel *The Jungle* is a vivid portrait of the fate of working-class women and households in turn-of-the-century Chicago.

10. Carroll D. Wright, *Pullman: A Joint Report* (Boston: Wright and Potter Printing, 1884), 9–10; Ely, "Pullman," 461–63.

11. James B. Gilbert, *Perfect Cities: Chicago's Utopias of 1893* (Chicago: University of Chicago Press, 1991), 131–68, ties these assumptions to Pullman's experiences, emphasizing Mrs. Pullman's ideas of middle-class families and her wish to apply those ideas to Pullman residents.

12. Buder, *Pullman*, 120–22, details the prohibition on taverns. However, alcohol was easily accessible to Pullman workers. Beer wagons sold and delivered beer on the town's streets for years. See the testimony of Rev. Morris L. Wickman (and others), in United States Strike Commission, *Report*, 463.

13. Quote from the sermon "A Girl's Choice" preached at the Adams Street Church, the next parish at which he served, on November 12, 1899, and delivered at all his subsequent parishes. Carwardine emphasized these sentiments in his lecture tours after the strike. A letter from the Pullman Strike Committee included in his papers says, "He is respected by all and loved by many. We heartily indorse all that he writes about the present strike and town of Pullman and can vouch for

the truth of the statements he makes." Carwardine Papers, Garrett Theological Seminary, Evanston, Ill.

14. Nancy Fraser and Linda Gordon, "A Genealogy of Dependency: Tracing a Keyword of the U.S. Welfare State," *Signs* 19 (Winter 1994): 309–26. In times of economic stress workers regularly pointed to the different needs of married and single men and accused the company of favoring whichever status they were not.

15. When I presented an earlier version of this essay, an audience member explained how her great-grandmother had asked her great-grandfather to leave his job elsewhere in Chicago to move to Pullman for the opportunities for their children. Versions of that story abound among longtime Pullman families, as do stories of people taking the train into Chicago and seeing the beautiful little town of Pullman and deciding they wanted to live there.

16. Pullman workers regularly used the Chicago press to voice their concerns. An anonymous letter would appear in a newspaper purporting to give a "true" picture of Mr. Pullman's model town. The letter would often provoke a series of exposés on Pullman.

17. Quoted in unidentified newspaper, May 19, 1886, Town Scrapbooks, vol. 1, PANL. The newspaper is not indicated, but a reference to another article suggests that it appeared in the *Sun*.

18. Ibid.

19. Although dominated by wives of Pullman officials, wives of businessmen in Kensington and Pullman were also included.

20. A list of requests and services, in the Minute Books of the Women's Union, Archives, Historic Pullman Foundation, Chicago.

21. *Chicago Herald*, May 7, 1883, Town Scrapbooks, vol. 1, PANL. The only slight variation on the theme raised an even more complex issue. It pointed out that the Pullman Company had a better tenant, "a negro; but what difference did that make the Pullman Company?"

22. The dollar figures appeared in the *Arcade Mercantile Journal* (Pullman) 1 (December 7, 1889): 5. Boarding here clearly meant simply eating. The *Journal*, edited by Duane Doty, the town agent, served as a source of local news, an advertising organ of the Pullman Arcade that was increasingly challenged by stores in Kensington and Roseland, and a purveyor of uplifting commentary.

23. Mrs. Duane Doty, *The Town of Pullman: Its Growth with Brief Accounts of Its Industries* (Pullman, Ill.: T. P. Struhsacker, 1893), estimated that at least nine hundred families in Pullman took in boarders. Mrs. Doty indicated there were 1,855 tenements in Pullman (51).

24. *Chicago Daily News*, December 11, 1883, Town Scrapbooks, vol. 1, PANL.

25. Doty, *Town of Pullman*, 116.

26. As other jobs, particularly clerical, opened, laundry work became even less desirable, and it disappeared by World War I.

27. *Chicago Tribune*, May 20, 1888, Town Scrapbooks, vol. 1, PANL.

28. It is fair to say that some domestic violence in Pullman erupted over imagined or real incidents of marital infidelity with boarders, but these incidents were not reported as the logical result of boarding.

29. *Chicago Herald*, May 20, 1887, Town Scrapbooks, vol. 1, PANL.

30. During the 1994 strike centennial celebrations held in Pullman, an actress played Jennie Curtis and, from the front steps of Curtis's former home, told her story to thousands of visitors.

31. *Chicago Tribune*, September 20, 1888, Town Scrapbooks, vol. 2, PANL.

32. The *Chicago Times* reported her presentation on June 13, 1894.

33. W. T. Stead, *Chicago To-day: The Labour War in America* (New York: Arno Press and the New York Times, 1969), 187–88.

34. The Pullman payrolls document the general decrease in the work force. The payroll for the first half of May in 1893 had 4,643 names; for the first half of May in 1894 it had 3,289 names. Microfilms of the payrolls in Pullman Company Archives, Newberry Library.

35. Ibid. There were fifty seamstresses in 1893 and thirty-eight in 1894. The comparative numbers are calculated for all workers who were not seamstresses. This fact was publicized by Rena Michaels Atchison of the Equal Suffrage Association of Illinois, "Women Sufferers at Pullman," *Chicago Evening Post*, May 23, 1894. It reported that men's wages fell from 33 to 57 percent, while women's wages fell 50 percent and in many cases substantially more.

36. For a complete list of names and needs, see the Minute Books of the Pullman Women's Union. The Chicago papers' lists of the starving during the strike often noted that families were deeply in debt before the strike began.

37. Quoted in *Chicago Tribune*, May 17, 1894, Strike Scrapbooks, vol. 1, PANL.

38. Not all these publications supported the strike without criticism. But the stories of starvation also noted that the wealthy Pullman Company could probably have done something to alleviate it. There was also a sense of having been "taken." The Brickyard homes—wooden frame shanties—appeared in stories that earlier had showcased only the brick flats and public buildings. Women who had visited Pullman for social events in the past now expressed indignation that they had never see this "other side."

39. This difference between Roseland, Kensington, and Pullman is another important dimension of the strike that will be covered more fully in my forthcoming book *Manufacturing a Community: Pullman Workers and Their Towns, 1880–1981*. Estimates at the end of the strike suggested about half of the strikers lived inside Pullman and that the rest lived in one of the neighboring communities.

40. Hopkins's first individual gift came during the first week of the strike. See *Chicago Tribune*, May 17, 1894, Strike Scrapbooks, vol. 1, PANL. Several weeks later Hopkins led the city appeal. See *Chicago Tribune*, June 5, 1894, ibid. The local alderman was also active in seeking the support of the city council. The *Chicago Evening Journal* reported that city hall donated $2,000 of the approximately

$19,000 contributed to the Pullman Strike Fund by the middle of August. See "How the Case Stands," August 21, 1894, Strike Scrapbooks, vol. 8, PANL. Other gifts came from individuals and agencies. The Chicago Fire Department contributed $909 to the strike fund, and the Grand Crossing police gave $46. See William H. Carwardine, *The Pullman Strike* (1894; reprint, with an introduction and bibliography by Virgil J. Vogel, Chicago: Charles H. Kerr, 1973), 42–43.

41. *Chicago Tribune,* June 5, 1894, Strike Scrapbooks, vol. 1, PANL. The *Chicago Evening Dispatch,* August 22, 1894, reported that county employees had contributed $1,027.28 to the relief fund. Two days later the paper reported that "Chicago, Cook County, and the entire state of Illinois are bending their energies to keep these people [in Pullman] from starving to death." Strike Scrapbooks, vol. 8, PANL.

42. *Chicago Tribune,* August 21, 1894, described the fates of Mrs. O'Halloran, Mrs. O'Conner, and Mrs. Lengstone, whose families suffered a particularly grim fate, while the *Chicago Herald* used the governor's visit to inform readers that in Pullman "Larders are Empty," August 21, 1894. Even the largely unsympathetic *Chicago Evening Journal* editorial of August 21 admitted, "In the face of actual starvation, however, there is, of course, no room for argument, and this is particularly the case where the sufferers are innocent women and children." Strike Scrapbooks, vol. 8, PANL.

43. *Chicago Times,* August 24, 1894, reported that the donation of the beef was the result of the efforts of W. J. Bailey, a Kensington butcher. Other papers cited the Swift donation as an example of the greater Chicago effort to aid the starving at Pullman. Strike Scrapbooks, vol. 8, PANL.

44. The case of the Dutch workers in the strike had been complicated from the outset because of religious strictures against joining a union. A special Dutch branch had to be organized so that the out-of-work Dutch could also get relief.

45. *Chicago Evening Post,* July 21, 1894, Strike Scrapbooks, vol. 6, PANL.

46. *Chicago Tribune,* July 21, 1894, Strike Scrapbooks, vol. 6, PANL.

47. "Minions of the Duke, White Slaves of Pretty Pullman," *Chicago Herald,* May 31, 1890, Pullman Scrapbooks, series A, vol. 13 (1889–90), PANL.

48. Forty percent is the best estimate of how many names on the May (first half) 1895 payroll appeared on the May (first half) 1889, 1893, or 1894 payrolls. Microfilms of payrolls in the PANL.

49. *Chicago Evening Journal,* August 21, 1894, Strike Scrapbooks, vol. 8, PANL.

50. Ibid; *Chicago Times,* August 16, 1894; *Chicago Record,* August 17, 1894; *Chicago Tribune,* August 26, 1894, Strike Scrapbooks, vol. 8, PANL.

51. Addams, *Twenty Years at Hull-House,* 218–20, told of a man still suffering the effects of the blacklist ten years after the strike.

52. Theda Skocpol, *Protecting Soldiers and Mothers: The Political Origins of Social Policy in the United States* (Cambridge, Mass.: Belknap of Harvard University Press, 1992), and Linda Gordon, *Pitied but Not Entitled: Single Mothers and the History of Welfare, 1890–1935* (New York: Free Press, 1994), have sketched these ideas out quite clearly.

4

Photography and the Pullman Strike: Remolding Perceptions of Labor Conflict by New Visual Communication

Larry Peterson

Looking back from 1900, Americans would hardly have recognized illustrations of labor conflicts made just a quarter of a century earlier. The great railway strike of 1877 had been depicted according to the canons of narrative history painting. Strikes in the twentieth century were captured immediately through photojournalism. The 1877 strike belonged to a new kind of labor conflict, yet no style of illustration or communications technology could portray its novelty.[1] Twenty years later major newspapers adopted the halftone process and by 1900 replaced drawings with photographs.[2] Henceforth an industrialized medium represented the new forms of class conflict. The most important questions remained to be answered, however. What should be depicted? Who should produce it? How should it be portrayed?

Technology by itself did not create the new photographic image of labor. Rather, new photomechanical media selectively copied, then redefined, and ultimately replaced older imagery that had lost its credibility.[3] The Pullman strike is important because it shows how this credibility was lost and how it was restored. It raised new problems of industrial conflict at the moment when older forms of illustration could no longer be believed but new ones had not yet been formed. After 1900 the photographic image of workers appeared self-evident; all traces of its prephotographic origins were obliterated. In illustrations of the Pullman strike it is possible to see how photography created this new image out of the old.

The Communications Revolution and Industrial Conflict

Photomechanical media were originally intended only to reproduce existing forms of illustration more faithfully, but they inadvertently undermined traditional depictions of labor conflict. They multiplied the types of reproduction media, contrasted photographs directly with drawings on the printed page, and greatly increased the volume of illustrations. They thereby revealed the artistic conventions that underlay previous forms of illustration, discrepancies between fact and artistic imagination, and the failure of artists to develop forms to convey industrial conflict adequately. At first photography offered no clear-cut alternative. Its accomplishments had stimulated the search for more truthful illustrations reproduced more faithfully. But its methods were only partially adaptable to mechanical reproduction, and photographers did not know how to make better pictures. The halftone process therefore generally replaced wood engraving in magazines only after 1890. Process line engraving, a nonhalftone form of photomechanical reproduction, made it possible for newspapers from the 1880s to illustrate fully the news with line drawings but not with tonal sketches or photographs. Though the use of photographs both directly and as copy for sketches grew significantly by 1894, they were not obviously superior to drawings and did not replace them.[4]

The development of the new media between 1880 and 1900 coincided with social and economic changes that fundamentally altered class relations and industrial conflict. The Pullman strike was emblematic of these changes. It was the culmination of a series of smaller strikes between 1882 and 1894 that pitted previously autonomous groups of skilled workers, organized in craft unions, against the encroaching power of a single, large employer. It was therefore fought over the reorganization of the American economy around monopolistic corporations and a restructuring of the labor force that systematically reduced the position and role of skilled craftworkers in production. The Pullman Car Works was a mammoth, new factory, built to secure one corporation's domination over an entire industry. It consolidated the Pullman Company's control over the sleeping-car industry by expanding into the general railcar market and thus achieving economies of scale and vertical integration. To increase productivity and secure control within the factory, its management introduced a series of radical changes in production, especially a much more elaborate division of labor; proto-assembly line organization of work; "scientific" methods of measurement, such as time study; dilution of skilled tasks and where possible their substitution with unskilled labor; bureaucratic regulation of personnel; replacement of American-born workers with immigrants according to racial and ethnic criteria; and even the systematic use of photography to inventory materials, document finished products, and analyze production. Pullman also constructed a model company town to address the social problems caused by the rapid, unplanned growth of America's industrial cities. By paternalistically offering workers a healthy, beautiful environment and regulating their lives outside the factory, Pullman sought to resolve class conflict and reconcile labor to capital.

The Pullman Company adamantly refused, as a corollary of this strategy, to recognize or negotiate with workers' organizations and restricted their access to the factory and town. In disputes from 1882 to 1894 workers tried to reach compromises, presenting their grievances through successive types of organization—ad hoc strike committees, a general union (the Knights of Labor), and craft unions. After repeated failure, they sought the backing of a new kind of industrial union, the American Railway Union (ARU). When the Pullman strike broke out in 1894, the ARU adopted the new form of dynamic, mass industrial strike and, with the centralized backing of a single, national organization, expanded it beyond the scale of 1877. Its success in disrupting nationwide commerce provoked first fear and apprehension in the capitalist class and then contradictory interventions of the federal, state, and local governments to suppress the strike, regulate labor disputes, and break Pullman's monopoly.[5]

Traditional depictions of labor conflict were thus challenged by simultaneous communications and industrial revolutions. The Pullman strike, by its timing and scope, exposed the resulting crisis of representation. The American press reported the strike with vastly more pictures in more media juxtaposing more contradictory styles than in any previous labor conflict: in engravings of original sketches and of sketches based on photographs reproduced by prephotographic, photomechanical, and mixed technologies; in halftone reproductions of photographs both corrected by engravers and unretouched; in photographic prints sold singly, in albums, and as postcards; and in composite engravings based on mixed photographic and nonphotographic sources. Different kinds of illustration, sometimes uncredited or inaccurately credited, were reproduced not only in the same publications but also next to each other on the same page. They were produced before, during, and after events, on the spot and in the central offices of newspapers and magazines, with and without eyewitness knowledge of Chicago or Pullman. They ranged from impression-istic line sketches in newspapers and more substantial pen-and-ink wash drawings in magazines to architectural, panorama, portrait, and product photography. Moreover, while prephotographic conventions were rapidly dissolving, no new ones had been founded to replace them. The halftone process freed artist-illustrators to pursue individualized styles and made the craft of engraving technologically obsolete. But photojournalism did not yet exist as a profession; photographers had few formal ties to jour-nalists and did not know how to portray news events convincingly.[6] Fi-nally, corporations, unions, and government, all of whom relied on the print news media to depict their views and mold public opinion in their favor, were in the process of redefining how they represented themselves. Unable to tell by observation an illustration's source or method of repro-duction, how could viewers trust in its truthfulness?

Nevertheless, magazines in 1894 could reproduce photographs with a degree of verisimilitude that potentially deceived viewers into believing they were witnessing events themselves rather than representations of them. In 1893 the World's Columbian Exposition became the first major event to be reported overwhelmingly in photographs reproduced directly as photographs.[7] The participants in the Pullman strike experimented with different adaptations of traditional imagery to photography, directed at the public through different approaches to the pictorial press, to restore the appearance of truth to their views of labor conflict.

The Pullman Company: The Public Relations of a Model Town

The Pullman Company was the most visually sophisticated partici-pant in the strike. From the building of the Pullman Car Works and model town in 1880 its public relations were insistently modern and photo-graphic. Its huge cash reserves allowed it first to employ a regular pho-tographer and then in 1888 to create a photography department, as well as pay for the most advanced reproduction technologies.[8] Between 1883 and 1893 it published four comprehensively illustrated photographic books on the model town, progressing from hand-mounted prints to photogravure to halftones, and supplied a steady stream of photographs of the town and new Pullman cars to the news media.[9] In them Pullman adapted the dominant urban grand style of photography to the depiction of modern industry and urban reform, comprising the ultramodern factory, mass production, new products and the work teams that produced them, aesthetically distinguished public architecture and landscaped parks, well-groomed workers' families, and company-controlled recreation (see figure 1).[10]

Pullman's radically new corporate image derived its power from the photographic transformation of traditional visual models. In particular it translated the codes of perspectival drawing and Renaissance concepts of verisimilitude, especially the establishment of human scale, three-dimensional space, and hierarchy of value through architecture, to the technical capabilities of the camera. Pullman was so successful that its photographs were easily transformed back into credible drawings to illustrate magazine articles before direct reproduction was possible (see figure 2).[11]

Pullman used the visual symbolism of architecture to represent hierarchical social relations. The monumental factory and public buildings dominated sequences on the town. Workers' houses and popular customs appeared only as barely legible background details in panoramas and product shots.[12] Workers and factory were linked instead in the new image of the factory work force as an industrial army under the command of corporate management, regulated by the factory gate and clock tower (see figure 14, p. 112).[13] Pullman portrayed the model town as a structured

Figure 1. Lake Vista, administration building, and erecting shops looking toward the town of Pullman. Photograph by T. S. Johnson, in Johnson's *Pullman Illustrated*, 1883. (Courtesy of Illinois State Historical Library)

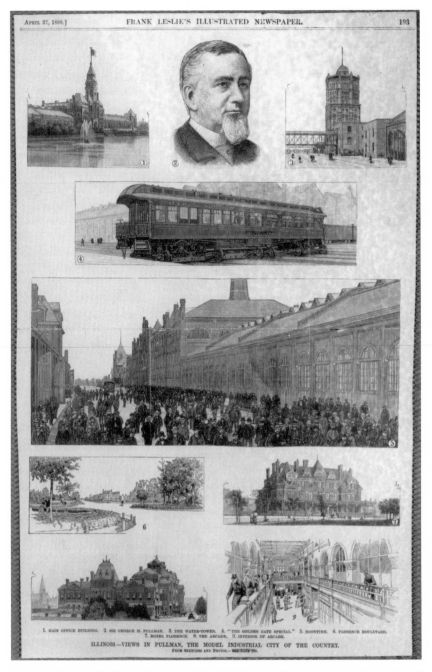

1. MAIN OFFICE BUILDING.   2. SIR GEORGE M. PULLMAN.   3. THE WATER-TOWER.   4. "THE GOLDEN GATE SPECIAL."   5. NOONTIME.   6. FLORENCE BOULEVARD.
7. HOTEL FLORENCE.   8. THE ARCADE.   9. INTERIOR OF ARCADE.

ILLINOIS.—VIEWS IN PULLMAN, THE MODEL INDUSTRIAL CITY OF THE COUNTRY.

Figure 2. Views of Pullman, from *Frank Leslie's Illustrated Newspaper*, April 27, 1889. All views are redrawn from photographs. (Courtesy of Chicago Historical Society, ICHi 01914)

whole with hierarchically integrated functional parts and then publicized the perfection of its machine-like beauty and order as the solution to class conflict. Through photography Pullman's industrial and social experiment appeared as both real utopia and eternal capitalist order.

Pullman achieved almost complete control over imagery of the town. The company encountered only two problems. First, the prephotographic and semiphotographic reproduction media of magazines and newspapers inevitably translated its starkly photographic vision into less realistic illustrations, sometimes with garbled results but more often in conventionally embellished drawings.[14] Pullman solved this problem by publishing its own books.

Second, other photographers produced competing books and portfolios. The company's first book, however, had been so comprehensive, photographically successful, and widely disseminated that all later works refined but did not substantively revise it. The local neighborhood photographer, Henry R. Koopman, added workers' housing and popular recreation;[15] Chicago's leading architectural photographer, J. W. Taylor, perfected architectural shots.[16] But both copied the company's basic views and style. Even critics of Pullman, such as Richard Ely, illustrated their articles with the company's photographs.[17] In 1893 the Pullman Company trumped its competitors by distributing thousands of free copies of *The Story of Pullman, Pullman Illustrated,* and *The Town of Pullman* to visitors during the Columbian Exposition.[18] On the eve of the Pullman strike the American public had seen only one side of the story of Pullman, and an impressive number had seen it through the company's photographs.

During the strike Pullman capitalized on its previous illustrative monopoly to drive home one overriding message: the striking workers foolishly and irrationally rejected the beauty and benefits of the model town. It permitted sympathetic magazines to reprint its photographs to reinforce the public's positive prestrike opinions of the town and to counteract negative publicity about mass layoffs, wage cuts, and exorbitant rents during the depression of 1893. In its biggest coup *Harper's Weekly* used six of the twelve photographs in *The Story of Pullman* in the two-page center spread reserved for art quality engravings.[19] Pullman also provided the sympathetically paternal portrait of George M. Pullman used originally as the frontispiece of both *The Story of Pullman* and *The Town of Pullman,* again playing on established visual associations of the company's benevolence and generosity to workers.[20]

Pullman produced only one new type of illustration during the strike:

pictures of the National Guard troops that occupied the town.[21] Just as it offered the Pullman Building in Chicago as central headquarters and Pullman palace cars as mobile quarters for the occupying troops, so it dispatched the company photographer to garner the National Guard's goodwill. His photographs did not report news events; since the occupation of Pullman passed without serious incident, the only subjects to portray were officers, military parades, drills, and camp life. Nor with rare exceptions did they resemble modern photojournalism; the company photographer carried out his assignment in the same styles he used to portray work teams, railcars, and factory architecture. However, some of his photographs may have been provided to sympathetic newspapers to serve as copy for line sketches,[22] and in at least one instance he created an anecdote of camp life—two inebriated, disheveled guardsmen—whose staging and manipulation were worthy of twentieth-century photojournalism (see figure 3).[23] Dozens of line drawings of similar nonevents exploited popular humor and sentiment to bolster sympathy for the military, some

Figure 3. Two inebriated National Guardsmen during the occupation of Pullman, July 1894. Photograph taken by the Pullman Company photographer. (Courtesy of Chicago Historical Society, ICHi 04917)

probably redrawn from photographs. A staple of the sketch artist was thus successfully adapted to photography, which, because of the limitations of reproduction technology, then had to be translated back into line drawings. A clearer example of how photography copied, adapted, influenced, and finally transformed familiar prephotographic imagery could hardly be found. Nor was there a better example of how photojournalism from the very beginning carefully crafted and edited photographic "reality."

Mostly, however, the Pullman Company relied on its established public relations practices. It recycled prestrike photographs of the model town and worked behind the scenes to have sympathetic magazines and newspapers reprint them as "news." It did not exploit the innovation of its own photographer to systematically shape illustrations of the strike itself. Though its message was internally consistent, visually coherent, and readily understood, the underlying strategy was too conservative and its implementation too informal to compete with the wealth of new images produced during the strike.

Workers and the Labor Movement

The American Railway Union had the least developed means to influence public opinion visually in 1894. American unions had limited experience in approaching the public through pictures, and little of it was relevant in a mass industrial strike.[24] Moreover, they did not control mass circulation publications that could compete with the innovative reproduction capabilities of the commercial press.

Workers were unquestionably familiar with photography and adopted it to depict themselves as eagerly as corporations like Pullman did, but they used it within their family and community. In the mid-nineteenth century workers commonly posed for portraits in work clothes, holding tools to symbolize their trades.[25] Starting in the 1860s larger employers appropriated this style of portrait for corporate purposes.[26] Simultaneously, technological innovations transformed or destroyed many of the traditional crafts that workers had so proudly displayed. As this form of portrait lost its original meaning and became associated with employers, workers replaced it with formal studio portraits in which they commemorated milestones in their family lives. By the 1880s workers in major urban areas posed for portraits only in their holiday best. Thus, from the building of Pullman the Pullman Company completely monopolized individual portrayals of workers as workers, while its workers preferred the new imagery of family life.[27]

For group portraits, in contrast, workers appropriated the company's style. Early company portraits of work teams conveyed the autonomy enjoyed by Pullman's predominantly skilled work force (see figure 4).[28] Workers began to lose their visual independence about the time of the Pullman strike. First women, then departments with predominantly immigrant workers, and finally the entire work force were visually regimented.[29] Only a handful of highly skilled workers, such as locomotive drivers on Pullman's industrial rail line, maintained their freedom in front of the camera into the twentieth century.[30] Workers preferred the company's original, freely posed style and adopted it for group portraits of labor organizations.[31]

The neighborhood photographer Henry R. Koopman sought to bridge the conflicting viewpoints of workers and company by fostering local patriotism. Dependent on Pullman workers, he readily showed aspects of working-class life in his book on Pullman. But as a local merchant depen-

Figure 4. Pullman No. 6 and some of the crowd that built it. Photograph by T. S. Johnson, 1884.

dent at times on the Pullman Company, he never contested its overriding vision. His photographs encouraged cross-class neighborhood ties that aided the strikers when they sought community support and relief in 1894.[32]

Labor organizations in the late nineteenth century used imagery primarily to reinforce group solidarity. Here, too, Pullman's workers stood at the midpoint of a major visual transformation. Older unions, such as the railway brotherhoods, mixed traditional craft, classical, and republican symbols with naturalistic depictions of their trades derived from prephotographic technical illustration.[33] The AFL unions were only beginning to depict themselves photographically, especially by adapting parade illustration dating back to artisans' associations to Labor Day. However, they eliminated cross-class symbolism and depicted each union as a unit identified by its banners, thereby transforming a popular tradition through photographic prints and Labor Day souvenir books into a memento of workers' occupational pride and trade union solidarity. Koopman photographed the brickmakers' union at Pullman in this way on the Fourth of July in 1892 (see figure 5).[34] Craft imagery, however, was too esoteric and exclusive for a general industrial union. With time the American Railway Union might have developed an image of workers that transcended craft, but its main

Figure 5. Pullman Brickmakers' Union No. 4, Fourth of July 1892. Photograph by Henry R. Koopman. (Courtesy of Paul Petraitis)

strategy was to promote the photographic image of Eugene Debs combined with a minimum of fraternal and republican symbols to simplify and personalize industrial unionism for workers.[35]

Few ARU pictures of the Pullman strike itself have been preserved, probably because few were made. Most important was one portrait of the young, handsome Debs (see figure 6), paired repeatedly in the pictorial press with one portrait of the graying, paternal George Pullman. These two photographs had already taken on symbolic meaning before 1894. Debs was the young labor firebrand who had left a moderate, craft-oriented railroad brotherhood for a new type of militant industrial union founded to unite the entire working class. His dignified portrait still betrayed his respectable origins, but it also challenged the establishment with his youthful vigor, idealistic gaze, and charismatic good looks. Pullman's portrait, in contrast, was the well-known frontispiece of *The Story of Pullman* and *The Town of Pullman*. In it he appeared as the somewhat distant but caring father and benefactor of his workers, the capitalist as progressive businessman and urban reformer. During the strike these portraits, originally photographs, were reproduced in every available medium and type of publication.[36] They personalized the promise of the model town and the industrial union. The strike also loaded them with further meaning. Eugene Debs and George Pullman came to represent the struggle over the nation's soul between the competing visions of the labor radical and the monopoly capitalist. The real Debs and Pullman were lost behind the mythical proportions of the conflict to which their stylized images alluded. Halftone reproductions of photographs initially offered a democratic medium whose realism and immediacy could bring public figures closer to the people, but the news media quickly learned to reify them. As in classical portraits of kings and generals, idealized photographs of distant leaders personified political events and substituted symbols of power and authority for real people and their social movements.

Beyond Debs the ARU relied on sympathetic third parties. The lack of public consensus on the strike created numerous openings for favorable—or at least not negative—portrayals of the union.[37] The *Chicago Times* used its illustrations to express support for the strike and ARU. The *Chicago Mail*, though Republican and not predisposed to the ARU, depicted workers' grievances sympathetically in May and gave the ARU convention neutral illustrated coverage in June. The *Evening Post* dignified ARU officials in the same large, formal portrait style it used for business leaders and military commanders but ridiculed George Pullman for leaving Chicago

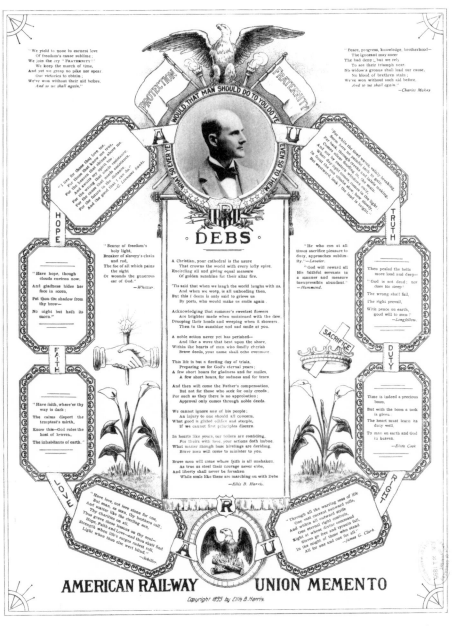

Figure 6. American Railway Union memento, 1895. (Courtesy of Library of Congress)

instead of meeting with workers. The *Chicago Record* and *Daily News* tried
to report impartially; their illustrations broadened public perceptions of
the strike's beginning and aftermath, in particular. In contrast the rabidly
antiunion *Chicago Tribune, Inter-Ocean,* and *Herald* illustrated the strike
only after the boycott began in late June and depicted primarily the rioting in July. Moreover, a new type of muckraking journalism found expression in the reporting of Ray Stannard Baker at the *Record* and of *Frank
Leslie's Illustrated Weekly.* Though not pro-ARU, they discredited the Pullman Company's publicity with documentation of the strikers' living conditions and thus implicitly bolstered the ARU's arguments.[38]

Although the ARU did not develop its own visual interpretation of events
to influence either workers' actions or public opinion, two examples produced in the local community suggested some elements of a union strike
imagery. In the first the local Pullman artist Karl Schliefmann illustrated the
Reverend William Carwardine's defense of workers in *The Pullman Strike*
with drawings of their living conditions, organization, and solidarity.[39] He
symbolized conditions through the destitution of a worker's family and
organization and solidarity through the architecture of the strikers' relief
headquarters. Moreover, he exposed Pullman's "front" view of the model
town with a "rear" view of workers' hovels, a socially critical contrast that
photography could express more trenchantly than art could.[40]

In the second example, a postcard of the occupying National Guard troops
in front of Pullman's Arcade Building, an unknown photographer conveyed
symbols of state and corporate repression in an inexpensive mass format
(see figure 7).[41] As recently as the Homestead strike in 1892, news photographs of strikes were disseminated primarily by national stereograph companies to a middle-class market.[42] The new photographic postcards suggested the potential power of formats that could reach into workers'
homes.[43] In style, though, this photograph combined a conventional architectural view identical to prestrike photographs of the Arcade Building with
an equally conventional depiction of a National Guard formation.

In sum the American Railway Union relied on the symbol of Debs and
sympathetic third parties. Favorable illustrations consequently were in-
consistent in form and content. The strikers' grievances were widely depicted as just, but the role of the ARU in defending them was portrayed
more critically. At the height of the boycott hardly a picture distinguished
the ARU's position from the rioting. The most effective images grew out
of the local working-class community. Surprisingly, in the light of the
ARU's limited resources and Pullman's power and connections, it had

Figure 7. Postcard of National Guard Troops in front of the Pullman Arcade Building in 1894. (Courtesy of Chicago Public Library, HPC 1.33)

enough allies—and Pullman enough enemies—to ensure that its views were illustrated as frequently as the company's. But the ARU also had to contend with the U.S. government, which tipped the scales in Pullman's favor.

Management of the News and the Federal Government

The federal government was vitally interested in the depiction of its military intervention, but the Pullman strike raised novel publicity problems that taxed the government's informal procedures for dealing with the pictorial press. The pretext for sending troops to Chicago—to ensure delivery of the mails—provided little material for compelling pictures. Yet the real reasons—to suppress the ARU and end the boycott on employers' terms—constituted an unprecedented abuse of governmental authority that could not be openly admitted. Moreover, illustrations of previous labor upheavals portrayed the National Guard and police rather than the army, which had its own, separate pictorial traditions derived from the Civil War and western expansion. Finally, the army command and the Justice Department were inexperienced in dealing with urban labor conflicts. Artist-illustrators who depicted the federal government relied heavily on stock portraits and architectural views of the Capitol and White House, which they combined in their art studios as political stories arose.[44] Leading officials could not expect this staid, prepackaged style of reporting to convey the government's position favorably in a nationwide labor crisis, yet they had no direct way of influencing news imagery except by providing portraits of themselves to journalists. The army, acting on its own, offered a fortuitous solution to the problem by drawing on its experience in working with photographers and illustrators.

During the Civil War and postwar geological surveys of the West the military employed its own photographers and artists and collaborated with private ones. The photographers, even those in military employ, were allowed to sell their work to the popular press, where it helped justify military actions and appropriations.[45] This arrangement proved mutually advantageous. During the wars to subjugate Native Americans in the West during the 1870s and 1880s the army further cultivated relations with photographers and artists by allowing them to tag along; in return they sent favorable images back east, most famously in the work of Frederic Remington.[46] This informal public relations strategy paid off fabulously for the army in 1894 through Remington's celebrated illustrations of the Pullman strike in *Harper's Weekly*.[47]

The Pullman strike consequently produced many images of the army but virtually none of the Justice Department officials who called the shots, and the army's reliance on photography nearly equaled the accomplishments of the Pullman Company.[48] Photographs of the military intervention mostly followed traditional subjects: portraits, panoramic views of the sites of events, and the aftermath of rioting but not events themselves (see figures 8 and 13, p. 111). Sketches were still needed to represent the government's action. They highlighted themes that stimulated public outcry against the boycott and support for the military, especially the confrontation with rioting mobs, clearing of the tracks, and protection of the first meat trains out of the stockyards. Remington frequently redrew photographs and used them in composite sketches, and his quick, prolific coverage of the strike suggests that he based some of his sketches on uncredited photographs of people and places he may not have personally witnessed. Realistic detail lent the imprimatur of truth to his imaginative narrative of heroic officers, steadfast infantrymen, and cowardly rioters.[49] In contrast to the stereotypes of violent mobs vignettes of camp life in sketches and snapshots humanized soldiers and appealed to veterans across the country. Indeed, true snapshots taken with Kodak cameras

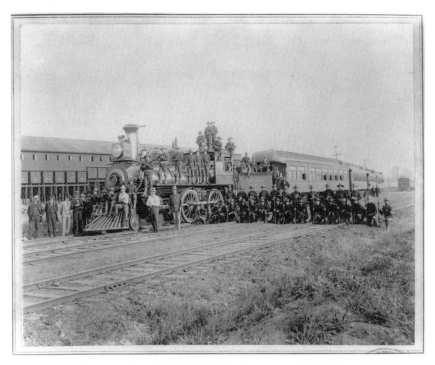

Figure 8. Special patrolling train, Rock Island Railroad, Company C, 15th U.S. Infantry, Blue Island, Illinois, July 1894. Photograph by Foss Etching and Photo Co., Chicago. (Courtesy of Library of Congress)

added an entirely new dimension to the Pullman strike: soldiers and citizens recording their own participation in the events.[50] Protection of the mail, incidentally, was almost completely forgotten. Also not shown were army headquarters in the Pullman Building and the cooperation of military commanders and Justice Department officials with the General Managers' Association.

The army's public relations encountered serious technical and logistical problems, however. Photographic panoramas of encampments and the aftermath of rioting lacked dramatic form and also contradicted sketches of heroic action.[51] Informative photographs lost their immediacy even when redrawn faithfully for reproduction.[52] Less interesting photographs were so heavily redrawn that they, too, lost their realism and fell back on captions to claim authenticity (see figure 9).[53] More seriously, photographs of soldiers ensconced in Pullman cars found their way through drawings

Figure 9. Camp of U.S. regular troops on the lakefront, Chicago, July 6, 1894, published in *Harper's Weekly*, July 21, 1894. Redrawn and embellished from two photographs by J. W. Taylor. (Courtesy of Library of Congress)

into local newspapers where they implied the collusion between the army and Pullman,[54] while the sheer number of vignettes of camp life belied the reasons given for federal intervention by suggesting that the troops spent more time posing for the camera than protecting rail traffic. The army's lack of strategic consensus and tactical unity also undercut its public relations; by dispersing poorly supervised contingents to key points throughout the city, it exposed them to enterprising but uncontrolled photographers.[55] Moreover, the intervention of U.S. marshals, the National Guard, and police led to the fusion of their pictorial traditions from earlier labor upheavals with the army's, thereby associating the army with the suppression of strikes. Fortunately for the army, the public saw only dramatic sketches of the restoration of rail traffic, not the boringly mundane photographs of the actual event (see figure 10).[56] Nevertheless, enough photographs were published or available for sale to challenge the veracity of both the old style of illustration and the government's justifi-

Figure 10. No. 3 Export Beef Train, Union Stockyards. The first meat trains left the stockyards on July 10, 1894, under escort of the U.S. Cavalry. Photograph by Brisbois Photo, Chicago. (Courtesy of Chicago Historical Society, IChi 04910)

cation for occupying Chicago, while their conflicting styles and hodge-podge of reproduction media prevented them from offering a fully convincing alternative.

In short the army's public relations strategy was promising but poorly adapted to the communications revolution and modern class conflict. The government could not, however, realize its potential until the private news media resolved their own crisis of representation.

The Photographic Transmutation of Prephotographic Strike Imagery

The Pullman Company, the American Railway Union, and the government all turned to the commercial print media to publicize their views. While most of the press closed ranks against the boycott, it was divided deeply over the issues raised by the strike. However, it shared a common

pictorial heritage and faced a common problem in deciding how to adapt
it to the new visual communications media.

Traditionally the news media composed illustrations of strikes through
the perspective, figure studies, and frozen action of neoclassical and
neobaroque narrative history painting.[57] They relied on equally conventional symbols, in particular scenes of rioting and destruction. So unified
were style and symbolism that drawings of the burning of freight cars,
explosions, and workers stopping trains during the Pullman strike were
indistinguishable from earlier ones.[58]

As early as 1877 magazines claimed photographic sources for some strike
reports; however, the actual illustrations disclosed prephotographic pictorial conventions. For technical reasons alone strike action could not have
been photographed. For example, in 1877 *Harper's Weekly* prominently credited a photographic source for a cover illustration of the Maryland National
Guard as it opened fire on rioters in Baltimore during the railway strike.
However, this drawing faithfully followed conventions of military battle
illustration dating back to the eighteenth century and earlier. For a photograph to achieve the same effect, it would have had to have been taken with
a bulky large format camera on a tripod set up directly in the National
Guard's line of fire. Moreover, because of the weak sensitivity of photographic emulsions and the need to use a small aperture to keep the architectural background (a narrow street in shadow) in sharp focus, the exposure would have had to have been at least several seconds and probably
longer. Finally, the photographer would have had to use the cumbersome
and time-consuming wet-plate process. In short the photographer would
have needed an hour or more to set up the camera, prepare the negative,
then take the picture, and develop it before the plate dried, which would
have further required a fully equipped darkroom nearby. Under these circumstances the split-second action of violent conflict could not have been
successfully photographed (and would have been life threatening to the
photographer). The "event" would have appeared as no more than an un-
intelligible blur.[59] Most likely, a Baltimore photographer supplied a stock
architectural photograph of the street where the event occurred; *Harper's*
sketch artist then photographically reproduced it on a wood block, redrew
the background from the photograph, and added the soldiers and rioters
according to the illustrative conventions governing military subjects.[60]

The veracity of such photographic attributions was open to question at
the time because the public could compare composite drawings with
strike and architectural photographs reproduced especially as stereo-

graphs. By the 1870s stereographs (and to a lesser extent *cartes de visite*) revolutionized the way Americans viewed urban life and news events. Stereo viewers were as common in middle- and upper-class homes as television sets are today; stereo cards, reproduced by the millions, were readily available throughout the United States. Architectural views depicted a serenely unpopulated, monumental urban landscape (unpopulated because long exposures prevented passers-by from being recorded on the film). For major conflicts, such as the 1877 railway and 1892 Homestead strikes, enterprising photographers produced stereographic series for public sale. However, they were unable, for the technical reasons discussed earlier, to photograph action and instead depicted the destructive aftermath of riots, as well as quiet moments when strikers and the National Guard could be posed.[61]

Between 1877 and 1894 three types of strike illustration thus competed for public acceptance: sketches following traditional artistic conventions; hybrid drawings that combined photographic backgrounds with conventional figure compositions and were produced by an equally hybrid—part photomechanical, part hand engraving—technique; and photographs taken just before or just after major events. The hybrid type was especially important as a transitional form, for it attempted to combine the sketch artist's ability to define context and convey meaning through composition and symbolism with the photographer's concern for capturing a particular time and place. Grand style photographs of the cities where events occurred replaced the classicized architecture of academic history painting and introduced a real stage on which to superimpose the stereotypical battle between destructive mobs and the forces of civilized order. But its failure, when compared with drawings and photographs, to integrate old and new forms undermined the veracity of traditional illustration by exposing its conventions, heightened confusion about what was real, and spurred illustrators to develop more convincing alternatives.

The Homestead, Coeur d'Alènes, and other strikes in the summer of 1892 marked the pictorial turning point. A network of professional photographers throughout the country could by then take and sell pictures of strikes, and national magazines could reproduce them in halftone within a few weeks of the events.[62] Photography began to subsume the themes and symbols of traditional strike imagery and transform them, first through the photographic adaptation of prephotographic illustration but then in specifically photographic forms.

The first step can be seen in the many engravings of the Pullman strike that drew on prephotographic themes and symbols but were based not on original sketches as in the past but on photographs. For example, portraits and pictures of the sites of events, two staples of strike imagery, were now redrawn from photographs.[63] For the reading of the injunction against the boycott, a symbolic image derived from illustrations of the reading of the riot act, the *Chicago Herald* also redrew photographs (see figures 11 and 12).[64] To depict the poverty of workers, the *Chicago Times* and the *Chicago Record* published drawings of laundry hanging outside one of Pullman's tenements. Jacob Riis had incorporated this prephotographic symbolism into photography in the 1880s,[65] and the *Times* and *Record* now based their drawings on a snapshot by Ray Stannard Baker.[66] The intertwining of art and photography was most obvious in depictions of the destruction of railroad cars. A photograph of the wreckage at Burnside Crossing copied almost exactly the composition of the foreground of a drawing of Pittsburgh made during the 1877 railway strike.[67] A second photograph by J. W. Taylor of the Panhandle yards, published in *Harper's Weekly*, was redrawn, transposed, for the *Inter-Ocean*.[68]

Figure 11. Reading the injunction to the strikers, Blue Island, Illinois, July 1894. (Courtesy of Chicago Historical Society, IChi 23697)

Figure 12. Deputy Allen reads the injunction to the strikers. Drawing published in *Chicago Herald*, July 3, 1894.

The translation of artistic subject matter, style, and symbolism into photography and then back into art perpetuated but transformed prephotographic strike imagery. In the first step photographers learned how to represent its conventions believably through the selective use of the camera. The artist's imaginative interpretation of generic strike iconography became interchangeable with photographs of actual strikes. The biases inherent in drawings could henceforth be expressed in images taken from real people and things.

Artist-illustrators actively mediated this transition. They were influenced by photographic vision and helped define photojournalistic style. For example, in the drawings of the reading of the injunction and Pullman's tenements the artist radically cropped the original photographs to edit out extraneous detail and focus exclusively on the main subject. Photographers in 1894 still thought their task was to depict the broad context of events.

Newspaper sketch artists, not photographers, introduced the fragmented close-ups that later became a hallmark of photojournalism.

Photomechanical technologies also allowed artist-illustrators to experiment with new styles. In magazines the halftone process freed them to work in pen-and-ink wash drawings and thus achieve an illusionistic tonality far beyond the capabilities of black line wood engraving.[69] In newspapers process line engraving often made line sketches seem more truthful than wash drawings because direct reproduction of the sketches' notational code suggested that the artist witnessed the story, captured it in quick strokes of the pen, and conveyed it without mediation to viewers. Both styles anticipated photojournalism—wash drawings through gradations of tonal values and line sketches through immediacy.

Artist-illustrators influenced photojournalism more directly, however. Some newspapers, such as the *Inter-Ocean,* printed sketches of raw news captured fleetingly, the way a camera might have if one had been available.[70] Others, most notably the *Chicago Tribune,* interpreted the strike in highly finished, prepackaged drawings that mimicked well-composed photographs.[71] Some of the *Inter-Ocean*'s sketches exhibited remarkably photographic, flattened, and off-balanced composition, while the *Tribune* published a fake mock-up of imaginary snapshots. Innovative magazine and newspaper artists thus defined photojournalistic style before a mechanical process could regularly reproduce actual photographs.

In the next step photography removed the intermediary of the artist altogether. Mechanically reproduced pictures replaced hand engravings and thus eliminated all visible signs of subjective human intervention. Then, having learned how to make news illustrations from artistic models, photographers stripped conventional iconography of artistic embellishment and simplified it to the bare reflections of real objects. For example, in summing up the cost of the Pullman strike, *Harper's Weekly* published in halftone three photographs of burned railroad cars, cropped and laid out repetitiously for emphasis (see figure 13).[72] *Harper's* had consistently supported Pullman and the government in melodramatic drawings of riots, the destruction of property, and the military restoration of law and order. Through photographs it could now convey the loaded symbol of labor violence as simple, brutal, irrefutable fact. Once halftone reproductions of photographs superseded drawings, the public could no longer discern the artistic origins of such illustrations and easily mistook their tendentious message for objective reporting of the news.

Only two groups of photographs seized on the camera's potential to

Figure 13. Burned freight cars during Pullman strike. Photographs published in *Harper's Weekly*, July 28, 1894. (Courtesy of Library of Congress)

express class conflict and investigate its causes. One photograph of a group of workmen in front of the factory's main gate (see figure 14) was faithfully reproduced as a line drawing in the *Chicago Times* during the strike's sixth week, shortly before the start of the boycott (see figure 15).[73] Easily mistaken in this context as a depiction of the strikers, it inverted one of the Pullman Company's original photographs from *The Story of Pullman*, which was reprinted during the strike by *Harper's Weekly* (see figure 16).[74] The company's industrial army, pouring out of the main gate at the sound of the evening whistle, became the union's line of pickets, barring entry to the factory. Ray Stannard Baker then completely subverted the meaning of Pullman's grand urban utopia in a powerfully subtle photograph that broke all the rules for a "good" picture (see figure 17).[75] Taking a photograph with tilted perspective and poor depth of field that lacked clear focus or detail in the sole shadowy figure, the light of the setting sun illuminating the blurred factory buildings in the background but enshrouding the main gate, brightened only by fading posters for long past performances at the Arcade Theater, Baker transformed the vision of the model town into a symbol of emptiness and decline. It is unlikely that anyone, including Baker, understood what he had taken. Using uniquely photographic means, he refuted one false photographic message with another photograph. He thus left the prephotographic world entirely behind him.

Figure 14. Workmen in front of the main gate of the Pullman Car Works, 1891(?). (Courtesy of Chicago Public Library, HPC 1.13)

Figure 15. Line drawing in *Chicago Times,* June 19 and 20, 1894. (Courtesy of Chicago Historical Society, IChi 27330)

Figure 16. "Main Gate to Works," in *The Story of Pullman,* 1893.

Figure 17. Main gate of the Pullman Car Works. Photograph by Ray Stannard Baker, 1894. (Courtesy of Library of Congress).

Toward the end of the strike *Frank Leslie's Illustrated Weekly* sent a reporter to investigate its causes and ran in halftone a full page of photographs to accompany his article (see figure 18).[76] *Leslie's* juxtaposed portraits of the three members of the federal commission appointed to investigate the strike, one photograph from *The Story of Pullman,* and six unique photographs of workers' living conditions, fortuitously included only because the Pullman Company refused the request for architectural plans of the model houses. Against the "front view," seen by millions of rail passengers from the comfort of their Pullman cars as they traveled to and from Chicago, *Leslie's* contrasted the rear entrance tenements, crowded housing conditions, the dismal water closets, and flimsy wood cottages near Pullman's paint sheds. Moreover, the sophisticated layout suggested how the problems raised by the strike could be solved: by the activist intervention of the federal government to discover the causes of class conflict and propose reforms to resolve them.

This new, critical use of photography did not, however, extend to those groups that had traditionally been excluded from strike imagery. As in

Figure 18. The homes and wages of the Pullman operatives. Photographs published in *Frank Leslie's Illustrated Weekly,* August 9, 1894. (Courtesy of Library of Congress)

earlier strikes, immigrant, African American, and women workers were barely recognized in 1894 and continued to be ignored in the early years of photojournalism. The pictorial conventions of ethnicity and gender developed separately from those of labor conflict.[77] They intersected in a very minor way during the Pullman strike without influencing each other. Stereotyping immigrants by physical type, costume, and consumption of alcohol; African Americans by servile occupation and mannerisms; and women as housewives or harridans concealed and distorted their true roles in the strike and boycott. At most, one photograph of an unemployed black man in a shantytown near one of Chicago's rail yards, taken by Ray Stannard Baker along with other photographs of unemployed white workers, may have introduced a critical note (see figure 19).[78] It probably depicts one of the unemployed who burned freight cars and confronted the army and National Guard. By illuminating not only social conditions in Chicago but also apparently friendly relations between black and white workers, it implicitly contradicts sketches of rioting white mobs and obsequious black servants. Baker's images of the unemployed upset too many stereotypes to be published in any form during the strike.

The photographs by Baker and *Leslie's* revealed the extent of public dis-

Figure 19. Living conditions in Chicago during the 1893 depression and 1894 Pullman strike. Photograph by Ray Stannard Baker, 1894. (Courtesy of Library of Congress)

agreement over the strike. Unlike *Harper's Weekly* and the *Chicago Tribune*, they did not manipulate their reports by hiding the content of old imagery in the new forms of photography. Rather, they directly confronted the social problems raised by the strike. They were critical rather than narrative, emphasized causes and solutions, not drama and morality, and created uniquely photographic symbols from ordinary working-class life. Their snapshot quality only enhanced their meaning. Artlessly composed, they were probably taken with amateur cameras, concealed to prevent detection by Pullman's guards, while the photographers were on the run and using available light. But they could not affect the strike's outcome. The photographs of the factory gate were never published as photographs, and those in *Leslie's* appeared after the strike was defeated. Nevertheless, they alone fluently spoke the new language of industrial conflict.

Conclusion: Toward a New Image of Labor Conflict

If Chicago's newspapers are any guide, the Pullman strike stimulated a permanent increase in news illustration.[79] After 1894 magazines reported strikes primarily in photographs. Illustrators were already so influenced by photography and photographers had learned to adapt enough traditional imagery to the camera that the next logical step was to dispense with artists and illustrators altogether. The juxtaposition of different kinds of images and media, brought to a head by the unprecedented outpouring of news illustrations during the Pullman strike, underscored the need to resolve the confusion raised by the communications revolution. More specifically, the participants in the strike drew far-reaching lessons from their experiences.

The strike shattered the promise of the model town and with it Pullman's photographic vision. After 1894 the Pullman Company retreated into the new fields of advertising and especially industrial photography, which its photographers helped create. The next time it tried to influence labor conflict, after 1910, it applied photography even more ambitiously and intrusively but focused on industrial imagery to mold workers' attitudes. Its guards also made sure that no photograph critical of Pullman was ever again taken on company property, and its public relations department worked more successfully than its informal predecessors in 1894 to suppress critical stories and images.[80]

The American Railway Union's reliance on sympathetic third parties, surprisingly effective in 1894, was continued by other unions. To foster internal ties, unions noticeably increased their use of photographs. Koopman's still novel photograph of 1892 became a recognized symbol of AFL trade union organization and solidarity by 1900. Eugene Debs cultivated his personification first of industrial unionism and then of socialism, and later the Industrial Workers of the World (IWW) assembled the elements of union strike imagery into a coherent photographic narrative of class oppression, workers' community, union organization, strike mobilization, and industrial solidarity.[81]

The U.S. government gradually adopted, regularized, and institutionalized the army's informal approach to photographers. By President William McKinley's second inauguration the coincidental practices of 1894 became a function of government, providing photojournalists routine but structured and controlled access to governmental actions and events.[82]

Finally, the news media learned how to make original news photographs. In 1894 *Leslie's* was unusual in employing a fully credited staff photographer. In 1895 George Bain founded the first news photo agency, and by 1900 an entirely new profession with its own institutions, photojournalism, sprang up to supply the nation's newspapers and magazines.[83] The reporting of strikes now took on its twentieth-century form. Before 1894 major strikes were profusely illustrated classical tragedies in three acts: caused by workers' flawed character, climaxing in violence and destruction, punished in swift denouement. Already during the Pullman strike the news media neglected the first and last acts in favor of the climax and garbled the details and chronology of the boycott because of the incompatible production times of different media. After 1900 illustration of even major strikes declined drastically. Newspapers and magazines henceforth ran a handful of sensational but ephemeral photographs to symbolize, in the guise of eyewitness reporting, only the most dramatic moments of conflict.[84]

The Pullman strike exposed a crisis in the representation of labor conflict by discrediting older visual forms and messages without clearly producing new ones. This crisis of representation in turn deepened the social fissures exposed by the strike by revealing the artistry that had veiled social cleavages, the lack of consensus on class conflicts, and the manipulation of public opinion. It remained unresolved until new styles, contents, and institutions adapted to the technical potential of the communications revolution created new, plausible images of labor. From the competition of corporations, unions, government, and the news media over representations of labor conflict emerged the photographically "realistic" image of twentieth-century workers. But for a brief moment the Pullman strike revealed both the extent of class divisions and the ways images of labor conflict were made to conceal them.

Notes

Portions of this essay previously appeared in Larry Peterson, "Pullman Strike Pictures: Molding Public Perceptions in the 1890s by New Visual Communication," *Labor's Heritage* 8 (Spring 1997): 14–33, 48–56.

1. See Philip S. Foner, *The Great Labor Uprising of 1877* (New York: Monad, 1977); and Shelton Stromquist, *A Generation of Boomers: The Pattern of Railroad Labor Conflict in Nineteenth-Century America* (Urbana: University of Illinois Press, 1987). On the new type of mass strike, see Friedhelm Boll, *Arbeitskämpfe und Gewerkschaften in Deutschland, England und Frankreich: Ihre Entwicklung vom 19. zum 20. Jahrhundert* (Bonn: J. H. W. Dietz Nachf., 1992).

2. See Robert Taft, *Photography and the American Scene: A Social History, 1839–1889* (New York: Dover, 1964), 419–50; and Ulrich Keller, "Photojournalism around 1900: The Institutionalization of a Mass Medium," in *Shadow and Substance: Essays on the History of Photography in Honor of Heinz K. Henisch, ed. Kathleen Collins (Bloomfield Hills:* Amorphous Institute Press, 1990), 283–303.

3. My approach differs from Neil Harris, "Iconography and Intellectual History: The Halftone Effect," in *New Directions in American Intellectual History,* ed. John Higham and Paul K. Conkin (Baltimore: Johns Hopkins University Press, 1979), 196–211. Harris misunderstands the argument made by Estelle Jussim, *Visual Communications and the Graphic Arts: Photographic Technologies in the Nineteenth Century* (New York: R. R. Bowker, 1974), when he argues that photomechanical reproduction was a "nonmediated" type of information transfer. Jussim's book demonstrated the opposite: that photomechanical technologies mediated information transfer by developing a new set of codes to replace those of older media. My argument demonstrates that the subjects, symbolism, styles, and messages of prephotographic imagery were then systematically translated, adapted, and ultimately transformed through photography to conform to the new media.

4. See Taft, *Photography and the American Scene;* and especially Jussim, *Visual Communications and the Graphic Arts.* On the birth of photojournalism, see Keller, "Photojournalism around 1900." On the "invention" of photography as a pictorial form, see Joel Snyder, "Inventing Photography," in *On the Art of Fixing a Shadow: One Hundred and Fifty Years of Photography,* by Sarah Greenough, Joel Snyder, David Travis, and Colin Westerbeck (Boston: Little, Brown, 1989), 3–38.

5. Stanley Buder, *Pullman: An Experiment in Industrial Order and Community Plan-*

ning, 1880–1930 (New York: Oxford University Press, 1967); Almont Lindsey, *The Pullman Strike: The Story of a Unique Experiment and of a Great Labor Upheaval* (Chicago: University of Chicago Press, 1964); James Gilbert, *Perfect Cities: Chicago's Utopias of 1893* (Chicago: University of Chicago Press, 1991).

6. Jussim, *Visual Communications and the Graphic Arts;* Keller, "Photojournalism around 1900."

7. Jussim, *Visual Communications and the Graphic Arts,* 279–95; James Gilbert, "Fixing the Image: Photography at the World's Columbian Exposition," in *Grand Illusions: Chicago's World's Fair of 1893,* by Neil Harris, Wim de Wit, James Gilbert, and Robert W. Rydell (Chicago: Chicago Historical Society, 1993); Peter B. Hales, *Constructing the Fair: Platinum Photographs by C. D. Arnold of the World's Columbian Exposition* (Chicago: Art Institute of Chicago, 1993); Julie K. Brown, *Contesting Images: Photography and the World's Columbian Exposition* (Tucson: University of Arizona Press, 1994).

8. Henry Koopman, "Pullman's Photographic Department," *Pullman Car Works Standard* 4 (August 1919): 12; "Pullman Incorporated: 105 Years of Photography—From Glass Plates to Video Tape," *Professional Photographer* 99 (May 1972): 53–55; John H. White Jr., *The American Railroad Passenger Car* (Baltimore: Johns Hopkins University Press, 1978), 245–66.

9. T. S. Johnson, *Pullman Illustrated* (Pullman, Ill.: n.p., 1883); T. S. Johnson, *Photos of Pullman* (Pullman, Ill.: n.p., 1885); *The Story of Pullman* (Chicago: n.p., 1893); Mrs. Duane Doty, *The Town of Pullman: Its Growth with Brief Accounts of Its Industries* (Pullman, Ill.: T. P. Struhsacker, 1893).

10. See the Pullman collections in the Chicago Historical Society, Chicago Public Library, Pullman Research Group, Illinois State Historical Library, and Smithsonian Institution; Peter B. Hales, *Silver Cities: The Photography of American Urbanization, 1839–1915* (Philadelphia: Temple University Press, 1984); and Larry Peterson, "Producing Visual Traditions among Workers: The Uses of Photography at Pullman, 1880–1980," *Views: The Journal of Photography in New England* 13 (Spring 1992): 3–10, 25.

11. Compare Richard T. Ely, "Pullman: A Social Study," *Harper's Monthly* 70 (February 1885): 452–66, and "Illinois: Views in Pullman, the Model Industrial City of the Country," *Frank Leslie's Illustrated Newspaper* [hereafter referred to as *Leslie's*], April 27, 1889, 193, with Johnson, *Pullman Illustrated.* On perspective, see Peter Galassi, *Before Photography: Painting and the Invention of Photography* (New York: Museum of Modern Art, 1981), 12–19; John Szarkowski, *Photography until Now* (New York: Museum of Modern Art, 1989), 15–59; Weston Naef, "Daguerre, Talbot, and the Crucible of Drawing," *Aperture* 125 (Fall 1991): 10–15; and Snyder, "Inventing Photography." I disagree with the modernist interpretation of Galassi and Szarkowski that the essence of camera vision is fundamentally opposed to Renaissance concepts of perspective. They argue that artists use perspective to create the illusion of three-dimensionality on a two-dimensional surface, whereas

photographers reduce three-dimensional objects to the two-dimensional film plane. I argue that photography can be successfully manipulated to achieve different ends. Architectural and industrial photographers deliberately adapted the pictorial effects of Renaissance perspective to the technical requirements of the camera to convey a specific content and meaning. For their models, see Francis D. Klingender, *Art and the Industrial Revolution,* rev. ed. (New York: Schocken Books, 1970); Klaus Schrenk, "Industriedarstellungen in der Mitte des 19. Jahrhunderts and Aspekte ihres gesellschaftlichen Charakters," *Kritische Berichte* 3, nos. 5–6 (1975): 13–31. For their adaptation to photography, see Allan Sekula, "Photography between Capital and Labor," in *Mining Photographs and Other Pictures, 1948–1968: A Selection from the Negative Archives of Shedden Studio, Glace Bay, Cape Breton,* ed. Don Macgillivray and Allan Sekula (Halifax: Press of Nova Scotia College of Art and Design, 1983); Alan Thomas, *The Expanding Eye: Photography and the Nineteenth Century Mind* (London: Croom Helm, 1978), 127–29, 132–33; Jack Simmons, *Image of the Train: The Victorian Era* (Bradford, U.K.: National Museum of Photography, Film and Television, 1993); and Henning Rogge, *Fabrikwelt um die Jahrhundertwende am Beispiel der AEG Machinenfabrik in Berlin-Wedding* (Cologne: DuMont, 1983).

12. Johnson, *Pullman Illustrated;* Pullman Photographic Collection, Smithsonian Institution, for example, Pullman neg. no. 1435.

13. "Main Gate to Works," in *Story of Pullman;* "Noontime," *Leslie's,* April 27, 1889, 193.

14. *Graphic* (Chicago), June 17, 1893; *Buffalo Illustrated Express,* July 15, 1894; Ely, "Pullman"; *Leslie's,* April 27, 1889.

15. Henry R. Koopman, *Pullman: The City of Brick* (Roseland, Ill.: Henry R. Koopman, 1893); also in the Chicago Historical Society, Chicago Public Library, and Pullman Research Group.

16. J. W. Taylor portfolio, Art Institute of Chicago; Illinois State Historical Library.

17. Ely, "Pullman."

18. Mr. Fritch to George M. Pullman, Reports on the World's Fair Exhibit 1893, George M. Pullman Collection, Chicago Historical Society; Buder, *Pullman,* 147; Gilbert, *Perfect Cities,* 136.

19. *Harper's Weekly,* July 21, 1894, 684–85. The top half of the spread was a large illustration of the ruins of the World's Columbian Exposition after a panoramic photograph by J. W. Taylor, taken after a fire destroyed the Court of Honor during the Pullman strike. The fire was probably set accidentally by homeless, unemployed squatters and thus was unrelated to the strike, but the ruins, when contrasted with the model town then under siege, suggested the senseless destruction of the nation's urban-industrial ideals by mob violence. See also Gilbert, *Perfect Cities,* 209–13. These illustrations were a good example of the confusion caused by different reproduction media when used side by side. The top picture

was a redrawn photograph, while the Pullman pictures were probably copied from silver prints of the photogravures in *The Story of Pullman*, both reproduced by the halftone process. The reader could not tell either their complex derivation or photography's role in making and reproducing them.

20. Pullman regularly supplied information to the news media and tried to manipulate its use. For example, *Leslie's*, August 25, 1877, April 27, 1889, and *Graphic*, June 17, 1893, among others, are lightly edited, Pullman Company publicity materials; Duane Doty, a Pullman town manager, worked as a sometimes anonymous Pullman publicist. For the Pullman strike a suggestive line of pictorial and written evidence connects the Pullman Company with the *Inter-Ocean*, *Chicago Herald*, *Chicago Tribune*, and *Harper's Weekly*. See *Story of Pullman*; Events, Demonstrations, Strikes, Ill-Chgo, 1894-Pullman I, Prints and Photographs Department, Chicago Historical Society; *Inter-Ocean*, July 10, 1894; *Chicago Herald*, July 12, 1894; *Chicago Tribune*, July 11, 1894; and *Harper's Weekly*, July 14, 1894, 655, July 21, 1894, 684–85, 689.

21. Pullman Strike I, Chicago Historical Society. These photographs originally belonged to the Pullman family. See also Cary T. Ray, "A Short Resume of Service in Company 'D' First Infantry Illinois National Guard," Box 289/Folder 1, 8–9, Cary T. Ray Papers, Chicago Historical Society.

22. See, for example, *Inter-Ocean*, July 10, 1894; and *Chicago Herald*, July 12, 1894.

23. "Two Guardsmen," Pullman Strike I, Chicago Historical Society.

24. This subject has not been studied. Most important was probably the union label and boycotts of nonunion products sometimes propagated through pictures. This approach worked well for craft unions that produced goods bought by workers but was inapplicable to an industrial union in the railcar industry. In the Pullman boycott the ARU called on workers to refuse to handle Pullman cars. Since only the well-to-do rode on Pullman cars, a consumer boycott was pointless.

25. Harry R. Rubenstein, "Symbols and Images of American Labor: Badges of Pride," *Labor's Heritage* 1 (April 1989): 37–41.

26. Ronald Filipelli and Sandra Stelts, "Sons of Vulcan: An Iron Workers Album," in *Shadow and Substance*, ed. Collins, 105–9.

27. See Pullman collections, Smithsonian Institution; Pullman Research Group; and Peterson, "Producing Visual Traditions among Workers." Workers in isolated work environments, such as mining and lumber, continued to pose in work clothes well into the twentieth century. See Ralph W. Andrews, *This Was Logging: Selected Photographs of Darius Kinsey* (West Chester: Schiffer Publishing, 1984); and *The Mining Town of Morococha: Photographs of Sebastian Rodriguez and Fran Antmann* (New York: Museum of Contemporary Hispanic Art, 1987).

28. See, for example, a photograph of a group of workers in front of the erection shops by T. S. Johnson, ca. 1885, in the Pullman Research Group collection; and group portraits from the 1880s and early 1890s in Historic Pullman Collec-

tion, 1.28, Chicago Public Library; *Pullman Car Works Standard* 2 (July 1917, December 1917); and *Pullman News* 7 (August 1928, January 1929).

29. Peterson, "Producing Visual Traditions among Workers."

30. Pullman neg. nos. 15738 (1913), 16901 (1914), Pullman Photographic Collection, Smithsonian Institution.

31. Peterson, "Producing Visual Traditions among Workers."

32. Paul W. Petraitis, "Henry Ralph Koopman II: The Life and Times of a Neighborhood Photographer," *Chicago History* 7 (Fall 1978): 161–77.

33. See, for example, a banner of the Brotherhood of Locomotive Firemen, reproduced in Stromquist, *Generation of Boomers*, following 62. See also Rubenstein, "Symbols and Images of American Labor," 41–46; and Howard B. Rock, "'All Her Sons Join in One Social Band': Visual Images of New York's Artisan Societies in the Early Republic," *Labor's Heritage* 3 (July 1991): 4–21.

34. Henry R. Koopman, "Pullman Brickmakers' Union No. 4, Fourth of July 1892," Pullman Research Group. See also Rubenstein, "Symbols and Images of American Labor," 44–46; and Rock, "'All Her Sons Join in One Social Band,'" 14–15.

35. See, for example, American Railway Union Memento, ca. 1895, LC-USZ62-43971, Prints and Photographs Lot 4403, Broadside Collection, Library of Congress.

36. See, for example, *Harper's Weekly*, July 14, 1894, 656; and *Chicago Evening Post*, June 30, 1894 (Debs), July 2, 1894 (Pullman).

37. The following is based on an analysis of Chicago's illustrated daily newspapers from April 1894 to February 1895. See also David Paul Nord, *Newspapers and New Politics: Midwestern Municipal Reform 1890–1900* (Ann Arbor: UMI Research Press, 1981), esp. 28–32.

38. Ray Stannard Baker, Prints and Photographs Lot 4069, Library of Congress; *Chicago Record*, August 1 and 2, 1894, Pullman Company Scrapbooks, series 03, Vol. 7, 87, 105, RG No. 12, Pullman Company Archives, Newberry Library, Chicago. *Leslie's*, July 26, 1894, 54, August 9, 1894, 86. For an analysis of these illustrations, see below. *Leslie's* vehemently opposed the boycott but also found the strikers' grievances justified and broke with the Pullman Company over its treatment of workers.

39. William Carwardine, *The Pullman Strike* (Chicago: Charles H. Kerr, 1894).

40. Photographic contrasts became a staple of such social reformers as Lewis Hine and of the socialist and radical press. See Margaret F. Byington, *Homestead: The Households of a Mill Town* (New York: Russell Sage Foundation, 1910; reprint, Pittsburgh: University of Pittsburgh Press, 1974), photographs opposite 23, 56, 60, 85, 152; and *Chicago Daily Socialist*, 1908–12.

41. Historic Pullman Collection, 1.33, Chicago Public Library.

42. "Strikers Watching for Scabs, Homestead 1892," LC-USZ62-12996, and "Homestead—Strikers on the Look-out 1892," LC-USZ62-98267, Prints and Photographs Lot 7105, Library of Congress.

43. Paul J. Vanderwood and Frank N. Samponaro, *Border Fury: A Picture Postcard Record of Mexico's Revolution and U.S. War Preparedness, 1910–1917* (Albuquerque: University of New Mexico Press, 1988), esp. 1–5; Gisèle Freund, *Photography and Society* (London: Gordon Fraser, 1980), 99–100.

44. For the construction of such illustrations, see Szarkowski, *Photography until Now*, 181–82; and Michael L. Carlebach, *The Origins of Photojournalism in America* (Washington, D.C.: Smithsonian Institution Press, 1992), 15–17. *Leslie's* used this style as late as the early 1890s to report the opening of Congress and major debates.

45. Taft, *Photography and the American Scene*, chaps. 13–15; Carlebach, *Origins of Photojournalism in America*, chap. 3; Alan Trachtenberg, *Reading American Photographs: Images as History, Matthew Brady to Walker Evans* (New York: Hill and Wang, 1989), chaps. 2–3; Joel Snyder, *American Frontiers: The Photographs of Timothy H. O'Sullivan, 1867–1874* (Millerton, N.Y.: Aperture, 1981).

46. Carlebach, *Origins of Photojournalism in America*, 139; Jussim, *Visual Communications and the Graphic Arts*, chap. 7.

47. *Harper's Weekly*, July 21, 1894, July 28, 1894, August 11, 1894.

48. The following is based on an analysis of photographs and prints of the strike in the Chicago Historical Society; Library of Congress; *Harper's Weekly; Leslie's;* and Chicago daily newspapers. Similar photographs of U.S. troops were taken outside Chicago. See the photograph of troops protecting a train in Montana during the boycott, reproduced in Stromquist, *Generation of Boomers*, following 62.

49. Jussim, *Visual Communications and the Graphic Arts*, 204–14; Peter H. Hassrich, *The Frederic Remington Studio* (Seattle: University of Washington Press, 1995).

50. Ferdinand Schapper, "Southern Cook County before the Civil War: Views of Blue Island, Index of Early Settlers, Their Families, Etc.," vol. 3 (typescript, 1917), 1018, 1020, Chicago Historical Society; Harry Jebsen Jr., "The Role of Blue Island in the Pullman Strike of 1894," *Journal of the Illinois State Historical Society* 67 (June 1974): 275–93.

51. For example, see Ralph D. Cleveland, "Troops Encamped on Lakefront, 1894" and "Burned Railroad Cars on Side Tracks between Burnside Crossing and 104th Street, Looking Northeast, July 15, 1894," Pullman Strike I, Chicago Historical Society.

52. Compare "Troops Encamped by Courthouse, R.R. Strike of 1894," Pullman Strike I, Chicago Historical Society, with "Two Companies of U.S. Regulars Guarding U.S. Subtreasury, Post Office Building," *Chicago Tribune*, July 11, 1894; "United States Troops Encamped in front of the Post-Office and Sub-Treasury, July 10th," *Harper's Weekly*, July 21, 1894, 689; and "Camp of Illinois State Militia at Post-Office, Clark and Adams Street, Chicago," *Leslie's*, July 19, 1894, 40.

53. Compare two views of "Troops Bivouaced Looking South to 12th Street I.C. Station," Album of Troops 1894, Pullman Strike II, Chicago Historical Society; and

"Camp of United States Regular Troops on the Lake Front, July 6th," drawn by T. Dart Walker from a photograph by J. W. Taylor, *Harper's Weekly*, July 21, 1894, 688. Walker's drawing actually combined both photographs. To frame the picture with the architectural symbols of the Auditorium Building and the Illinois Central's Twelfth Street Station, the artist compressed the perspective, difficult if not impossible in a single photograph even with a wide-angle lens. A similar photograph was published in *Buffalo Illustrated Express*, July 15, 1894, Pullman Company Scrapbooks, series 03, vol. 5, 91, RG No. 12, Pullman Company Archives, Newberry Library.

54. "Privates Schantz, Simpson, Belt, Matthews, Payne, and Ray of Company D Quartered at Pullman during 1894 Strike," Pullman Strike I, Chicago Historical Society; "Lieutenant-Colonel Kavanaugh's HQ inside a Pullman Palace Car," *Chicago Daily News*, July 12, 1894; Ray, "Short Resume."

55. Clayton D. Laurie, "Antilabor Mercenaries or Defenders of Public Order?" *Chicago History* 20 (Fall–Winter 1991–92): 4–31.

56. Compare "First Export Beef Train to Leave Stockyards during R.R. Strike of 1894," Pullman Strike I, Chicago Historical Society; and "The First Meat Train Leaving the Chicago Stock-Yards under Escort of United States Cavalry, July 10, 1894," *Harper's Weekly*, July 28, 1894, 701. See also Ray, "Short Resume," 5.

57. For examples from the 1877 railway strike, see *Harper's Weekly*, August 11, 1877, 628; and *Leslie's*, August 4, 1877, 372–73. See also Harry R. Rubenstein, "Symbols and Images of American Labor: Dinner Pails and Hard Hats," *Labor's Heritage* 1 (July 1989): 34–49; Judith Ayre Schomer, "New Workers in a New World: Painting American Labor, 1830–1913," *Labor's Heritage* 3 (January 1991): 36–47; John Gladstone, "Working-Class Imagery in *Harper's Weekly*, 1865–1895," *Labor's Heritage* 5 (Spring 1993): 42–61; Edward Lucie-Smith and Celestine Dars, *Work and Struggle: The Painter as Witness 1870–1914* (New York: Paddington, 1977); and Karl Janke and Monika Wagner, "Das Verhältnis von Arbeiter und Maschinerie im Industriebild," *Kritische Berichte* 4 (1976): 5–26.

58. Compare "Steeple View of the Pittsburgh Conflagration: Burning Freight Trains, Pennsylvania Railroad," *Harper's Weekly*, August 11, 1877, 624–25, with "Burning of Six Hundred Freight-Cars on the Panhandle Railroad, South of Fiftieth Street, on the Evening of July 6th," *Harper's Weekly*, July 21, 1894, 677; "The Disaffected Workmen Dragging Firemen and Engineers from a Baltimore Freight Train at Martinsburg, July 17th," *Leslie's*, August 4, 1877, 373, with "Police Driving Back the Mob from a Train Blocked by Obstructions on Track near Forty-third Street," *Harper's Weekly*, July 21, 1894, 677; and "Haymarket, May 4, 1886," in Michael Schaack, *Anarchy and Anarchists: A History of the Red Terror and the Social Revolution in America and Europe* (Chicago: F. J. Schultz, 1889), with "Scene at the Instant of the Terrible Caisson Explosion in Grand Blvd.," *Chicago Tribune*, July 17, 1894.

59. "The Sixth Maryland Regiment Fighting Its Way through Baltimore," attributed to a photograph by D. Bendann, *Harper's Weekly*, August 11, 1877, cover. To

be taken even today, this picture would have to posed and reenacted, as in a Hollywood movie. A photographer using a 35mm camera could (with luck) capture the split-second action but not the architectural view.

60. Even more egregious was *Harper's Weekly*'s claim that its illustration of the Haymarket bombing in 1886 was drawn partly from photographs. See "The Anarchist Riot in Chicago: A Dynamite Bomb Exploding among the Police," drawn by T. de Thulstrup from sketches and photographs furnished by H. Jeanneret, *Harper's Weekly*, May 15, 1886, 312–13. The composition closely followed Mannerist and Baroque models; the chiaroscuro was obviously Rembrandtesque; the symbolism and codes for the explosion copied engravings of fireworks and gun battles. *Harper's* expected viewers to believe that its photographer was able to take a split-second, stop-action picture at night without artificial street illumination and that, without prior knowledge that a bomb would be thrown, he positioned himself for the best angle to view the event and, without an automatic shutter release, timed the exposure to coincide with the explosion. As in 1877, the artist probably drew only the background from photographs of the Haymarket. Such photographs, taken during the day, were available in stock series of urban views and could be bought from Chicago photographers. See Prints and Photographs Department, Chicago Historical Society. I disagree with the analysis by Gladstone, "Working-Class Imagery in *Harper's Weekly*, 1865–1895," 56–57, who claims photographic influence for this illustration. Some twentieth-century news photographs are similar but only because photojournalists learned to render prephotographic effects and symbolism with the camera. For a similar example from the Pullman strike, see "The Striker's Wife: Left Helpless and Despairing," credited as drawn from a photograph by H. Reuterdahl, *Leslie's*, July 26, 1894, cover.

61. For S. V. Albee's forty-two stereographs of the 1877 railway strike in Pittsburgh, see Carlebach, *Origins of Photojournalism in America*, 158–59. For Homestead, see LC-USZ62-98267 and LC-USZ62-12996, Prints and Photographs Lot 7105, Library of Congress. See also William C. Darrah, *The World of Stereographs* (Gettysburg: W. C. Darrah, 1977); William C. Darrah, *Cartes de Visite in Nineteenth Century Photography* (Gettysburg: W. C. Darrah, 1981); and Hales, *Silver Cities*.

62. Patricia Hart and Ivar Nelson, *Mining Town: The Photographic Record of T. N. Barnard and Nellie Stockbridge from the Coeur d'Alènes* (Seattle and Boise: University of Washington Press and Idaho State Historical Society, 1984), 49–69; *Harper's Weekly*, July 30, 1892, August 27, 1892.

63. Compare portraits of the members of the federal commission appointed to investigate the Pullman strike in *Leslie's*, August 9, 1894, 86, with August 15, 1894, Scrapbook on the Pullman Strike in Chicago, 335, Chicago Historical Society, and clippings from August 14–18, Pullman Company Scrapbooks, series 03, vol. 8, RG No. 12, Pullman Company Arhives, Newberry Library; and "U.S. Troops Encamped at Lake Front," Pullman Strike, Chicago Historical Society, with "Bird's

Eye View of the Military Camp in the Chicago Lake Front," *Chicago Tribune*, July 10, 1894.

64. Compare "Scene from 1894 Pullman Strike," Pullman Strike, ICHi 23697, Chicago Historical Society, with "Deputy Allen Reads the Injunction to the Strikers," *Chicago Herald*, July 3, 1894.

65. Maren Stange, *Symbols of Ideal Life: Social Documentary Photography in America, 1890–1950* (Cambridge: Cambridge University Press, 1989), chap. 1; Jacob A. Riis, *How the Other Half Lives: Studies among the Tenements of New York* (New York: Dover, 1971). See also Hales, *Silver Cities*, 233–41.

66. Compare Ray Stannard Baker, LC-USZ62-24878, Prints and Photographs Lot 4069, Library of Congress, with "One of the Model Homes," May 26, 1894, Scrapbook on the Pullman Strike in Chicago, 17, Chicago Historical Society, and with "Fulton Street Tenement House," *Chicago Record*, August 2, 1894, and "Children of Pullman Tenements" and "A Row of the Workmen's Houses," *Chicago Record*, August 1, 1894, Pullman Company Scrapbooks, series 03, vol. 7, 87, 105, RG No. 12, Pullman Company Archives, Newberry Library.

67. Compare "Burning of the Round-House at Pittsburgh," sketch by John W. Beatty, *Harper's Weekly*, August 11, 1877, 628, with "Burned Railroad Cars on Side Tracks between Burnside Crossing and 104th Street, Looking Northeast, July 15, 1894," Pullman Strike I, Chicago Historical Society.

68. "Inside the Panhandle Railroad Yards," from a photograph by J. W. Taylor, *Harper's Weekly*, July 28, 1894, 704; "Panhandle Yards from Sixty-third Street North," *Inter-Ocean*, July 9, 1894.

69. Jussim, *Visual Communications and the Graphic Arts*, chap. 4, esp. 235–36.

70. See, for example, "When the Meat Train Was Ready to Start," *Inter-Ocean*, July 6, 1894; and "Wrecking Car Clearing Fort Wayne Tracks," *Inter-Ocean*, July 7, 1894.

71. See, for example, "Sunday Scenes in the Big Strike of the American Railway Union," *Chicago Tribune*, July 2, 1894; and "Lake Shore Train Loaded with Artillerymen Stopped by the Mob at 40th and Halsted Street," *Chicago Tribune*, July 5, 1894.

72. *Harper's Weekly*, July 28, 1894, 704, after photographs by J. W. Taylor and R. D. Cleveland. For an original print of Cleveland's photograph, see Pullman Strike, ICHi 21816, Chicago Historical Society. For a similar example, see *Railroad Gazette* (New York), August 3, 1894.

73. Historic Pullman Collection, 1.13, Chicago Public Library; "Main Entrance to the Pullman Works," June 19, 1894, Scrapbook on the Pullman Strike in Chicago, 45, Chicago Historical Society; *Chicago Times*, June 20, 1894, Pullman Company Scrapbooks, series 03, vol. 1, 133, RG No. 12, Pullman Company Archives, Newberry Library. This photograph has long been considered the only extant photograph of the striking Pullman workers, an attribution I also initially made. In fact, it was taken no later than August 1891, when a different, equally faithful

line drawing based on it illustrated a newspaper article on Pullman. "Two Model
Towns: Roseland and Pullman Thriving, Rushing Places," *Chicago Evening Post,*
August 18, 1891, Pullman Company Scrapbooks, series 01, vol. 14, clipping, RG No.
12, Pullman Company Archives, Newberry Library. See also miscellaneous clippings from December 29, 1890, to May 24, 1891. The photograph may nevertheless have depicted striking workers. The Pullman Car Works was hit by a series
of small strikes against wage cuts from December 1890 to May 1891. Groups of
strikers left the factory (through the gate depicted in the photograph) on their
way to nearby Kensington, outside the model town, where they held strike meetings and assembled pickets at the Illinois Central's Kensington Station to turn
back arriving strikebreakers. This photograph may have been taken of a group of
strikers leaving the factory. It is a good example of how a photograph's meaning
often depends more on the context in which it appears than on its true subject
matter (in this case unknown). While the *Chicago Evening Post* used it to illustrate
an article that helped restore the Pullman Company's favorable public image after the 1891 strikes, the *Chicago Record*'s recycling of it in 1894 suggested that it
depicted striking workers. In this latter guise it helped establish twentieth-century
labor iconography, in which strikes are routinely symbolized in photographs by
picket lines in front of factory gates.

74. "Main Gate to Works"; *Harper's Weekly,* July 21, 1894, 684–85.

75. Ray Stannard Baker, LC-B31-141, Prints and Photographs Lot 4069, Library
of Congress. A faithful line drawing based on this photograph was published as
"Employes Gateway at Pullman," *Chicago Record,* July 30, 1894, Pullman Company
Scrapbooks, series 03, vol. 7, 61, RG No. 12, Pullman Company Archives, Newberry
Library.

76. *Leslie's,* August 9, 1894, 86. See also sketches of the same subject in *Leslie's,*
July 26, 1894, 54.

77. For an early photographic example, see Sigmund Krausz, *Street Types of Chicago: Character Studies* (Chicago: M. Stern, 1891). Photographs of ethnic and racial types in the U.S. combined prephotographic stereotypes with portraits of
"street types" modeled after the work of John Thomson. See John Thomson and
Adolphe Smith, *Street Life in London* (London: Sampson Low, Marston, Searle, and
Rivington, 1877); Hales, *Silver Cities,* 224–33; Stephen White, *John Thomson: A Window on the Orient* (Albuquerque: University of New Mexico Press, 1985); and Robert W. Rydell, "A Cultural Frankenstein? The Chicago World's Columbian Exposition of 1893," in Harris et al., *Grand Illusions,* 143–70.

78. Ray Stannard Baker, LC-USZ62-24836 and LC-USZ62-80337, Prints and Photographs Lot 4069, Library of Congress. Only a handful of illustrations in Chicago newspapers at the beginning of the strike alluded to the active support
women in the Pullman community and work force gave the strike.

79. Prior to the Pullman strike, Chicago's daily newspapers were heavily illustrated in the Sunday edition but only lightly during the week. During the strike

even the weekday editions were profusely illustrated with line drawings related to the events. After August the number of illustrations returned to the prestrike pattern but with more during the week.

80. Peterson, "Producing Visual Traditions among Workers."

81. For Labor Day, see Historic Pullman Collection, 1.60, 1.61, 1.62 (1901 in Pullman), Chicago Public Library; and Chicago Building Trades Council, *Labor Day Illustrated* (Chicago: Chicago Building Trades Council, 1897). See also Peterson, "Producing Visual Traditions among Workers."

82. Keller, "Photojournalism around 1900."

83. Ibid.

84. Conclusion based on a comparison of illustrations in the Chicago press of Pullman strike of 1894 and the rail shop craftworkers' strike of 1922. For a good study of news reporting on labor unions in the twentieth century, which unfortunately does not discuss photography, see William J. Puette, *Through Jaundiced Eyes: How the Media Views Organized Labor* (Ithaca, N.Y.: ILR Press, 1990). Most of the kinds of media bias Puette discusses were already common in 1894, but the overall mix—how stories on labor were put together in a coherent narrative—differed between the nineteenth and twentieth centuries.

5

Advocate for Democracy:
Jane Addams and the Pullman Strike

Victoria Brown

WHEN THE PULLMAN STRIKE began in May of 1894, Jane Addams had been at the helm of the Hull-House settlement in Chicago for less than five years. She was only thirty-four years old, but she stood at the center of a neighborhood enterprise destined to expand from three buildings, a playground, and a bathhouse in 1894 to a complex of thirteen buildings, which by 1907 would encompass an entire square block of Halsted Street in the Nineteenth Ward. Press clippings indicate that at the time of the Pullman strike Addams was an object of public interest and respect both in Chicago and around the country. But she was not yet the most famous and most powerful woman in America; John Burns's claim that she was "the first saint America produced" lay years in the future, as did her leadership role in the Progressive party and the National American Woman Suffrage Association, public rebuke for her pacifism during World War I, and her subsequent receipt of the Nobel Peace Prize.[1]

In the spring of 1894 Addams was still establishing herself as a member of Chicago's reform community, simultaneously burdened by and benefiting from the media image of her as a selfless maiden who had sacrificed personal wealth and happiness to live and work among the poor. Feature stories about Addams, which were plentiful in the early 1890s, devoted most of their attention to the domestic, nurturing aspects of daily life at Hull-House: the kindergarten, the children's clubs, the teas for immigrant women, the play groups, the art groups, the university extension classes, and the community kitchen. These articles might make passing mention of other Hull-House activities, the clubs for political and economic debate, the trade union meetings, the political campaigns, and the legislative lobbying, but in the early 1890s these more partisan efforts never dominated the public image of Hull-House. Though the press strained to assert that Addams herself was a Christian, much was made of the fact that Hull-House had no explicitly religious mission and therefore presumably had no agenda beyond community service.[2]

The journalistic insistence on depicting Addams as a disinterested, secular nun certainly made her activities appear less threatening to the Chicago establishment and undoubtedly gained her access to some of the city's most powerful, wealthy families. But it says much about the tenacity of nineteenth-century definitions of both womanhood and social reform that Addams and her project continued to be viewed in terms of sacrificial service. This image persisted even though Addams brought Hull-House to public attention in the 1890s by delivering speeches, publishing articles, and giving interviews in which she explicitly disavowed any philanthropic purpose, insisting that the Hull-House settlement was not a charity but a neighborhood center, where people could gather for fellowship and to organize ways of meeting community needs. "It represents an attempt to make social intercourse express the growing sense of the economic unity of society," she wrote in 1892, "to add the social function to democracy."[3]

Addams had put Hull-House on the nation's reform map in 1892 with two articles in *Forum* magazine in which she argued that work with the poor and laboring classes benefited privileged women like herself as much as, if not more than, it did those ostensibly receiving help, that such work gave her and her fellow settlement residents a purposeful life.[4] Addams thus began her settlement house with an unsentimental assertion of mutual benefit rather than noble sacrifice in all reform endeavors. Though the press quoted those assertions and the public applauded them, cultural tradition—and probably Addams's own personal style—continued to cast her in the public eye as "a girlish figure with a refined and sympathetic face glowing with the beauty of purpose that has no thought of self."[5]

Because of this public image, it is tempting to tell the story of Jane Addams's involvement in the Pullman strike as a dramatic turning point in her political evolution, as a jolting end to her innocence and the beginning of her realization that urban, industrial reform was going to demand that she be much more than a friendly neighbor. It is also tempting to argue that the Pullman strike exposed Addams's limitations as a reformer, that her conduct during the strike and her subsequent analysis of the strike reveal her as a timid, temporizing member of the middle class. Allen Davis, her most critical biographer, has pointed to the Pullman strike to support his belief that Addams's "habit" of seeing both sides in a conflict prevented her from ever "becoming the impassioned advocate of any cause." With this logic, the Pullman strike can be employed to support Davis's claim that Jane Addams "never followed the logic" of her prolabor position onto a picket line or into the Socialist party, that in the face of a violent strike she "preferred to stand aside and interpret rather than get involved in the fray," and that this pattern of behavior was, at the very least, regrettable, calling into question the depth and sincerity of Addams's commitments.[6]

The examination of Jane Addams and the Pullman strike presented here is designed to plead against these interpretive temptations. The Pullman strike did not mark a dramatic turning point in Addams's reform thinking, nor was her reaction to it timid or temporizing. Instead, the evidence makes clear that by the time the strike occurred, Addams had been thoroughly immersed in Chicago's community of union activists and labor theorists; she was hardly innocent of knowledge about the potential for brutal obstinacy lying just beneath Chicago's veneer of capitalist civility. In this context Addams's reaction to the strike bespeaks not her political timidity in the mid-1890s but her rather impressive philosophical maturity and independence. Though still relatively young, fairly new to social reform, and strongly influenced by and deeply committed to her friends in the labor and socialist movements, Addams demonstrated remarkable ability to follow the logic of her own thinking and thereby carve out her own unique stance toward the Pullman strike in particular and the "labor question" in general.

The argument here is that Addams defined an independent position on the labor question precisely because she was the "impassioned advocate" of a cause: the cause of mediated conflict through democratic process. Her friends and colleagues in social reform did not always appreciate or understand that cause; like many modern historians, they wanted Jane Addams fighting in their corner, not serving as the referee. But the record demonstrates that Addams stood her ground out of conviction, not timidity. The record further demonstrates that in her daily life in Chicago in the 1890s, Addams acted on her conviction by mediating a continual, democratic dialogue between the city's concentric and overlapping circles of civic activists. Finally, the record demonstrates that Addams conducted her personal relationships as she did her public ones: with an unsentimental regard for mutual benefit and a democratic insistence on respect for personal autonomy.

It is important to make clear at the outset the very thing that Jane Addams made clear in her testimony before the U.S. Strike Commission investigating the Pullman strike: she was not anywhere near the center of the strike's storm. There is no need to exaggerate Addams's practical role in the strike in order to establish the significance of Addams's relationship to the strike. That Addams tried—and failed—to arbitrate the strike says a great deal about the climate for U.S. labor mediation in 1894. On the one hand, Addams's efforts signal tremendous optimism among some members of the Chicago business community and some members of the labor community that cooperation in achieving mutual aims could be accomplished within industrial capitalism. On the other hand, Addams's ultimately marginal role in the strike serves as a reminder that optimism about peace in labor-capital relations in 1894 was premature, to say the least. To say that Addams was prematurely optimistic, however, is not to say that she was timid, temporizing, or even naive. It is to say that she had a very particular vision of how to solve the problems inherent in industrial capitalism, a vision that required optimism, and she was doggedly persistent in articulating that vision. Addams was so persistent that almost twenty years after the strike she was still sufficiently invested in her view of it to publish a long-suppressed essay on George Pullman, which would serve to frame the strike in her unique terms for decades to come.

Addams appeared before the three-member U.S. Strike Commission on August 18, 1894, six weeks after the end of the strike. She explained at that time that she was drawn into the strike in her capacity as a member of the board of trustees of the newly formed Civic Federation of Chicago and, more specifically, as a member of the federation's Industrial Committee and its Board of Conciliation. Three months before the Pullman strike began, the Civic Federation had announced that its purpose was to energize "the public conscience of Chicago" by serving as the "non-political, non-sectarian center of all the forces that are now laboring to advance our municipal, philanthropic, industrial and moral interests" and to "serve as a medium of acquaintance and sympathy" between the diverse members of the Chicago community.[7] It is noteworthy that when Jane Addams signed on as one of the fifteen "incorporators" of the Civic Federation in February of 1894, she put herself on the federation's Industrial Committee. She did not join the Philanthropic Committee, whose immediate concern was relief for those devastated by that winter's economic depression. Nor did she join the Municipal Committee, whose focus was corruption in City Hall, or the Morals Committee, whose concern was urban vice.

Rather, Addams chose to join the Industrial Committee, whose task was to harmonize labor relations in Chicago by encouraging cooperation and arbitration between workers and employers. Within days of the strike vote in Pullman, the Civic Federation appointed the special Board of Concili-ation, chaired by A. C. Bartlett, a successful businessman in wholesale hardware, to investigate arbitration possibilities.[8] The federation's mem-bers probably viewed the strike as an opportunity to demonstrate what enlightened public discourse could accomplish.

Jane Addams was on the Civic Federation's Board of Conciliation, and, according to her testimony before the strike commission, "the gentlemen on the board" asked her to "find out as near as I could the attitude of the strikers toward arbitration."[9] This assignment occasioned a trip to the town of Pullman sometime in the latter half of May. She squeezed this trip in between the daily demands of her duties at Hull-House, a speaking engagement and presidential reception at the University of Wisconsin in Madison, and another trip to Cincinnati, Ohio, where she spoke to teach-ers about "the Socialistic Settlement Idea."[10] According to Addams her visit to Pullman included "supper with some of the girls working there," a tour of homes with members of the Pullman Relief Committee, and conversations with Thomas Heathcoate, the president of the local chap-ter of the American Railway Union (ARU), and George W. Howard, the national vice president of the ARU. Addams reported back to the Board of Conciliation that the leaders of the strike were "very friendly toward the notion of arbitration."[11]

Since so many of her colleagues in the Civic Federation were prominent Chicago businessmen who favored arbitration of labor disputes, Jane Addams was not fanciful in imagining that such a course was possible in the Pullman case. Numerous other strikes in Chicago had been settled by arbitration in recent years; Hull-House itself had arbitrated a strike at the Star Knitting Works in April of 1892.[12] But if Jane Addams felt optimistic about the chances for arbitration as she took leave of Heathcoate and Howard that May evening in Pullman, the feeling did not last long. By June 1 the *Chicago Mail* was reporting that George Pullman had ignored Ad-dams's letters asking for arbitration. On that particular day Addams had even attempted to meet with the company's vice president, Thomas Wickes, but was told he was out.[13] Jane Addams—the young woman who had enjoyed almost five years of sustained applause from such city lead-ers as George Pullman, the young woman who had just recently received a one-minute standing ovation when she spoke at Chicago's prestigious

all-male Sunset Club about working "WITH the masses, not FOR them"—
was now rudely left to cool her heels in the Pullman Company's foyer.[14]
When Vice President Wickes finally did consent to receive Addams on
June 2, he flatly informed her that there was "nothing to arbitrate."[15]

In her August testimony before the Strike Commission, Addams insisted
that executives of the Pullman Company "were always courteous to me,"
but back in June she had not felt so generous.[16] In an uncharacteristically
sharp remark quoted in the *Chicago Herald* on June 2 Addams had described the Pullman strike as "a struggle between one of the great monopolies on earth and the most powerful organization in railway labor. It
is worthwhile for the Civic Federation to settle this question if it can. But
Mr. Pullman . . . will not consent. And if the Civic Federation, representing all the best elements in the community, cannot effect so desirable a
result, it cannot justify its existence."[17] If these were the stakes as Addams
perceived them, one can imagine her dismay when she read in the *Chicago
Times* on June 7 that Lyman Gage—the president of the First National Bank
in Chicago, the former president of the board of directors of the World's
Columbian Exposition, and at the time of the strike the president of the
Civic Federation—had sharply rebuffed a solicitation for the Pullman
strikers' Relief Fund, reputedly barking that "people who voluntarily leave
good work deserve to suffer."[18] Kate Bradley and Fanny Kavanaugh, Jane
Addams's colleagues from the Illinois Women's Alliance, were the objects
of Gage's scorn, and they repeated their charges of ill-treatment on June
8 in response to a printed denial from Gage.[19] The following week the press
reported that the ARU had voted to close the Relief Fund's account at
Lyman Gage's bank.[20] This peculiar story about Gage, whatever its veracity, may well have undermined Addams's credibility with both the strikers and the Pullman company. After all it was Lyman Gage's plan for ini-
tiating arbitration on the matter of rents in Pullman town that Addams
was trying to put on the negotiating table.[21]

Against all odds Addams persevered in her efforts, meeting once with
Eugene Debs and traveling alone to Pullman for a meeting on the evening
of June 14 to discuss arbitration strategies with "between fifty and sixty
delegates from the local union." It was all for naught. As Addams told the
Strike Commission, it was "impossible to come to any understanding with
the Pullman company" on the matter of arbitration, "and it was dropped."
In the end, said Addams, "we considered the effort a failure."[22]

Addams's exasperation notwithstanding, the Civic Federation did not
take this defeat as evidence that it could not "justify its own existence."

By November the organization's members—including Jane Addams—
would recoup its losses on the labor front. During the same week that the
U.S. Strike Commission issued its finding that the Pullman strike should
have been settled by arbitration, the now-vindicated Civic Federation was
convening its two-day Congress on Industrial Conciliation and Arbitration.[23] The November congress brought together an impressive array of
labor activists, legislators, reformers, and government officials. Even
Carroll D. Wright, the U.S. commissioner of labor who had headed the U.S.
Strike Commission in the Pullman case, accepted the Civic Federation's
invitation to speak and was interrupted by applause when he predicted a
day in the future when Americans would voluntarily submit their disputes
to arbitration and "the man or the corporation who so conducts—or
rather who so misconducts—his affairs as to permit a strike will receive
the same disgrace at the hands of public opinion as the fraudulent bankrupt does today."[24] As a result of that congress, the Civic Federation sponsored legislation, which was enacted by the Illinois General Assembly in
1895, to establish the state Board of Conciliation and Arbitration, empowered to mediate labor disputes—when both parties in the dispute agreed
to such mediation.[25] For all practical purposes the bill was useless, but it
represented a symbolic victory for the Civic Federation.[26] George Pullman
may have ignored Jane Addams and the federation of civic reformers she
represented, but at least the state of Illinois had placed its imprimatur on
the principle of voluntary, civilized arbitration that Addams and the Civic
Federation espoused.

None of these developments affected the outcome of the Pullman strike
itself, of course. That outcome was decided on the ground in late June and
early July, when a national melee of railway strikers, the unemployed, and
ultimately the military combined to create a transportation snarl of unprecedented proportions. By that time Jane Addams was out of the picture. On June 20, the day before the American Railway Union voted to
support the Pullman strikers, Addams was in Cleveland, Ohio, delivering
the commencement address to the female graduates of Case Western
Reserve. Without ever mentioning the Pullman strike Addams took the
occasion to criticize the "selfishness" and "narrow individuality" of those
"leaders in society in our large cities" who lacked "that broad conscience
which takes in those around them."[27] Three days later, in one of the very
few letters that have survived from this month in Jane Addams's life, she
told her former teacher Sarah Anderson about the strain the economic
depression of 1893–94 had put on Hull-House's resources, but she made

no mention of the Pullman strike.[28] By the following week, when the Pullman strike was at its peak, when 125,000 workers were out and twenty railroads were shut down, Jane Addams was rushing to the bedside of her beloved older sister, Mary Linn, who was dying of heart failure in Kenosha, Wisconsin.

Fifteen years later Addams recalled in her autobiography that she had been able to reach Kenosha from Chicago "at once" but that Mary Linn's husband and children had encountered "every possible obstacle of a delayed and blocked transportation system" as they struggled to reach Mary's bedside "from a distant state."[29] As with most of the stories in Addams's autobiography, this one blends fact and fiction into an effective parable. Mary Linn's family had to travel only to Kenosha from Winnebago in northern Illinois—hardly a distant state. Still, it is quite likely that they encountered difficulty if they tried to travel by train during that chaotic week. What is less likely is the autobiography's purported exchange in which Mary, while dying, assured her younger sister that she bore no resentment toward the strikers who were depriving her of a last glimpse of her husband and children. "I don't blame anyone," Addams quoted Mary saying, "I am not judging them." Addams chose to immortalize her deeply religious sister in this Christ-like role to make the point that labor strikes inevitably create "lasting bitterness" in the hearts of those less devout than her sister and that even a righteous cause can be sullied if it injures or alienates too many innocent bystanders.[30]

The fatally high cost of "barbaric" conflict was the main lesson that Jane Addams carried with her from the wreckage of the Pullman strike. She had stood foursquare in favor of cooperation over conflict before the strike, but in the months and years following the event she drew upon her memories to develop a powerful indictment of those—on the left as well as on the right—who used ultimatums, confrontation, and violence in the name of social progress or community welfare. At the same time she used the circumstances surrounding the Pullman strike to teach a complementary lesson about the arrogance of unilateral philanthropy and, hence, the need for democratic process and a cooperative spirit in all public affairs. Ultimately Jane Addams viewed a whole array of social relations—from philanthropy to industry—as civic matters best adjudicated through the democratic state.

In the year following the strike Addams wove these lessons into a compelling speech that depicted George Pullman as "a modern Lear." It is because of this speech, not her failed effort at arbitration, that Jane

Addams's name has been historically linked to the great railway strike. There were other speakers, other writers who used the strike to call for labor arbitration; Addams was not unique in her advocacy of that specific policy. But Addams was unique in the way she captured both the human drama and the abstract issues salient to the event, and Addams was unique in the sympathetic but independent position she staked out between the various players in the Pullman drama and amidst the numerous issues that drama brought to light.

In the three years prior to the Pullman strike Addams had been delivering a series of semiautobiographical commentaries on the struggle between college-educated daughters and their parents caught in a generational shift from one set of expectations to another. Parents, reared in an era "when there was absolutely no recognition of the entity of woman's life beyond the family," were shocked by the educated, adult daughter's individuality, independence, and interest in public life, or what Addams called "the social claim." A tragic struggle ensued, said Addams, when these parents—in the name of love—asserted their generation's values by insisting that the daughter put aside her generation's ambition and submit to the traditional dictates of "the family claim."[31]

Reflecting on the Pullman strike, Jane Addams discerned a notable similarity between gender struggles she had analyzed in the family and labor struggles she had observed in industry. From this she drew her comparison of George Pullman and King Lear. In "A Modern Lear" Addams argued that the plight of the modern industrial worker was analogous to the plight of the modern educated daughter. Employers, like fathers, simply refused to recognize, much less respect, their subordinates' autonomy; employers, like fathers, were blind to the possibility that a worker, like a daughter, might be "moved by a principle" that went beyond mindless duty to the job or the family.[32] The result of such paternal intransigence, said Addams, was industrial and domestic tragedy. In some cases the subordinates submitted to the authority, to that "one will" that was "insisting upon its selfish ends at all costs." The costs, Addams asserted, were the mental and physical health of both workers and daughters, whose "vitality" was "consumed by vain regrets and desires."[33] In other cases, such as the Pullman strike, the subordinates rebelled, dissolving the familial or industrial bond, leaving behind "distrust and bitterness" and thereby destroying all "mutual interest in a common cause."[34] Neither outcome was acceptable to Addams; with submission came the destruction of the individual, with rebellion came the destruction of community.

As a full participant in her era's search for balance between the rights of the individual and the needs of the community, Jane Addams refused to accept the conservatives' call for subordination or the radicals' call for rebellion.[35] This stance had the potential of creating conflict between Addams and her more partisan friends in the labor movement.

Even the most sentimental feature stories on Jane Addams in the 1890s acknowledged that Hull-House was "on the side of unions."[36] Addams justified this degree of partisanship on the grounds that in her experience unions were much more open to arbitration than business was and the "masses" she wished to reach were in unions. As Addams herself put it, "If the design of the settlement is . . . fraternal cooperation with all good which it finds in its neighborhood, then the most obvious line of action will be organization through the trades-union."[37] Note the emphasis here on "fraternal cooperation." It was this, not the choosing up of sides, that shaped Addams's thinking on the resolution of modern industrial conflict.

Addams's writings on the labor movement in the 1890s make clear that she understood and accepted the necessity of labor strikes. "The labor movement is bound," she said in 1895, "to work for shorter hours and increased wages and regularity of work" so that workers would have the time and energy to contemplate "the larger solidarity" and "higher motives."[38] Her 1899 article in the *American Journal of Sociology*, "Trades Unions and Public Duty," was a brilliantly clever defense of the use of the boycott, the demand for shorter hours and limited apprenticeships, the sympathy strike, and strikers' hostility to scabs. Even as she mounted this defense, however, Addams argued that workers should not have to be engaging in these adversarial actions; they were doing the work the state should be doing.[39] Only the state reflected the collective will of all the people, only the state was bound to democratic process, and therefore only the state—not labor unions, not individual paternalistic employers—could bring about industrial conditions in which citizens enjoyed autonomy and individual dignity but were not isolated from one another or from one another's interests.

"A Modern Lear" was not as explicit about the role of the state in resolving labor conflict as some of Addams's other commentaries, but the essay left no doubt that Addams placed her faith in shared participation in the democratic process; no one in the community could be shut out. "The emancipation of working people will have to be inclusive of the employer from the first or it will encounter many failures, cruelties and reactions," she warned her friends in labor. "The doctrine of emancipation must be strong enough in its fusing power to touch those who think they lose as well as those who think they gain." For Addams the purpose of the entire enterprise was "to touch to vibrating response the noble fiber in each man, to pull these many fibers, fragile, impalpable and constantly breaking, as they are, into one impulse."[40]

The sine qua non of Jane Addams's political vision was the connectedness of all individuals in a community, and the democratic process was for her the only means of realizing that vision. This was her impassioned cause. As she would later explain in *Democracy and Social Ethics*, Addams viewed democracy "not merely as a sentiment which desires the well-being of all men, nor yet as a creed which believes in the essential dignity and equality of all men." In other words, democracy was not the sole province of either communitarians or individualists. Rather, she said, we must think of democracy as a process that "affords a rule of living" and a means of negotiating between our competing impulses. Finding equilibrium between the needs of the community and the individual, she said, "consists of processes as well as results, and . . . failure may come quite as easily from ignoring the adequacy of one's method as from selfish or ignoble aims."[41]

Addams's devotion to democratic process meant that she was willing to accept a half-measure, the "feasible" over the "absolute right," if it represented the common ground on which the whole community could stand. Addams admitted in "A Modern Lear" that compromise—what she called "Mr. Lincoln's 'best possible'"—often left her with the "sickening sense" that she had sold out. But that sense was outweighed by her much stronger sense that slow, collective progress was more permanent than a coerced victory.[42] Labor leaders would succeed where George Pullman had failed, said Addams, if they recognized that no solution could be imposed by a ruling party and if they embraced the necessity for democratic process and consent of the whole community.

Contrary to what her critics have charged, Jane Addams did not subscribe to these views because she entertained the illusion that capitalists, approached rationally, would willingly sacrifice personal wealth and political privilege for the commonweal. On the contrary she understood only too well that the King Lears and the George Pullmans of the world were bent on resistance, even violent resistance. That was her whole point. Violent confrontation between capitalists and workers—whatever the outcome—would only further rend the social fabric, making her goal of community cohesion and cooperation ever more elusive. Better, said Jane

Addams, to chip away at the capitalists' position, wear them down, erode their resistance, and build their support bit by bit, law by law, contract by contract, so that their children and their children's children would gradually come to share a communalistic commitment to "universal kinship" and would feel no urge to avenge the death of capitalist power. In this way the broadest, most excellent gains of the labor movement would become permanent.[43]

Addams's argument in "A Modern Lear" was suffused with the assumption that the conflict between labor and capital was an inevitable product of historical evolution and that the rise of an organized labor movement was equally inevitable. The day for individualism was over, she said; whatever the "personal ambition" of men like Lear and Pullman may have accomplished in the past, "it is certainly too archaic to accomplish anything now."[44] Her announcement that "we are all practically agreed that the social passion of the age is directed toward the emancipation of the wage-worker" was vintage Addams.[45] She typically enacted her aversion to conflict by presenting her position as one on which "we are all practically agreed." Addams chose to assert, rather than argue, that respect for workers (and daughters) was the era's "new code of ethics." Such historical relics as George Pullman had simply "failed to catch the great moral lesson which their times offered them."[46] All that remained in doubt was whether subordinates' emancipation would come through conflict or cooperation, whether it would destroy the community or unite it, and whether it would be temporary or permanent.

Where Addams carved out her independent ground, however, was not in her support for the rights of labor, for she shared that position with many others. Her independence emerges in her hope that labor and capital alike would accept the historical imperative of the moment, take the long view, and keep in mind that the ultimate goal was a unified, cooperative community, not a partisan victory. She cast George Pullman into the larger historical tableau provided by the Lear story to make the evolutionist's point that "we may in later years learn to look back upon the industrial relationships in which we are now placed as quite as incomprehensible and selfish, quite as barbaric and undeveloped, as was the family relationships between Lear and his daughters."[47] Every generation, said Addams, was charged with the task of enlarging, ennobling, and adapting old virtues to fit new conditions. "Individual virtues" were now "archaic"; the thoughts "at least of this generation," she announced, "cannot be too much directed from mutual relationships and responsibilities."[48] If workers as well as employers could learn from the "dramatic failure" of both Lear and Pullman and if they could adopt a generous, cooperative, democratic approach to their conflicts, then, she declared, "we may possibly be spared useless industrial tragedies in the uncertain future which lies ahead of us."[49]

Addams began framing this argument on Pullman and Lear soon after the strike was over. It appears that she delivered an early version of the essay to the Chicago Woman's Club and the Twentieth Century Club of Boston in the fall of 1894. She addressed the subject again at a New York conference of settlement workers in May of 1895 in what one newspaper called a "striking characterization of Pullman."[50] When she submitted the essay for magazine publication early in 1896, however, she hit a wall of resistance. In quick succession Addams received rejection letters from the *Forum,* the *North American Review,* and the *Atlantic Monthly.*[51] When she asked Henry Demarest Lloyd to return his copy of the article to her after reading it, she added wryly that "in doing that you will be following the example of the most illustrious magazines in the country."[52] In the end "A Modern Lear" did not get into print until 1912, almost two decades after the Pullman strike in 1894—and George Pullman's death in 1897.

Given the ease with which all of her previous writings had been accepted for publication, and given her popularity in the press, it seems likely that Jane Addams was surprised by initial rejection of the Pullman essay. She lived in a political climate in the 1890s that would have encouraged her to expect that an article calling for community cooperation, civic unity, and evolutionary progress would be enthusiastically received. Coming off the World's Columbian Exposition in 1893, Chicago was thick with civic pride and reform activism. It is true that when the British reformer William Stead visited Chicago in 1893, he was shocked by the city's filth, poverty, vice, and corruption. But it is also true that when Stead called a mass meeting at the Central Music Hall to protest these conditions, hundreds of respectable Chicagoans came to be berated by Stead and other reformers for their civic failings, and dozens stayed to form the Civic Federation.[53] The Civic Federation was hardly alone in attempting to build a larger sense of public community that could unite Chicago's diverse interests. After all the federation's own statement of purpose referred to "all the forces that are now laboring to advance our municipal, philanthropic, industrial, and moral interests." Those forces included, obviously, the settlement houses—Hull-House, the University Settlement, the Chicago Commons, and other smaller efforts—as well as the Chicago Woman's

Club, the Chicago Ethical Society, the Sunset Club, the Woman's Christian Temperance Union, the Society for Christian Socialists, the United Labor party, the Illinois Women's Alliance, and the Municipal Voters' League, as well as the city's dozens of labor organizations, mutual aid societies, and ethnic clubs, to name just a few of the organizations active in Chicago civic reform in the 1890s. When Jane Addams cried out for a "larger solidarity" in 1895, hers was not the voice of a lone wolf.[54]

The publishing fate of "A Modern Lear" suggests, however, that there was something different about Jane Addams's insistence on unity, cooperation, and mediation in Chicago civic life in the 1890s, something a bit discomfiting. While others talked about making room at the civic table for all points of view, Jane Addams actually did it. While others talked about putting a human face on industrial conflict, Jane Addams actually did it. This made her both a noble figure in Chicago and an irritating one. As she herself admitted in her autobiography, the "desire to bear independent witness to social righteousness often resulted in a sense of compromise difficult to endure and at times it seemed that we were destined to alienate everybody."[55]

It is on this very matter of alienating everybody that "A Modern Lear" invites a final bit of scrutiny. Examining the essay for ways in which she might have offended a wide spectrum of readers, including close friends and colleagues, helps in appreciating Jane Addams's sturdy independence within the various circles of Chicago's reform community.

Some of her wealthier colleagues, those Addams referred to privately as "the swells," would likely have been offended by her treatment of George Pullman himself.[56] Addams probably saw her treatment as sympathetic; after all, she said that the comparison with King Lear had "modified and softened" all her judgments of the man. She credited Pullman with an "honest desire to give his employees the best surroundings" and with reaching "the height of sacrifice" for his unfortunately ill-conceived plan to control workers' lives.[57] Since Addams's intent was to write a universal human story, she made sure that every criticism of Pullman took broad aim at every employer, philanthropist, and parent who had ever succumbed to the arrogance of power. This is precisely why "A Modern Lear" would have made a number of Addams's colleagues in the Civic Federation—such colleagues as Lyman Gage, for example—profoundly uncomfortable. Many members of such Chicago organizations as the Civic Federation, the Municipal Voters' League, the Chicago Bureau of Charities, and the City Club were motivated by the same principles of elite stewardship and the same desires for social control that motivated George Pullman. While they might have regretted his conduct of the strike, they were ideologically sympathetic to his claims to the prerogatives of private ownership.[58] Jane Addams managed to work with Chicago's reform-minded "swells" in the post-mugwump 1890s and won their respect in the process, but she had no compunction about exposing their faults on occasion. It was not, after all, Jane Addams who kept "A Modern Lear" under wraps until 1912; it was the editors of elite magazines.

The longest and most telling rejection letter that Addams received regarding "A Modern Lear" was from Horace Scudder, the editor at the *Atlantic Monthly* (and, coincidentally, the uncle of Vida Scudder, the Christian socialist founder of New York's College Settlement). Scudder's letter is worthy of note because it shows the size of the ideological gap between Addams and many of those in the upper crust with whom she maintained cordial working relations. While protesting his "very great . . . respect" for Addams and the "skill . . . earnestness . . . and impressiveness" of her article, Scudder found that Addams's argument in "A Modern Lear" "fell to the ground" because she assumed George Pullman's intent was philanthropic when, in fact, said Scudder, his intent was to "get a good investment on his capital."[59] Apparently, in Scudder's view, philanthropy required some deference to democratic process, but capitalism did not. Scudder did not consider the possibility of amending the laws of capitalism and completely missed Jane Addams's point that all human relations—whether charitable or profitable—required deference to democratic process.[60]

If publication of "A Modern Lear" in 1896 would have offended Jane Addams's reform colleagues in elite circles, it would just as likely have offended her friends in the labor movement and the socialist movement, for not only did Addams presume to lecture George Pullman on the conduct of his affairs, she also preached to her friends in the working class. In arguing for the primacy of democratic process and inclusiveness, Addams bemoaned "the fatal lack of generosity in the attitude of workmen" toward employers and their "narrow conception of emancipation." The labor movement, she feared, was as susceptible to the seductions of power and wealth as the capitalists it sought to replace; workers ran "an awful risk" of selling out "for the sake of fleshpots, rather than for the human affection and social justice" requisite for true emancipation.[61]

If Addams's vision of "affectionate interpretation" in the worker-employer dialogue did not offend those workers who had battled the militia at the height of the Pullman strike, surely the faith she placed in the state as the ultimate arbiter of industrial conflict would have made many unionists uneasy. Workers in the 1890s—from Samuel Gompers on down the ranks—expressed serious reservations about empowering a heretofore procapitalist government to manage their affairs.[62] Addams, who put the state at the center of her plan for a more just economy, regarded the unions' suspicion of government as proof that labor could be as stubborn and hidebound as George Pullman. In fifty years, she said, opponents of state-run arbitration in labor crises like the Pullman strike "will be looked upon with amazement, perhaps with contempt."[63]

But at the same time that she sought recourse in the political arena, Addams rejected the socialist solution. Like Eugene Debs, Addams emerged from the Pullman strike convinced that the brute force of capital would always defeat strikes, and, like Debs, she looked to the ballot box for justice. But unlike Debs, Addams did not believe that social harmony could arise from the electoral defeat of the capitalist minority. As she said at the commencement speech she delivered in Cleveland at the height of the Pullman strike, "More wealth will not bring prosperity to the workingman any more than did the universal vote. It is only to be found in the widening of social life." Addams agreed with much of the Marxist analysis but not with the Marxist solution; she held firm to the belief that there were "principles, ideas" that existed independent of class relations and the cash nexus, and she held equally firm to the belief that "the emancipation of working people will have to be inclusive of the employer from the first."[64]

Over the course of her reform career Jane Addams distinguished herself by insisting on her independence from the elite, the labor movement, and the socialists while sustaining deep and abiding friendships with individuals in all three circles. Nowhere is this pattern more evident than in her relationships with Ellen Gates Starr, Henry Demarest Lloyd, and Florence Kelley. All three were vital influences in Addams's political development, and all three had strong partisan ties to the labor movement and socialism. Addams's management of those three relationships is one more indication of her admirable (and probably irritating) commitment to an unsentimental assertion of autonomy and mutual benefit in all relations, whether public or private.

In her eulogy to Lloyd in November 1903 Addams emphasized the similarity of their views when she recalled commiserating conversations about "the hard places into which the friends of labor unions are often brought

when they sympathize with the ultimate objects of a strike, but must disapprove nearly every step of the way taken to obtain that object." She
claimed that in their private talks Lloyd "referred with regret to the dis-
favor with which most labor men looked upon compulsory arbitration."
According to Addams's rendering in this final memorial to her dear friend
and mentor, Lloyd "himself believed that as the State alone has the right
to use force and has the duty of suppression toward any individual or
combination of individuals who undertake to use it for themselves, so the
State has the right to insist that the situation shall be submitted to an
accredited court, that the State itself may only resort to force after the
established machinery of government has failed."[65] All of this was true,
but it glossed over the fact that when Lloyd referred to "the State," he
envisioned a socialist state, and when Lloyd spoke publicly about labor
conflict, he used a much more adversarial voice than Addams's to indict
capital and defend labor.[66] Here, as usual, Addams dealt with difference
by emphasizing commonality.

Lloyd, Starr, and Kelley all shared Addams's dream of a unified, democratic community, but none of them conducted their daily political relations as Addams did. That is to say, none followed Jane Addams's strict
adherence to the rules of civility and cooperation that would pertain in
such an ideal community. For Lloyd, as for Starr and Kelley, the ethical
imperative of the day necessitated constant, combative assertions of industrial capitalism's immediate evils, not conciliatory gestures to common
ground. They admired Addams's belief, expressed in "A Modern Lear,"
that reform efforts "will be warped unless we look all men in the face, as
if a community of interests lay between them, unless we hold the mind
open, to take strength and cheer from a hundred connections."[67] But the
facts as Lloyd, Kelley, Starr—and most of Addams's other colleagues—saw
them were that a community of interests between labor and capital did
not yet exist, and no Jamesian leap of faith, no acting "as if," could change
that. So while Addams stood vigilant guard over the vision of "a larger
solidarity" and built civic ties to a "hundred connections," Lloyd refused
to join the Civic Federation because it had attracted too many businessmen, Kelley delivered fiery attacks on factory conditions and sweated labor and frantically tried to raise money for Eugene Debs's defense fund,
and Starr passionately sided with unionists in a series of strikes.[68] Addams
certainly shared Lloyd's doubts about the capitalists in the Civic Federation, Kelley's hatred of labor exploitation (though not her interest in Eugene Debs's defense), and Starr's concern for the plight of striking work-

ers and their families. She always kept the doors of Hull-House open to
union meetings and lent her considerable energies and personal resources
to the provision of relief funds during strikes. Indeed, by the early twentieth century, many in the Chicago business community had decided
Addams was too prolabor for their taste; from where they stood she
looked as partisan as her friends.[69] What these capitalists failed to see was
that Addams never shared her friends' zest for the fight; where they were
exhilarated by victories and crushed by defeats, Addams was only wea-
ried and saddened by the persistent quarreling all around her.

It is not surprising that the Chicago business community misunderstood
Jane Addams's prolabor version of nonpartisanship. The wonder is that
Addams's friends and colleagues on the left did not turn against her tire-
some evenhandedness. It appears that only Ellen Gates Starr ever lost
patience with Addams, exclaiming in the heat of one labor strike that "if
the devil himself came riding down Halsted Street with his tail waving out
behind him," Jane Addams would say "what a beautiful curve he had in
his tail."[70] But Starr is the exception, and her special frustration with
Addams on the matter of partisanship bore the marks of their especially
complex tie.[71] In every other relationship Addams maintained her own
and others' separate space, and her coworkers seem to have accepted her
insistence on standing independent of and, to some extent, above the fray.
They must have recognized the benefits her position gave them in the way
of political legitimacy and contacts to individuals they themselves did not
wish to cultivate, and they must have appreciated the programmatic autonomy Addams granted to others as she preserved it for herself.[72]

In the surviving record John Dewey's voice gives clearest expression to
the way in which Addams's friends understood her. Indeed, it is possible
that of all her reform friends in Chicago, Dewey—the philosopher—understood Addams best. Just weeks after the Pullman strike, right at the
time that Jane Addams was first crafting the essay that would become "A
Modern Lear," John Dewey wrote to his wife, Alice, of their stimulating
conversations. Addams had told Dewey that

> she had always believed, still believed, that antagonism was not only useless
> and harmful, but entirely unnecessary; that it lay never in the objective differ-
> ences, which would always grow into unity if left alone, but from a person's
> mixing in his own personal reactions—the extra emphasis he gave to the truth,
> the enjoyment he took in doing a thing because it was unpalatable to others
> or the feeling that one must show his own colors, not be a moral coward, or
> any no. of other ways. That historically only evil had come from antagonisms.

Dewey reported on his efforts to challenge Addams on this point, asking
her "if she didn't think that besides personal antagonisms, there were
[antagonisms] of ideas and institutions, as Christianity and Judaism, and
Labor and Capital, the Church and Democracy now and that realization
of that antagonism was necessary to an appreciation of the truth and to a
consciousness of growth and she said no."[73]

In her conversations with Dewey and in all her personal and political
dealings, Addams held steadfast to the view that antagonism was "always
unreal" and that "instead of adding to the recognition of meaning, it delayed and distorted it."[74] Dewey confessed to Alice that Addams had
forced him to reconsider his own assumptions: "I can see that I have always been interpreting the dialectic wrong end up—the unity as the reconciliation of opposites." In sharing their postmortems on the Pullman
strike in October of 1894, Addams had raised the possibility that opposites were not opposites at all but rather "unity in its growth." Addams,
the apostle of democratic process, "translated physical tension into a
moral thing."[75]

Attracted though he was to Addams's view, Dewey confessed that she
had "converted me internally, but not really, I fear." In the fall of 1894
Dewey simply could not bear the thought that "all this conflict . . . has no
functional value."[76] But two years later, when Addams was circulating "A
Modern Lear" among her friends, only Dewey was unreserved in his
praise. Insisting that "it is quite impossible to say anything in the way of
'criticism' or even of remark upon the Pullman paper," Dewey would say
only that "it is one of the greatest things I have read both as to its form
and ethical philosophy." Unlike those, including Henry Lloyd, who found
the essay too personal or too removed from current events, Dewey believed the essay avoided doing "harm" and "said exactly the things that
must be realized if the affair is going to be anything more than a . . . dis-
gusting memory."[77]

In many ways "A Modern Lear" did ennoble the Pullman strike. Though
some rejected the essay for publication in 1896 because the strike was old
news, the essay ultimately endowed the strike with a mythic, timeless
meaning. From the point of view of the partisans in the strike this may
have been regrettable. By writing and ultimately publishing what became
the strike's most enduring piece of literature, Addams got the final word,
and her final word was not about injunctions or militia or the first amendment or the rights of private property or any of the other serious points
of contention in the strike. Addams's final word was that all contention

would melt away if her fellow citizens would devote themselves first to "mutual interest in a common cause." She admitted that finding the "rhythm of the common heart-beat" was "no easy task." But, Addams insisted, "progress is impossible without it."[78]

Partisans in the strike might well have said that Addams was idealistic to think the conflict could be resolved with harmony. She would have said they were idealistic to think harmony would ever result from conflict. Her position may have been maddeningly detached. But it did not lack passion. And it was never timid.

Notes

1. John Burns quoted in "The Only Saint America Had Produced," *Current Literature* 40 (April 1906): 377.
Descriptions of physical expansion of Hull-House are in Mary Lynn McCree Bryan and Allen F. Davis, eds., *100 Years at Hull-House* (Bloomington: Indiana University Press, 1990), 7; and Helen Lefkowitz Horowitz, "Hull-House as Women's Space," *Chicago History* 12 (Winter 1983–84): 45. Press clippings on Jane Addams's early years at Hull-House can be found in the Hull-House Scrapbooks, 1889–94 (Clippings), Jane Addams Memorial Collection, University of Illinois, Chicago (hereafter JAMC); and Jane Addams Papers (hereafter JAP), microfilm edition, Addendum Reel 10 (frame numbers are not provided on the addendum reels).
2. Hull-House Scrapbooks, 1889–94 (Clippings), JAMC; JAP, Addendum Reel 10. For examples of such stories, see Mary A. Porter, "A Home on Halsted Street," *Advance*, April 11, 1889; "The Chicago Toynbee Hall," *Unity*, March 3, 1890; "She Gave Up Her Home: Noble Work Being Done: Miss Addams Turns Her House into a Useful Institution," *Chicago Journal*, May 17, 1890; "They Help the Poor: Jane Addams' and Ellen Starr's Self-Sacrificing Work among the Lowly," *Chicago Times*, March 23, 1890; "Two Women's Work: Little People Benefited," *Chicago Tribune*, May 19, 1990; "Pictures for the Poor," *Inter-Ocean*, June 21, 1891; "Noble Charity Work: Hull-House and What It Is Doing for the Poor: Miss Addams' Grand Success," *Chicago Post*, February 1, 1893; "Hull-House Chicago," *Record of Christian Work*, October 1893; and "One Day in Altruria: A Visit to Hull-House in Chicago: What Miss Addams Has Done," *San Francisco Chronicle*, February 4, 1894.
In an article that appeared shortly after the Pullman strike, one reporter referred to Hull-House as a "sort of non-Catholic convent" and described Jane Addams as "the gentle, the earnest, the noble woman" with "that spiritual face, almost wan in its intensity, still young and yet weighted with so many cares not her own." "A Social Settlement," *Citizen*, n.p., n.d., JAMC; JAP, Addendum Reel 10.
3. Jane Addams, "Hull-House, Chicago: An Effort toward Social Democracy," *Forum* 14 (October 1892): 226.

4. Ibid., 226–41; Jane Addams, "A New Impulse toward an Old Gospel," *Forum* 14 (November 1892): 345–58.

5. "Congress of Women: Doings at the Midwinter Fair: Bright Representatives of the Fair Sex in San Francisco Entertain Their Sisters from Other States: Miss Addams of Chicago Speaks of Hull-House," unidentified newspaper, n.d. [early February 1894], Clippings File, 1892–1960, JAMC; JAP, Reel 55, Frame 7.

6. Allen Davis, *American Heroine: The Life and Legend of Jane Addams* (New York: Oxford University Press, 1973), 110–11.

7. Quoted in Douglas Sutherland, *Fifty Years on the Civic Front* (Chicago: Civic Federation, 1943), 7.

Formation of the Civic Federation was prompted by a mass meeting in Chicago's Central Music Hall on November 13, 1893. William Stead, a crusading, prolabor journalist from Britain, organized the meeting with the aid of Chicago trades unionists. The aim of the meeting was to arouse Chicago citizens "of all grades, races, sects, and conditions" to the need for political, economic, and moral reform in the city. Following the meeting forty individuals—including Jane Addams—formed the organizing committee for the Civic Federation. The federation was formally incorporated in Springfield, Illinois, on February 3, 1894. See Sutherland, *Fifty Years on the Civic Front,* 4–7; and William T. Stead, *If Christ Came to Chicago: A Plea for the Union of All Who Love in the Service of All Who Suffer* (Chicago: Laird and Lee, 1894), appendix E, 465–67.

8. Jane Addams, testimony, in United States Strike Commission, *Report on the Chicago Strike of June–July, 1894* (Washington, D.C.: Government Printing Office, 1895), 645–47.

9. Ibid., 645.

10. Jane Addams Diaries, 1894–95, JAMC; JAP, Reel 29, Frames 209–14; "Miss Jane Addams of Chicago Explains the Socialistic Settlement Idea," Clippings File, 1892–1960, JAMC; JAP, Reel 55, Frame 21. The "socialistic settlement idea" was the title Addams gave to the talk despite her life-long resistance to being labeled as a socialist. See Jane Addams, *Twenty Years at Hull-House: With Autobiographical Notes* (New York: New American Library, 1961), 139.

11. Jane Addams, testimony, in United States Strike Commission, *Report,* 646.

12. Mina Jane Carson, *Settlement Folk: Social Thought and the American Settlement Movement, 1885–1930* (Chicago: University of Chicago Press, 1990), 80; "A Social Settlement," *Citizen,* Fall 1894, JAMC; JAP, Addendum Reel 10.

13. "He Will Not Act: Pullman Ignores the Efforts of Jane Addams on Behalf of Arbitration: She Makes Final Appeal," *Chicago Mail,* June 1, 1894, Pullman Company Scrapbooks, Newberry Library, Chicago.

14. "Invaded the Sunset Club: Bright Women Talk at the Regular Semimonthly Dinner," *Chicago Times,* February 9, 1894; "Sunset Club Talk," *Inter-Ocean,* February 9, 1894; "Aid for the Masses: The Sunset Club Gives the Subject Discussion,"

Chicago Tribune, February 7, 1894; "Uplift the Masses," *Chicago Daily News,* February, 1894, all in Clippings File, 1892–1960, JAMC; JAP, Reel 55, Frames 10–13.

15. "Pullman Is Stubborn: Flatly Refuses to Arbitrate with Striking Employees," *Chicago Times,* June 2, 1894; "Ready to Arbitrate: American Railway Union's Offer: Willing to Submit Its Grievances against the Pullman Company to the Civic Federation," *Chicago Herald,* June 2, 1894, Pullman Company Scrapbooks, Newberry Library.

16. Jane Addams, testimony, in United States Strike Commission, *Report,* 647.

17. "Ready to Arbitrate: American Railway Union's Offer: Willing to Submit Its Grievances Against the Pullman Company to the Civic Federation," *Chicago Herald,* June 2, 1894, Pullman Company Scrapbooks, Newberry Library.

18. Quoted in "Is Deaf to Appeal: Pullman Relief Committee Meets with Rebuff: Lyman Gage Has No Sympathy with the Strikers: Says He Will Not Give a Cent: Thinks Pullman Is a Dream and Its Plutocrat a Saint: Calls Strikers Lazy Loafers," *Chicago Times,* June 7, 1894, Pullman Company Scrapbooks, Newberry Library.

19. "Denial Is Useless: Lyman J. Gage's Exact Language Is Reiterated: Mrs. Bradley and Mrs. Kavanaugh Report Their Interviews: Banker Maligns Strikers," *Chicago Times,* June 8, 1894, Pullman Company Scrapbooks, Newberry Library.

20. "Acts on the Strike: American Railway Union Asks Pullman to Settle: Resolutions Passed Intending to Score Lyman J. Gage," *Chicago Tribune,* June 16, 1894, Pullman Company Scrapbooks, Newberry Library.

21. Jane Addams, testimony, in United States Strike Commission, *Report,* 646. According to Addams the strategy was to bring Pullman to the negotiating table to discuss the adjudication of rents in response to the decline in workers' incomes and to use that as a basis for arbitration on other, work-related, issues.

22. Ibid., 647.

23. "Minds Bent on Peace: Congress of Conciliation and Arbitration Opens," *Chicago Tribune,* November 14, 1894; "Hear the Big Guns: Congress of Conciliation Attracts Big Crowds: Labor Leaders in Line: Status of the Employer and Employee Discussed: Carroll D. Wright Gives His View of Arbitration: Gompers' Optimistic Address," *Chicago Tribune,* November 15, 1894; "Not Based on Facts: So Say Railway Men Anent the Strike Commission Report," *Chicago Tribune,* November 14, 1894.

24. Quoted in "Hear the Big Guns . . . Carroll D. Wright Gives His View of Arbitration . . . ," *Chicago Tribune,* November 15, 1894. For an even more interesting insight into Wright's reaction to the Pullman strike and his increasing willingness to argue for fairness in government involvement in the economy, see "The Chicago Strike," *Publications of the American Economic Association* 9, no. 5–6 (1894): 33–47.

25. Ray S. Baker, "The Civic Federation of Chicago," *Outlook,* July 27, 1895; Addams, *Twenty Years at Hull-House,* 161; Waldo R. Browne, *Altgeld of Illinois: A*

Record of His Life and Work (New York: B. W. Huebsch, 1924), 194–97; Donald David Marks, "Polishing the Gem of the Prairie: The Evolution of Civic Consciousness in Chicago, 1874–1900" (Ph.D. diss., University of Wisconsin–Madison, 1974); Ralph Easley, *The Civic Federation: What It Has Accomplished* (Chicago: Hollister Brothers, 1899), 14.

26. For example, the State Board of Conciliation and Arbitration was unable to settle a strike of the clothing cutters' union in March of 1896. Addams arranged meetings to "bring out clearly the issue of the strike, to insist further upon arbitration, and at the same time to increase the esprit-de-corps of the tailors." Jane Addams to Henry Demarest Lloyd, March 25, 1896, Henry Demarest Lloyd Papers, State Historical Society of Wisconsin, Madison; JAP, Reel 3, Frame 96. Addams reported in 1896 that "the failure of the State Board of Arbitration to accomplish an adjustment is a great disappointment. . . . All of us have a right to insist that the clothing manufacturers shall show the same fairness and willingness to abide by arbitration that the cutters' union has shown." *Hull-House Bulletin*, March 1896, 5; JAP, Reel 53, Frame 0522.

27. Quoted in "Not Lagging: Western Reserve University Keeps in the Vanguard: Eight Young Ladies Graduate from the Women's College," *Cleveland Leader*, June 20, 1894; JAP, Reel 55, Frame 023.

28. Jane Addams to Sarah Anderson, June 23, 1894, Rockford College Archives, Rockford, Ill.; JAP, Reel 2, Frame 1544–46.

29. Addams, *Twenty Years at Hull-House*, 160.

30. Ibid.

31. Jane Addams, "The College Woman and the Family Claim," *Commons* 3 (September 1898): 3–4. The larger biographical work of which this is a part argues against the view that Jane Addams was describing her relationship with her father in "A Modern Lear" and takes the position that in Addams's life it was other family members who sought to curb her independence. For the more traditional view that Lear and Pullman were surrogates for Jane Addams's father, see G. J. Barker-Benfield, "'Mother Emancipator': The Meaning of Jane Addams' Sickness and Cure," *Journal of Family History* 4 (Winter 1979): 395–420; and Louise W. Knight, "Biography's Window on Social Change: Benevolence and Justice in Jane Addams's 'A Modern Lear,'" *Journal of Women's History* 9 (Spring 1997): 111–38.

32. Jane Addams, "A Modern Lear," *Survey* 29 (November 2, 1912): 134.

33. Addams, "College Woman and the Family Claim," 4.

34. Addams, "Modern Lear," 134.

35. There is a rich literature tracing reformers' attempts in this era to formulate a satisfactory partnership between individualism and collectivism. See, for example, Chester Destler, *Henry Demarest Lloyd and the Empire of Reform* (Philadelphia: University of Pennsylvania Press, 1963); Carson, *Settlement Folk;* James T. Kloppenberg, *Uncertain Victory: Social Democracy and Progressivism in European and American Thought, 1870–1920* (New York: Oxford University Press, 1986); Peter J.

Frederick, *Knights of the Golden Rule: The Intellectual as Christian Social Reformer* (Lexington: University Press of Kentucky, 1976); Andrew Feffer, *The Chicago Pragmatists and American Progressivism* (Ithaca, N.Y.: Cornell University Press, 1993); and Robert B. Westbrook, *John Dewey and American Democracy* (Ithaca, N.Y.: Cornell University Press, 1991).

36. "A Social Settlement," *Citizen*, n.p., n.d., JAMC; JAP, Addendum Reel 10. Addams used this same phrase in "Hull-House: A Social Settlement," which was originally printed as a pamphlet in February 1893 and revised as an appendix to *Hull-House Maps and Papers* (Boston: Thomas Y. Crowell, 1895), 214. It is likely that the reporter for the *Citizen* lifted the phrase from the original pamphlet.

37. Jane Addams, "The Settlement as a Factor in the Labor Movement," in *Hull-House Maps and Papers*, 187–88. In an 1892 article Addams said, "I should like to make clear that we might as well expect the granite tower of the great Chicago Auditorium to float in mid-air . . . as to hope for any uplift in our civilization without the underpinning and support of the masses." "With the Masses," *Advance*, February 18, 1892; JAP, Addendum Reel 10.

38. Addams, "Settlement as a Factor in the Labor Movement," 195, 200–201.

39. Jane Addams, "Trade Unions and Public Duty," *American Journal of Sociology* 4 (January 1899): 448–62.

40. Addams, "Modern Lear," 137.

41. Jane Addams, *Democracy and Social Ethics* (New York: Macmillan, 1902), 6.

42. Addams, "Modern Lear," 137.

43. Addams, "Settlement as a Factor in the Labor Movement," 200. Throughout her life Addams expressed faith in the idea that the "excellent becomes permanent." See, for example, her diary entry at the time of her father's death in 1881, JAMC; and JAP, Reel 30, as well as the collection of public eulogies she had delivered over the years in Jane Addams, *The Excellent Becomes Permanent* (New York: Macmillan, 1932).

44. Addams, "Modern Lear," 137.

45. Ibid., 136.

46. Ibid., 134, 135.

47. Ibid., 132.

48. Ibid., 135, 137.

49. Ibid., 137.

50. "Likens Him to Lear: Miss Jane Addams' Striking Characterization of Pullman," unidentified newspaper, May 3, 1895; "Pullman Follows Lear: Miss Addams of Chicago Traces Their Histories in a Speech," unidentified newspaper, May 4, 1895; "Secret of Success: Efficacy of the College Settlement Depends on Cooperation: Hull House Worker Tells of the Danger She Sees," unidentified newspaper, May 4, 1895, all in JAMC; JAP, Reel 55, Frames 46–47.

Because she delivered the speech in May to a conference on settlement work at New York's United Charities Building, the news reports of the talk emphasized

Addams's warnings about the dangers of philanthropic arrogance. This was certainly a key theme in "A Modern Lear" but not the only theme. The current analysis regards Addams's criticism of condescending philanthropy as a subset of her larger criticism of all undemocratic social relations.

51. A. E. Keet to Jane Addams, February 1, 1896; Lloyd Bryce to Jane Addams, February 6, 1896; Horace Scudder to Mary H. Wilmarth, April 18, 1896, all in Swarthmore College Peace Collection; JAP, Reel 3, Frames 39–40, 45, 104–8.

52. Jane Addams to Henry Demarest Lloyd, February 10, 1896, Henry Demarest Lloyd Papers; JAP, Reel 3, Frame 49.

53. Graham Taylor, *Pioneering on Social Frontiers* (Chicago: University of Chicago Press, 1930), 29–34; Gary Scott Smith, "When Stead Came to Chicago: The 'Social Gospel Novel' and the Chicago Civic Federation," *American Presbyterian* 68 (Fall 1990): 193–205; Sutherland, *Fifty Years on the Civic Front*, 4–7; Stead, *If Christ Came to Chicago*, 466–67; Albion W. Small, "The Civic Federation of Chicago: A Study in Social Dynamics," *American Journal of Sociology* 1 (July 1895): 79–103.

54. There is a wealth of primary and secondary material testifying to the enthusiasm for civic and economic reform in Chicago in the 1890s. As Lyman Gage, the first president of the Civic Federation, put it in the federation's *First Annual Report* (Chicago: R. R. Donnelly and Sons, 1895), 25, the association was "a crystallization of sentiment slowly formed through long periods against civil and social abuses no longer tolerable." The most often cited causes of this wave of reform interest are the Columbian Exposition of 1893, the economic depression of 1893, and William Stead's dramatic "tour" of Chicago in 1893. The historical record makes clear, however, that there was considerable reform activity in Chicago before 1893. It is impossible to imagine that the young and inexperienced Jane Addams would have enjoyed such quick success in Chicago had there not been a ready climate for her "scheme" to uplift the masses. Jane Addams discusses this burst of civic energy in *Twenty Years at Hull-House*, chap. 9. See also Ray Ginger, *Altgeld's America: The Lincoln Ideal versus Changing Realities* (New York: Franklin Watts, 1973); and Thomas R. Pegram, *Partisans and Progressives: Private Interest and Public Policy in Illinois, 1870–1922* (Urbana: University of Illinois Press, 1992).

For a recent and highly persuasive discussion of the reform climate in Chicago prior to 1893, see Richard Schneirov, "Rethinking the Relation of Labor to the Politics of Urban Social Reform in Late Nineteenth-Century America: The Case of Chicago," *International Labor and Working-Class History* 46 (Fall 1994): 93–108. For discussions of the growth of the modern concept of the "public interest," see David Paul Nord, "The Public Community: The Urbanization of Journalism in Chicago," *Journal of Urban History* 11 (August 1985): 411–41; Maureen A. Flanagan, "Gender and Urban Political Reform: The City Club and the Woman's City Club of Chicago in the Progressive Era," *American Historical Review* 95 (October 1990): 1032–50; and Steven J. Diner, *A City and Its Universities: Public Policy in Chicago, 1892–1919* (Chapel Hill: University of North Carolina Press, 1980).

55. Addams, *Twenty Years at Hull-House*, 138–39.

56. Jane Addams to Henry Demarest Lloyd, December 1, 1894, Henry Demarest Lloyd Papers; JAP, Reel 2, Frame 1600.

57. Addams, "Modern Lear," 133–34.

58. For a discussion of the business orientation of the leaders of the Civic Federation, see Marks, "Polishing the Gem of the Prairie." For the conservatism of many businessmen involved in Chicago reform in the 1890s, see Ginger, *Altgeld's America;* Flanagan, "Gender and Urban Political Reform"; and Nord, "Public Community." For a discussion of the elitism of many academic reformers in the city, see Diner, *City and Its Universities.*

Two excellent examples of the conservative, elitist side of Chicago reform are Small, "Civic Federation of Chicago," 102, in which Small saluted the Civic Federation for conducting its business, "as a business man would," by using experts; and Lyman Gage's retort to criticism of the Chicago Board of Trade, in which he made clear his belief that the laws of capital were not susceptible to amendment— or in need of any—in Matthew Mark Trumbell, *Articles and Discussions on the Labor Question including the Controversy with Mr. Lyman J. Gage on the Ethics of the Board of Trade* (Chicago: Open Court Publishing, 1890), 216–22, 232–40.

59. Horace E. Scudder to Mary H. Wilmarth, April 18, 1896, Swarthmore College Peace Collection; JAP, Reel 3, Frames 104–8.

60. It appears that Jane Addams revised "A Modern Lear" at some point to make clearer her understanding that Pullman sought to make a 4 percent profit out of his operations in Pullman town. A typescript of an early, but undated, draft of the essay does not discuss Pullman's profit motive, as the published version does, nor does it include Addams's discussion of the "divergence between the social form and the individual aim," that is, between the profit motive and the communal motive. In the published version Addams argues that Pullman's plan "might have worked out" had Pullman been interested in an "associated effort" and willing to listen to his workers. It is not entirely clear from her discussion if Addams blamed the profit motive or Pullman's attitude for the failure of the model town. Nor does the record make clear if Horace Scudder saw a version that included Addams's revision or if her revision was in response to Scudder's comments. See Jane Addams, "A Modern Tragedy," typescript, 1895, JAP, Reel 46, Frames 0648–59, 266. See also Addams, "Modern Lear," 133.

61. Addams, "Modern Lear," 136–37.

62. John R. Commons, David J. Saposs, Helen L. Sumner, E. B. Mittelman, H. E. Hoagland, John B. Andrews, and Selig Perlman, *History of Labour in the United States,* vol. 2 (New York: Kelly, 1966); Philip S. Foner, *History of the Labor Movement in the United States,* vols. 2–8 (New York: International, 1972). See also the speeches delivered at the Congress of Conciliation and Arbitration in Chicago, *Chicago Tribune,* November 14–15, 1894; and the numerous testimonies from union members against compulsory arbitration in United States Strike Commission, *Report.*

63. "In Memoriam," to William H. Colvin, a businessman, labor supporter, and member of the Hull-House board of trustees, *Hull-House Bulletin*, October 15, 1896, 19; JAP, Reel 53, Frame 0557.

64. Quoted in "Not Lagging: Western Reserve University Keeps in the Vanguard," *Cleveland Leader*, June 20, 1894; Addams, "Modern Lear," 137. See also Addams, *Twenty Years at Hull-House*, 139.

65. Addams, *Excellent Becomes Permanent*, 44.

66. Destler, *Henry Demarest Lloyd and the Empire of Reform*; Frederick, *Knights of the Golden Rule*, chaps. 1 and 2; H. D. Lloyd, *The Safety of the Future Lies in Organized Labor*, paper presented at the Thirteenth Annual Convention of the American Federation of Labor, Chicago, December 1893 (Washington, D.C.: Press of Law Reporter Printing for Henry D. Lloyd, by authority of the convention, 1893), 3–8; H. D. Lloyd, "Strikes and Injunctions," speech delivered at Seventy-fifth Annual Meeting of the Sunset Club of Chicago, October 25, 1894, Chicago Historical Society.

Lloyd delivered his Sunset Club speech at the time Jane Addams was first crafting "A Modern Lear." Where Addams's essay was a parable, Lloyd's speech was a jeremiad. "Do not dream that the discontent can be dealt with by repressing its manifestations," Lloyd warned his audience of businessmen. "You do not cure but kill the small-pox patient when you drive in the eruption. . . . This discontent of the people is more righteous than the spirit which would repress without remedying the causes." While Lloyd's tone is dramatically different from Addams's, there is similarity in his call for a time when people "render equal service for service, and . . . make it so pleasant and profitable, so safe in love and justice to serve, that all hands and hearts will flow freely into deeds of reciprocal brotherliness." Lloyd's comfort with the prospect of social combat to achieve this loving end can be seen in a letter he wrote to Clarence Darrow in November 1894, in which he denounced "the fools of power" and the "aggressions of the enemy," predicting that the "radicalism of the fanatics of wealth . . . are likely to do for us what the South did for the North in 1861." Addams would not have shared Lloyd's "optimism" over the thought that capitalist intransigence would soon justify a decisive reaction from labor; in her view, the violence and bitterness of the Civil War had precluded a positive social outcome for blacks. Quoted in Caro Lloyd, *Henry Demarest Lloyd, 1847–1903: A Biography* (New York: G. P. Putnam's Sons, 1912), 145–46.

67. Addams, "Modern Lear," 137.

68. For a richly textured description of the heated climate in which Addams lived with Lloyd, Kelley, and Starr, see Kathryn Kish Sklar, *Florence Kelley and the Nation's Work: The Rise of Women's Political Culture, 1830–1900* (New Haven, Conn.: Yale University Press, 1995), part 3.

See also Florence Kelley's letters to Henry Demarest Lloyd at the time of Debs's imprisonment, July 18, 1894, and August 1, 1894, Henry Demarest Lloyd Papers. In the heat and chaos of the summer of 1894, when Addams had repaired to the

Rockford College Summer School for Chicago working women, Kelley confessed to Lloyd, "I would not be out of Chicago today for a thousand dollars an hour" (July 18, 1894). See also Ellen Gates Starr's letters to Lloyd at the time of the Chicago garment workers' strike in 1896, April 6, April 8, April 12, and April 21, 1896, Henry Demarest Lloyd Papers. When the strike collapsed, Starr wrote, "I feel a good deal like a funeral but let us hope it will count for something in the next fight" (April 21, 1896).

69. Davis, *American Heroine*, 116.

70. Quoted in ibid., 115.

71. The history of Addams's close personal relationship with Starr, beginning at Rockford Female Seminary, is beyond the scope of this discussion. Suffice it to say that the rifts that developed between the two founders of Hull-House in the 1890s were both emotional and ideological and were rooted in the two women's very different stances toward autonomy, partisanship, and self-revelation.

It is intriguing that Ellen Gates Starr taught a university extension course on *King Lear* at the Rockford College Summer School in 1891. Her syllabus for the course described the play as "a drama of retribution. 'Whatsoever a man soweth, that shall he also reap.'" Four years later Addams would try to argue for alternatives to this tragic outcome. See Hull-House Classes and Lectures, JAP, Reel 50.

72. For tributes to Addams for the respect and autonomy she granted Hull-House residents, see Bryan and Davis, eds., *100 Years at Hull-House;* Sklar, *Florence Kelley and the Nation's Work,* chap. 8; and Louise Knight, "Jane Addams Manages Hull House: A Study of an Early Nonprofit," *Nonprofit Management and Leadership* 2 (Winter 1991): 125–41.

The American Railway Union certainly understood Addams's utility as a civic leader who was perceived to be above the fray. According to the *Chicago Mail,* June 1, 1894, Pullman Company Scrapbooks, Newberry Library, "The strikers openly admit that they expect no result from the kindly endeavors of Miss Addams. But they want to put Mr. Pullman on record as refusing to arbitrate and they are glad to take this opportunity to prove it." Fifteen years after the Pullman strike Walter Rauschenbush, the social gospel minister, described Addams as "one of the invaluable people who combine velocity and stability, so that conservatives have to remain respectful toward you even while they are being dragged along." See Rauschenbush to Addams, February 24, 1910, JAMC, quoted in Davis, *American Heroine*, 119.

73. John Dewey to Alice Dewey, October 10, 1894, John Dewey Papers, Morris Library, Southern Illinois University, Carbondale, quoted in Westbrook, *John Dewey and American Democracy,* 80–81.

74. Ibid., 81.

75. John Dewey to Alice Dewey, October 9 and 10, 1894, John Dewey Papers, quoted in Feffer, *Chicago Pragmatists and American Progressivism,* 113. For an example of another Chicago intellectual who was working to create unity out of

dichotomy, see Small, "Civic Federation of Chicago," 91, where he comments that "it is only our stupidity which imagines that altruism and egoism are antithetical. They are complementary."

It is customary for scholars to assume that John Dewey influenced Jane Addams's thinking. It is less commonly understood that the influence was mutual. See Frederick, *Knights of the Golden Rule,* 17, for the typical assumption. Though her effort was not entirely successful, Mary Jo Deegan, *Jane Addams and the Men of the Chicago School, 1892–1918* (New Brunswick: Transaction Books, 1990), attempted to illustrate the mutuality in Jane Addams's intellectual relationship with a number of important Chicago intellectuals.

76. John Dewey to Alice Dewey, October 10, 1894, John Dewey Papers, quoted in Westbrook, *John Dewey and American Democracy,* 81.

77. John Dewey to Jane Addams, January 19, 1896, Swarthmore College Peace Collection; JAP, Reel 3, Frames 29–30.

78. Addams, "Modern Lear," 136, 137.

6

The Federal Judiciary, Free Labor, and Equal Rights

Melvyn Dubofsky

A RECONSIDERATION OF the Pullman strike of 1894 invites a rethinking of the relationship between labor and the law in the United States in the late nineteenth century. After all, the conflict between Eugene Debs, the American Railway Union, and the General Managers' Association of the midwestern railroads has long been considered the paradigmatic case of the national government's using the law to crush organized labor. The tale of how the railroad corporations worked hand-in-glove with Attorney General Richard Olney to break the strike has been told many times. So, too, have we learned how the strike taught Eugene Debs lessons about the relationship between the state and labor. Debs entered the strike a typical, perhaps even prototypical, exponent of the core values of nineteenth-century labor republicanism; he came away from it part way down the path that would carry him toward advocacy of international socialism and workers' revolution.[1] Today it has become almost commonplace to assert that the fate of the American labor movement was decided in the last two decades of the nineteenth century as a consequence of the clash between workers and the courts.

More than that an enormous new body of scholarly literature suggests that the law, meaning jurisprudential rules as interpreted and implemented by federal and state judges, governed the trajectory of workers' movements from the nineteenth century to the mid-twentieth century. Whether it is Christopher Tomlins and Robert Steinfeld exploring how judges established the categories of free labor and employment-at-will in the first half of the nineteenth century and in the process rendered workers subservient to employers;[2] or William Forbath, Victoria Hattam, and

Karen Orren explicating how judicial power produced both the "business unionism" and "labor liberalism" characteristic of the American labor movement;[3] or even David Montgomery, who, though somewhat more suspicious of the autonomy and power of law, concedes courts had a decisive impact on the labor wars of the late nineteenth century.[4]

For three years as a member of the American Historical Association's Littleton-Griswold Prize Committee and for one year as its chair, I devoted considerable time to reading legal history. The best of the nominated books that I read impressed me with their emphasis on the power of language to shape reality. Nearly all of them, especially those written by former or putative leftists (Marxists), reversed the classical Marxist dictum that "social reality shapes human consciousness"; instead, they stressed that consciousness, as mediated through language, created reality. A similar tale repeated itself in Tomlins's legal history of the early nineteenth century and Forbath's on the last decades of the century. Through the language of treatise books, law professors, and judges, the legal profession molded a singular culture that grasped inordinate power. The discourse of legal culture enabled its practitioners to construct a reality that simultaneously diluted labor's power and caused workers to parrot the words uttered from the bench. According to these scholars the language of the law created capitalist hegemony (by that they mean workers' submission to their own disempowerment).

It struck me as odd to discover how the scholarly methods dominant in cultural studies and literary criticism successfully colonized legal studies. It is not that "discourse" or the "linguistic turn" is absent from contemporary history but rather that many historians better resist the imperialism of other disciplines. It almost seems that the current focus on language flows from the political impotency of the Left. The United States in the last decade of the twentieth century lacks a vibrant labor movement and effective political parties on the left. Its historians, literary scholars, cultural studies mavens, and legal scholars, however, all work with language. Words are their coin of the realm, and the more of them such scholars possess and the better they use them, the more power they amass, if not in society at large at least in academia's professional guilds and on its separate campuses or research institutes.

In this essay I revisit terrain already well explored by several generations of scholars: the site where workers, employers, and judges struggled to define the meaning of labor's rights in a "democratic republic." As has now become the custom, I pay due obeisance to the power of language and its role in the making of legal culture. But I also stress how jurisprudence echoed beliefs and values that resonated through broader spheres of popular culture. I suggest that the power of the law flowed as much from the ability of judges to express key aspects of a nonjurisprudential cultural consensus as from their power to use language to shape a new reality.

Three narratives tell the tale of labor's encounter with the law in the late nineteenth century. What I call the "old" narrative, a product of the legal realism that emerged during the Progressive Era and blossomed fully during the New Deal years, described how state and federal courts legitimated the rule of capital. Judges moved from private commercial practice and newer forms of corporate law to state and federal benches, where they applied the values of corporate capitalism to jurisprudence. The law in a most direct and instrumental manner served as handmaiden to the accumulation of capital.[5] It has been succeeded by what I would characterize as a "new" old narrative, one that accords the law a measure of autonomy, asserts that judges seldom served businesspeople directly or instrumentally, and yet insists that the language and rules of legal culture ensnared workers in the bonds of wage slavery. This narrative can be found in the writings of Forbath, Tomlins, Steinfeld, Hattam, and Orren, among many others, who were influenced greatly by the school of "critical legal studies," whose exponents found "legal realism" crude and naive. Finally, we have scholars who borrow from both "legal realism" and "critical legal studies" and compose what I would characterize as a third or mixed narrative, one that accords judges partial autonomy from the rules of capitalism, takes legal culture and language seriously, and explores how the law simultaneously promoted corporate capitalism and restrained its worst tendencies to exploit workers and consumers.[6]

I lean toward the mixed narrative. Especially for the decades of the 1880s and 1890s the law, as explicated by judges, wove a mixed tapestry for employers and employees. Most judges, whether self-educated through apprenticeships in law offices or formally instructed in schools of law, imbibed what Daniel Ernst calls a Victorian legal culture that deified individualism, demanded personal rectitude, policed private practices in the interest of community well-being, and lauded natural law. Under the Victorian legal code neither employers nor employees could act to diminish the rights of others; group or collective interests had no standing in law. Private property rights did not cede businesspeople the power to restrain competition, impair free markets, or exact monopoly prices from consumers. The "free labor" doctrine and its concomitant, employment-at-will, denied workers an unlimited right to withhold their labor (i.e., strike or boycott) if such action infringed on the rights of other workers, harmed the community, or "illegally" diluted the value and use of employers' private property. Courts issued rulings and injunctions that restrained both employers and workers from acting to injure others through combinations (collective or group action) that violated the rules of the marketplace. Finally, judges schooled in Victorian legal culture insisted that public actors lacked the authority (right) to enact legislation that violated natural law (law that most judges considered to be divinely inspired; legislatures and executives, unlike kings, had no divine right to rule; they, too, must obey the commands of natural law).[7]

The view that judges are more responsible, perhaps more ethical, than legislators and are worthy guardians of enduring individual and community values has shown great durability. As recently as 1993 an eminent legal scholar in a book published by a major university press could write bluntly that "the risk of judicial abuse is an acceptable price to pay to control the legislative abuses that all too often do occur."[8] Unlike elected legislators who bent to the will of special interests or powerful classes, judges, especially those on the federal bench who served without fear of popular removal, dispensed evenhanded justice, prescribing the same rules for the rich and the poor, corporations and unions, capital and labor.

In practice, however, Victorian legal culture operated inequitably, exacting a far higher price from workers than from employers. Well before the Pullman conflict federal courts had established rules that prefigured court rulings during the strike and boycott of 1894. It was already a consistent legal principle, established in a series of cases brought by railroads in receivership, that federal courts would not tolerate private parties "taking the law into their own hands." The fear that workers acting through unions illegitimately usurped the function of public law was an old one in American legal history. It had been at the root of judicial rulings in the first half of the nineteenth century that condemned strikes for closed shops and minimum wages as criminal conspiracies.[9] Comparable anxieties concerning private individuals acting collectively and taking the law into their own hands underlay the tendency among state and federal judges in the late nineteenth and early twentieth centuries to issue injunctions against strikes and boycotts. Judges believed, for example, that they had no choice except to protect employers, nonunion employees, and the public from the power to call strikes "by any set of irresponsible men under the sun."[10] On the eve of the Pullman strike Judge William Howard

Taft ruled that the clause in the constitution of the Brotherhood of Locomotive Engineers requiring members to quit in solidarity with brothers
on strike "make[s] the whole brotherhood a criminal conspiracy against
the laws of their country."[11]

Fear that unions acted as private associations to make public law
prompted state and federal judges to outlaw boycotts, strikes for the closed
shop, and sympathy walkouts. Their language repeatedly echoed the same
themes. For example, in an 1891 case a federal district court ruled a boycott by a Cincinnati local of the printers' union to be a form of illegal coercion. In support of a strike against a newspaper in Covington, Kentucky,
the local had asked all its members and supporters to boycott the newspaper and its advertisers until the publisher agreed to hire only union
members. Such action, ruled the court, "was an organized conspiracy to
force the complainant to yield his right to select his own workman, and
submit himself to the control of the union, and allow it to regulate prices
for him, and determine whom he should employ and whom discharge."
The closed shop and boycotts to enforce it, the decision asserted, ceded
unions the power to dictate another's business practices and to damage
economically enterprises that refused to accede to union demands. Society, represented by the judicial arm of the state, must neither concede nor
tolerate such class-motivated behavior intended to enforce alternative law,
the court contended.[12] The following year, 1892, a circuit court of appeals
in Idaho ruled similarly in a case that concerned a collective withdrawal
of labor but not a boycott. To concede to unions the right to determine
whom employers might hire (the closed shop), declared the court, would
cause enterprises to cease and idleness to replace activity. In this country, proclaimed the court, "every owner of property may work it as he will,
by whom he pleases, at such wages, and upon such terms as he can make;
and every laborer may work or not, as he sees fit, for whom, and at such
wages as, he pleases; and neither can dictate to the other how he shall use
his own, whether of property, time, or skill. Any other system cannot be
tolerated."[13]

Judges, to be sure, conceded that law must respect the natural and also
constitutional right of "men" to work or cease working as they chose and
even to act collectively to forward their interests, "provided they do no
violence to others' rights, or commit no violation of law." For far too many
judges, however, strikes, by definition, wreaked harm on the community
and, in the case of railroads in receivership, unlawfully interfered with
management in stark contempt of the court.[14] These principles were enun-

ciated quite clearly in a railroad strike case decided in 1888 in which federal judges ruled that the courts could not prevent strikes or deny workers the right to leave their places (or compel them to return). Yet these judges insisted "a line must be drawn which the employees may not pass." Railroad workers could not force increases in their wages (what the judges defined as "private profit") at the expense of the public. "To redress the small wrongs of a few they [strikers] inflict irreparable injuries upon the many," the court declared.[15]

In the years immediately preceding the Pullman strike federal court precedents limiting collective action multiplied and hardened. Judges acted in what they deemed to be the "public interest" and in behalf of fundamental constitutional and natural rights. In theory workers remained free to withdraw their labor voluntarily, whether individually or collectively. To decide otherwise would be to legitimate involuntary servitude and thus to violate the "free labor" doctrine and the results of the Civil War. Yet judges persistently ruled that if a strike harmed the community, improperly infringed an owner's right to use property freely, or violated the rights of nonparticipating workers, it could be ruled illegitimate. Many federal judges rarely hesitated in using their equity power to offer injunctive relief to parties allegedly injured by strikers. As one federal judge ruled in a case in 1893, citing the words of David J. Brewer, an associate justice of the Supreme Court, "I believe . . . that the powers of a court of equity are as vast, and its processes and procedures as elastic, as all the changing emergencies of increasingly complex business relations and the protection of rights can demand."[16] This meant that judges decided if and when strikes infringed on basic rights.

Also in 1893, in a case concerning a teamsters' strike in New Orleans that spread into a citywide general walkout, federal judges decided that the Sherman Anti-Trust Act applied to combinations of labor as well as business. The legislators, asserted the court, acted to condemn evil, whatever its source, and their manifest intention was to include "combinations which are composed of laborers acting in the interest of laborers." The strikers in New Orleans thus acted illegally and evilly by insisting that unless their demands were met, they would prevent *everybody* from moving the commerce of the country.[17]

On the eve of the Pullman conflict, then, the most commonly accepted jurisprudential rules curbed workers' right to act collectively against the railroads. Man, asserted Judge Taft, has an inalienable right to his own labor, but only so long as he does not use that right to induce or compel other laborers to commit a criminal act. "Neither law nor morals can give a man the right to labor or withhold his labor" when such rights harm other innocent parties, whether workers, employers, or members of the community.[18] These were precisely the principles that judges, including Taft himself, would enunciate and implement during the Pullman conflict.

In 1893–94, a moment of exceptional discontent and conflict, federal judges saw themselves as guardians of the public interest against the depredations wrought by battles between employers and employees. The most antilabor judges insisted that it was not their role or function to participate in struggles between capital and labor; but courts must act, they said, to restrain warring factions from disrupting society and disturbing its peace and, most important, to ensure "that individual and corporate rights may not be infringed." Judges in the federal court for the eastern district of Wisconsin in early 1894 compared railroad strikers to surgeons ceasing work in the middle of an operation. "Liberty and license," the court declared, "must not be confounded. Liberty is not the exercise of unbridled will, but consists in freedom of action, having due regard for the rights of others." Strikes, asserted the judges, represented license not liberty, for, as used by railroad workers, they coerced the community and innocent nonunion workers in order to achieve goals that the strikers could not win fairly. "It is idle to talk of a peaceable strike," the court asserted. "None such ever occurred. The suggestion is impeachment of intelligence. . . . A strike is essentially a conspiracy to extort . . . by violence . . . I know of no peaceable strike."[19]

When members of the American Railway Union walked out in sympathy with their union brothers and sisters who were involved in a struggle against the Pullman Palace Car Company, the principles of the federal courts were crystal clear. Whether under the Sherman Anti-Trust Act, the Interstate Commerce Act, the constitutional mandate of the federal government to regulate interstate commerce and the federal mails, or the elastic equity power of the judiciary, a union-initiated boycott of the railroads in sympathy with the Pullman strikers was an illegal conspiracy. In the words of William Howard Taft, "The gigantic character of the conspiracy of the American Railway Union staggers the imagination. . . . Certainly the starvation of a nation cannot be a lawful purpose of a combination, and it is utterly immaterial whether the purpose is effected by means usually lawful or otherwise." No matter how just the claims of the Pullman workers and how right union labor's insistence on social reform, ruled other judges, labor may not enforce its rights "by violence and lawlessness. . . . neither the torch of the incendiary, nor the weapon of the insurrectionist, nor the inflamed tongue of him who incites to fire and sword is the instrument to bring about reforms."[20]

No doubt judicial language and rhetoric in the late nineteenth century associated organized labor and strikes with incendiary images.[21] It is also certain that most federal judges assumed the following to be unassailable natural rights: employers' freedom to use their property as they chose provided no irreparable harm was done to the community; individual workers' unimpeded right to labor on whatever terms they preferred, even if such choices diluted the equally legitimate right of other workers to withdraw their labor; and the public's right to be protected when labor and capital clashed. None of these assumptions, however, was peculiar to the judiciary in the late nineteenth century, the claims of Forbath and others notwithstanding. I find little convincing evidence to suggest that judicial language and reasoning altered popular thought concerning labor's rights and far more evidence that jurisprudence reflected attitudes that resonated across popular culture. Certainly judges shared a legal culture, but it never operated insulated from the larger society; and when legal rules clashed with more common or consensual values, the rules lost. Recall that Andrew Jackson refused to implement Chief Justice John Marshall's ruling in favor of the claims of the Cherokee Nation; that Dwight Eisenhower was reluctant to endorse the Warren Court's decision in *Brown v. Board of Education of Topeka* (because law cannot change people's hearts); or that for ten years after the Brown decision school desegregation proved the exception not the rule. The implementation of judicial rulings required consensus and coercion. Injunctions and other decisions were not self-enforcing; without the police power represented by municipal law officers, sheriffs, state militia, federal marshals, and, as an ultimate resort, the U.S. Army, judges were powerless to enforce their decisions. Elected public officials implemented court rulings because they shared the judicial values concerning the "natural" rights of employers, individual workers, and the community, and they assumed that such beliefs echoed across the voting populace. David Montgomery is absolutely correct when he writes that "it would be misleading . . . to depict the judiciary as the bulwark of capitalists' interests, single-handedly protecting the unfettered marketplace against persistent attempts by elected officials to aid the workers."[22]

Judges, elected public officials, and the citizens they claimed to represent shared a common commitment to principles of what might be termed *civic republicanism.* Civic republicanism, as it was understood in the late nineteenth century, assumed that the community (the public interest) had rights (interests) that must be protected against the selfish claims of organized private interest groups, whether composed of business people or working people. A corollary principle implied that individuals retained inalienable rights that neither the community nor the state could impair. Political debate, especially in the halls of Congress, rang with claims that American workers were the basis of all civilization and progress, that they were "the foundation on which this Government rests, the creator of wealth, and with . . . [their] welfare is linked the welfare of all the citizens of this country." Yet when "statesmen" alluded to labor as the source of all wealth, they were referring to an elastic category, one that encompassed nearly all citizens who engaged actively in a remunerated occupation or profession, for they insisted, "We have no classes here . . . the great prizes of life are open to . . . [all] citizens."[23] The same congressional members who defended the right of workers to combine in unions to redress their unequal bargaining power against corporate employers asserted that precisely the same principle demanded "that an equal right be secured to those workmen who desire to keep aloof from the combination and dispose of their labor with perfect individual freedom." In other words, neither trade unionists nor capitalists should have the power to restrain free choice among individual workers.[24] Senator Henry Teller of Colorado expressed the "free labor" doctrine in perhaps more popularly appreciated language than any federal judge did:

> No power should interfere to prevent the free exercise of this right [free contract], and no laboring man for a moment should surrender that right, either to the State, to his fellow-workmen, or to capital. His labor is valuable to him only as it is at his uncontrolled disposal, both as to whom he will sell it, and when he will sell it. Any interference by his fellow workmen of the same trade or any other in the disposal of his labor is an invasion of his right. . . . The difference between a slave and a freeman consists mainly in the fact that the freeman may freely dispose of his labor . . . on the terms fixed by himself.
>
> What the American laborer needs is individualism, freedom from the control of others . . . what the American laborer wants is freedom from control, either of capital or his fellow workmen, independence, individuality, the right and disposition to take care of himself untrammeled, either by legislation, the rules of guilds, associations, trades unions, or other conditions that deny him the free control of his labor.

Then in language redolent of the rhetoric of Jacksonian Democracy and the later Lincolnian "free labor" doctrine, Teller proclaimed, "The laboring man of today who claims and exercises the uncontrolled right to dispose of his labor on his own terms is very likely to be the capitalist of tomorrow. To-day an employe, to-morrow an employer."[25]

It is also vital to remember that antipathy toward combination, concentration, and collectivism resonated among ordinary people, whether workers or farmers. The two most massive popular movements of the late nineteenth century, the Knights of Labor and populism, shared a split vision. A large scholarly literature asserts that both exemplified popular hostility toward corporate capitalism, commitment to collective or communal action, and a turn to radical politics.[26] An equally impressive array of scholars, however, contend that both Knights and populists also swayed to the rhythms of antimonopolism, distrusted class-based collective solutions, and preferred such central aspects of the "old-time republicanism" as the free labor ideology to which Senator Teller had appealed.[27] Whether we want to characterize those who held fast to such principles as slaves to capitalist hegemony or adherents of a broad social consensus, it remains true that substantial numbers of common citizens shared the principles enunciated by jurists in the late nineteenth century and early twentieth.

Although many members of Congress, most federal judges, and innumerable ordinary citizens endorsed the "free labor" doctrine, "republican" platitudes, and "natural rights" philosophy, those principles never reigned unchallenged. Christopher Tomlins in his history of labor law in the early Republic and Sean Wilentz in his study of antebellum workers in New York City delineate popular and more radical republican traditions that sanctioned collective action by labor and repudiated the capitalist principle that the law of the market should regulate labor.[28] More to the point, the labor movement, as exemplified by the trade unions that joined together in 1886 to form the American Federation of Labor, challenged the hard individualism that underlay the doctrines of "free labor" and natural law. Trade unions, no matter how conservative many may have appeared, practiced solidarity and sought to repeal the "natural" laws of the marketplace.[29] It was their struggle for collective rights and repeal of laissez-faire that brought workers and their unions into conflict with the courts as well as employers. It was those same struggles that illustrated how judge-made rules concerning industrial relations required a coercive state (police, militia, and regular troops) for their enforcement, as happened during the Pullman strike, which intensified conflict and heightened a sense of class among aggrieved workers.

Trade unionists, however, were not alone in the late nineteenth century in speaking the language of organization, collective action, and even class. In the academy, in corporate boardrooms, and even on the state and federal benches new and younger leaders began to stress the indeterminacy of life, the mutability of society (Darwinism had reformist and radical as well as conservative implications when applied to humans), and the need for a "visible hand" to govern human affairs. Along with this new sensitivity to the contingency of social existence came a thirst for hard evidence, data that could be accumulated, collated, and manipulated statistically. Traditions, precedents, moral certainties must give way to reality, to the hard facts as disclosed by social science research. In the famous adage of Oliver Wendell Holmes Jr. logic must concede to experience (by which he meant history and evidence). The investigative state emerged to put these new principles of social science into practice.[30]

It was partly to abate the rising intensity of class conflict and dilute the strength of class sentiments that the writers of legal treatises, law professors, and judges began to apply the new knowledge to the law and to bid goodbye to the age of Victorian certainty and hard individualism.[31] A minority of judges began to rule in favor of workers and collective action. In a case in the federal court for the western district of Georgia the judge ruled that the receivers for the Central Railroad of Georgia had to sign a contract with the Brotherhood of Locomotive Engineers (BLE) concerning wage rates and seniority rules (the judge also applied the contract terms to engineers who were not members of the BLE). Unlike Taft, who ruled that the BLE's Rule 12 made the union ipso facto a criminal conspiracy, the Georgia judge declared that Rule 12 did not mitigate against binding contracts because a host of federal laws already interdicted illegal actions. For this judge collective rights did not clash with individual rights.[32] A year later in the Court of Appeals for the Seventh Circuit Judge John Marshall Harlan lifted an injunction aimed at a strike by the railroad brotherhoods against the Northern Pacific Railroad. Harlan ruled that collective withdrawals from work in the absence of contracts denying the right to cease work were legal; if employers were free to discharge labor without cause, employees, as individuals or as a group, were equally free to leave personal service at any time. Harlan thus declared that strikes were legal and unless they resulted in specific forms of otherwise unlawful activity were not enjoinable.[33] Earlier that same year, in April 1894, a district judge in Nebraska issued a ruling against the receivers of the Northern Pacific Railroad even more favorable to labor's collective rights:

> In this country, it is not unlawful for employees to associate, consult, and confer together with a view to maintain or increase their wages, by lawful and peaceful means, any more than it was unlawful for the receivers to counsel and confer together for the purpose of reducing their wages. A corporation is organized capital; it is capital consisting of money and property. Organized labor is organized capital; it is capital consisting of brains and muscle. What is lawful for one to do is lawful for the other to do. . . . Both act from the prompting of enlightened selfishness, and the action of both is lawful when no illegal or criminal means are used or threatened.

Furthermore, added the judge, the legality and utility of labor organizations were beyond question. In a sharp critique of free market economics he opined, "Sound public policy, no less than justice . . . requires that they [railroad workers] be paid a rate of wages that will enable them to live decently and comfortably. . . . Some corporations may pay their employees a less rate of wages . . . but a court of equity will not follow their bad example."[34]

As a dissenter in 1896 on the high court for the state of Massachusetts, Oliver Wendell Holmes illustrated particularly well how the new attitudes and the new social science had begun to enter legal discourse:

> One of the eternal conflicts out of which life is made up is that between the effort of every man to get the most he can for his services and that of society, disguised under the name of capital, to get his services for the least possible return. Combination on the one side is patent and powerful. Combination on the other is the necessary and desirable counterpart, if the battle is to be carried on in a fair and equal way. . . . I can remember when many people thought that, apart from violence or breach of contract, strikes were wicked, as organized refusals to work. I suppose that intelligent economists have given up that notion today. I feel pretty confident that they equally will abandon the idea that an organized refusal by workmen of social intercourse with a man who shall enter their antagonist's employ is wrong, if it is disassociated from any threat of violence, and is made for the sole object of prevailing if possible in a contest with their employer about the rate of wages. The fact, that the immediate object of the act by which the benefit to themselves is to be gained is to injure their antagonist, does not necessarily make it unlawful, any more than when a great house lowers the price of certain goods for the purpose, and with the effect, of driving a small antagonist from the business.[35]

These new judicial attitudes sometimes appeared in the strangest places. In 1902, for example, in the U.S. District Court for the Southern District of Texas, a region noted for its sympathy for unhindered economic development, the court enjoined the Southern Pacific Railroad from interfering with its employees' "right to organize in the manner that they please, so long as they are not influenced and coerced by the employer." Moreover, said the judge, the railroad unions had the right to ensure that their members "work and . . . continue to work under arrangements which will insure fair wages and working conditions."[36]

One of the clearest expositions of this alternative legal discourse occurred in Judge Learned Hand's Circuit Court of Appeals in 1914 in a decision endorsing the right of the United Mine Workers to try to unionize miners who had signed yellow-dog contracts, a decision subsequently overruled by the Supreme Court. The struggle between labor and capital, Hand and his colleagues ruled, "is a condition and not a theory." The union had a legitimate right to pursue a closed shop for its members, the court declared, because "[t]his is an age of co-operation through organization. . . . Such being the case, it is just as essential and perhaps more important, that the laboring people should organize for their advancement and protection, than it is for any of the vocations we have mentioned [doctors, lawyers, teachers, bankers, and manufacturers]."[37] Just as the antilabor judges borrowed beliefs and language from a broader American popular culture that extolled individualism, free labor, and the right to contract, the judges who chose to legitimate collective action absorbed a new language and legal, social, and economic principles borrowed from the academy, the corporate world, and the labor movement.

Precisely the same influences made themselves felt even more strongly in the universe inhabited by elected public officials. In the midst of the Pullman conflict members of Congress and executive officials rethought the labor question and the judiciary's role in industrial relations. As early as the spring of 1894 the House Judiciary Committee had concluded, after an investigation of a district court antistrike injunction, that Congress should limit the power of federal judges to issue injunctions and to punish for contempt.[38] Attorney General Richard Olney, who had orchestrated the legal offensive against the American Railway Union, suddenly decided that public policy should create a less antagonistic relationship with trade unions. Olney drafted legislation that legitimated unionism as practiced by the railroad brotherhoods and proffered voluntary arbitration as an alternative to industrial conflict.[39] After three years of desultory congressional debate concerning the rights of railroad workers Olney's proposal manifested itself in the Erdman Act of 1898. Congress for the first time recognized the legitimacy of independent unionism on the interstate railroads, outlawed the yellow-dog contract, and created a voluntary federal arbitration board as an alternative to strikes. In the words of one congressman, "It recognizes organized labor and puts them in a position to assert their rights in behalf of their members."[40]

Four years later the final report of President McKinley's Industrial Commission validated the approach Congress had taken in the Erdman Act. The commission's majority recognized that the typical wageworker "is worse off in several respects than the seller of almost any physical product. His commodity is in the highest degree perishable. That which is not sold today disappears absolutely. . . . If he refuses an offer, the next comer will probably accept it, and he is likely to be left destitute." Under the conditions that actually governed the labor market, reported the commission, "the result of free competition is to throw the advantage of the bargain into the hands of the stronger bargainer [meaning the employer]."[41] Such realities led the commission's investigators and a minority of its members to endorse union-shop contracts.[42]

Still the appeal of individual rights and the fear of class influences on public policy remained so strong that the best a majority of commission members could agree to was the endorsement of the following principles: (1) federal and state courts should use their power to enjoin strikes more sparingly and less punitively; (2) uniform state laws should be enacted to regulate child labor and the maximum workday and to ensure an eight-hour day for public employees; (3) Congress should regulate working conditions and industrial relations on the railroads as well as the transport of "strikebreakers" across state boundaries; and (4) states should enact uniform laws to protect the right of individual workers to obtain employment regardless of union membership (i.e., no yellow-dog contract; no union or closed shops) yet also grant labor "every facility . . . to organize if it desires, and the last vestige that trade unions are a criminal conspiracy should be swept away."[43] Despite the commission majority's pointed repudiation of any legislation or public policy that smacked of class legislation, a minority condemned the recommendations because "the unwise limiting of the hours of work by law we believe to be fraught with danger. The future prosperity of this country as the leading manufacturing nation of the world demands the greatest freedom of contract between labor and capital."[44]

From the late nineteenth century to the present the clash between the rights of citizens as individuals and their rights as members of groups has remained unresolved. Beginning with the Erdman Act and continuing through the recommendations of the Industrial Commission (1902), the Commission on Industrial Relations (1913–15), the Railway Labor Act of 1926, the Norris–La Guardia Act of 1932, the Wagner Act (1935), and the Dunlop Commission (1994), public policy has endorsed collective action by workers as the best means to promote democracy in all spheres of life—industrial as well as political, private as well as public—and to distribute income and wealth more equitably. Yet by stressing the right of individual workers to choose freely whether to unionize, public policymakers implicitly sanctioned the jurisprudential principles enunciated by a federal judge who enjoined picketers in 1898 because they impaired the ability of "scabs" (the judge's term) to work. Yesterday's version of replacement workers, he ruled, are "guaranteed to them by the law of every free country . . . the right to work as one pleases, and the right to contract for labor as one chooses. . . . It is the right not so much of property as of liberty which every man enjoys in this country as his birthright. . . . In this country, this right to contract in business is a constitutional right, which not even state legislatures can impair; and certainly not strike organizations, for surely they cannot lawfully do what the legislature may not."[45]

The tension between the rights of workers (citizens) as individuals and as members of a collective (unions), between liberty as a product of limiting public power and as the consequence of a positive state, and between the elected public government and private voluntary governance that burst on the national scene so dramatically during the Pullman strike of 1894 has since existed precariously in the law, the state, and society. In the 1990s the term *special interests* replaced *private state* or *private law*, but the meaning remained the same, and the connotation was equally reprehensible. Today, as yesterday, popular attitudes and legal consciousness question collective actions that diminish individual rights. The age of Victorian legal culture may be long dead and the antistrike injunction of the late nineteenth century a relic, but the right of individual workers to cross picket lines (even when they are members of the striking union), to serve as replacement labor (strikebreakers), and to claim a right to work regardless of union membership (right to work laws) remains alive and well. It lives not because judges and the law that they declare create reality but because the appeal of individualism and the desire for liberty resonate across a wide spectrum of society. I leave it to readers of this essay to de-

termine whether that hard fact of life in the United States results from the
rulings of judges cocooned within an hegemonic capitalist culture or from
a far longer, deeper, and popular traditional system of beliefs.

Notes

1. For typical narratives of the Pullman conflict, see Ray Ginger, *The Bending
Cross* (New Brunswick, N.J.: Rutgers University Press, 1951); Nick Salvatore, *Eugene V. Debs: Citizen and Socialist* (Urbana: University of Illinois Press, 1982); Gerald
G. Eggert, *Railroad Labor Disputes: The Beginnings of Federal Strike Policy* (Ann Arbor: University of Michigan Press, 1967); and Gerald G. Eggert, *Richard Olney:
Evolution of a Statesman* (University Park: Penn State University Press, 1974). On
"labor republicanism," see, among other works, Leon Fink, *Workingmen's Democracy: The Knights of Labor and American Politics* (Urbana: University of Illinois Press,
1983); Victoria Hattam, *Labor Visions and State Power: The Origins of Business Unionism in the United States* (Princeton, N.J.: Princeton University Press, 1993); Kim
Voss, *The Making of American Exceptionalism: The Knights of Labor and Class Formation in the Nineteenth Century* (Ithaca, N.Y.: Cornell University Press, 1994); David
Montgomery, *Citizen Worker: The Experience of Workers in the United States with Democracy and the Free Market during the Nineteenth Century* (New York: Cambridge
University Press, 1993); and Sean Wilentz, *Chants Democratic: New York City and
the Rise of the American Working Class, 1788–1850* (Princeton, N.J.: Princeton University Press, 1984).

2. Robert Steinfeld, *The Invention of Free Labor* (Chapel Hill: University of North
Carolina Press, 1991); Christopher Tomlins, *Law, Labor, and Ideology in the Early
American Republic* (New York: Cambridge University Press, 1993).

3. Hattam, *Labor Visions and State Power;* and William Forbath, *Law and the Shaping of the American Labor Movement* (Cambridge, Mass.: Harvard University Press,
1991), assert that AFL unions, as a result of their encounters with the judiciary,
turned away from political action toward voluntarism and its by-product, "business unionism." In contrast, Karen Orren, *Belated Feudalism: Labor, the Law, and
Liberal Development in the United States* (New York: Cambridge University Press,
1991), asserts that judicial antipathy toward unions and welfare legislation made
workers more active politically and the key actors in the coalition that produced
"Modern American liberalism." Stephen Skowronek, *Building a New American
State: The Expansion of National Administrative Capacities, 1877–1920* (New York:
Cambridge University Press, 1982), does not deal directly with the labor question,
but he does stress the crucial role and power of the courts in the late nineteenth-
century U.S. polity.

4. Montgomery, *Citizen Worker.*

5. For examples of this narrative approach, see Benjamin R. Twiss, *Lawyers and
the Constitution* (Princeton, N.J.: Princeton University Press, 1942); Robert

McCloskey, *American Conservatism in the Age of Enterprise* (Cambridge, Mass.: Harvard University Press, 1951); and Arnold M. Paul, *Conservative Crisis and the Rule of Law* (New York: Harper and Row, 1969).

6. Among the best works in this category are Herbert Hovenkamp, *Enterprise and American Law, 1836–1937* (Cambridge, Mass.: Harvard University Press, 1991); Haggai Hurvitz, "American Labor Law and the Doctrine of Entrepreneurial Property Rights: Boycott, Courts, and the Juridical Reorientation of 1886–1895," *Industrial Relations Law Journal* 8, no. 3 (1986): 307–61; Melvin I. Urofsky, "State Courts and Progressive Legislation during the Progressive Era: A Reevaluation," *Journal of American History* 72 (June 1985): 63–91; and Daniel R. Ernst, *Lawyers against Labor: From Individual Rights to Corporate Liberalism* (Urbana: University of Illinois Press, 1995).

7. Ernst, *Lawyers against Labor,* and Hovenkamp, *Enterprise and American Law,* tell this story best.

8. Richard A. Epstein, *Bargaining with the State* (Princeton, N.J.: Princeton University Press, 1993), 19.

9. Tomlins, *Law, Labor, and Ideology in the Early American Republic,* chaps. 4–5.

10. Chicago, Burlington and Quincy Ry. v. Burlington, C.R. and N. Ry. Co. et al., *Federal Reporter* 34 (1888): 484.

11. Toledo, A.A., and N.M. Ry. Co. v. Pennsylvania Co. et al., *Federal Reporter* 54 (1893): 739.

12. Casey v. Cincinnati Typographical Union No. 3 et al., *Federal Reporter* 45 (1891): 135–47 (quote on 135).

13. Coeur D'Alene Consolidated Mining Co. v. Miners' Union of Wardner et al., *Federal Reporter* 51 (1892): 263.

14. In re Wabash Railroad Company, *Federal Reporter* 24 (1885): 220. See also Donald L. McMurry, "The Legal Ancestry of the Pullman Strike Injunctions," *Industrial and Labor Relations Review* 14 (January 1961): 256.

15. Chicago, Burlington and Quincy Ry v. Burlington, C.R., N. Ry et al. *Federal Reporter* 34 (1888): 482.

16. Toledo, A.A., and N.M. Ry. Co. v. Pennsylvania Co. et al., *Federal Reporter* 54 (1893): 751.

17. United States v. Workingmen's Amalgamated Council of New Orleans et al., *Federal Reporter* 54 (1893): 996.

18. Toledo, A.A., and N.M. Ry. Co. v. Pennsylvania Co. et al. *Federal Reporter* 54 (1893): 738.

19. Farmers' Loan and Trust Co. v. Northern Pacific Ry. Co. et al., *Federal Reporter* 60 (1894): 812–13, 821–22.

20. United States v. Elliott et al., *Federal Reporter* 62 (1894): 821; Thomas v. Cincinnati, N.O. and T.P. Ry. Co., ibid., 821 (first quote); United States v. Alger, ibid., 824–28; In re. Charge to Grand Jury, ibid., 829 (second quote).

21. See, for example, Dianne Avery, "Images of Violence in Labor Jurisprudence:

The Regulation of Picketing and Boycotts, 1894–1921," *Buffalo Law Review* 37 (Winter 1988–89): 3–117.

22. Montgomery, *Citizen Worker,* 152.

23. *Congressional Record,* 48th Cong., 2d sess., 1885, 1626; 49th Cong., 1st sess., 1886, 8030.

24. House, Select Committee, *Investigation of Labor Troubles in Missouri, Arkansas, Kansas, Texas, and Illinois,"* 49th Cong., 2d sess., House Report 4174, 1887, xxiii–xxiv.

25. *Congressional Record,* 49th Cong., 2d sess., 1887, 2375–76.

26. For scholars who stress the radical implications of the Knights and populism, see, among others, Fink, *Workingmen's Democracy;* Richard Oestreicher, *Solidarity and Fragmentation: Working People and Class Consciousness in Detroit, 1875–1900* (Urbana: University of Illinois Press, 1986); Voss, *Making of American Exceptionalism;* Forbath, *Law and the Shaping of the American Labor Movement;* Hattam, *Labor Visions and State Power;* Lawrence Goodwyn, *Democratic Promise: The Populist Moment in America* (New York: Oxford University Press, 1976); Norman Pollack, *The Populist Response to Industrial America* (Cambridge, Mass.: Harvard University Press, 1962); and Norman Pollack, *The Humane Society: Populism, Capitalism, and Democracy* (New Brunswick, N.J.: Rutgers University Press, 1990).

27. For example, although Hattam, *Labor Visions and State Power,* suggests that the Knights were more radical and political than the trade unionists in the American Federation of Labor who succeeded them, she concedes that the trade unionists thought and acted in terms of permanent classes while the Knights shunned class-based action in favor of a politics of equal rights for all and special benefits for none (see especially 76–111). For similar insights into the populists that suggest how a radical political movement could also harbor more traditional and conservative tendencies, see Robert McMath, *American Populism: A Social History, 1877–1895* (New York: Hill and Wang, 1993); and Robert McMath, *Populist Vanguard: A History of the Southern Farmers' Alliance* (Chapel Hill: University of North Carolina Press, 1976). The early chapters of Salvatore, *Eugene V. Debs,* also suggest how the free labor ideology and the concept of "every man his own creator" resonated in Debs's life during the 1870s and 1880s.

28. Tomlins, *Law, Labor, and Ideology,* esp. part 1; Wilentz, *Chants Democratic.* While I do not deny that the alternative traditions of republicanism that Tomlins and Wilentz stress had a following among some laboring people, I am unconvinced that sentiments of solidarity or collectivism stirred a majority of common people.

29. Montgomery, *Citizen Worker,* is an extended paean to precisely this point, as is much of the analysis in Paul Krause, *The Battle for Homestead, 1880–1892: Politics, Culture, and Steel* (Pittsburgh: University of Pittsburgh Press, 1992). Hattam, *Labor Visions and State Power,* inadvertently makes a similar point. She contrasts

the republican, radical, political, and popular democratic Knights of Labor to the voluntaristic, apolitical, conservative, class-conscious craft unionists in the AFL. By contrast, I think Forbath, *Law and the Shaping of the American Labor Movement*, is wrong when he suggests that the labor movement, meaning the AFL, adopted the rights language of the federal judiciary in seeking to liberate workers from judicial repression. By my reading, labor leaders always preferred positive law to natural law and sought vindication for collective rather than individual rights. It is also important to remember, however, that labor leaders did not always reflect the sentiments of the mass of workers. Like Nick Salvatore's Debs, who was perhaps the most popular of all working-class leaders yet could never win a substantial minority of workers to his socialist banner, labor leaders preached solidarity and collective action to troops, many of whom preferred individualism and prior to World War II seldom included more than 10 percent of workers in their union army. On the gap between popular labor leaders and American workers, see Salvatore, *Eugene V. Debs*. See also Nick Salvatore, "Against Exceptionalism," *International Labor and Working Class History* 26 (Fall 1984): 1–24; and "Wilentz Answers His Critics," in *International Labor and Working Class History* 28 (Fall 1985): 46–55, in which they disagree about the influence of organized labor as well as the commitment of rank-and-file workers to collective action and anticapitalism.

30. For the role played by social scientists and the academy in pushing legislators toward a more positive state and the recognition of trade unionism among other collective adaptations to modern society, see especially Clarence E. Wunderlin Jr., *Visions of a New Industrial Order: Social Science and Labor Theory in America's Progressive Era* (New York: Cambridge University Press, 1992); and Mary O. Furner, "Knowing Capitalism: Public Investigation and the Labor Question in the Long Progressive Era," in *The State and Economic Knowledge: The American and British Experiences*, ed. Mary O. Furner and Barry Supple (New York: Cambridge University Press, 1990), 241–86. Alfred D. Chandler, *The Visible Hand: The Managerial Revolution in American Business* (Cambridge, Mass.: Harvard University Press, 1977), makes wonderful use of the metaphor of the "visible hand" to portray the business world's shift from the proprietary and partnership firms of the antebellum era to the rationalized, bureaucratized, managerial enterprises that began to emerge in the era of the first great merger movement—circa 1897–1904 (precisely the moment that the AFL matured as a national labor organization). The same tendencies toward positive state action and collective forms of social and economic action are also portrayed in Martin J. Sklar, *The Corporate Reconstruction of American Capitalism, 1890–1916: The Market, the Law, and Politics* (New York: Cambridge University Press, 1988).

31. Ernst, *Lawyers against Labor*, is an astute analysis of the shift in law from an individual to a group approach in matters of employment and industrial relations. For a similar but more intellectual and formalistic approach to the same development, see Morton J. Horwitz, *The Transformation of American Law, 1870–1960:*

The Crisis of Legal Orthodoxy (New York: Oxford University Press, 1992), chaps.
1–5.

32. Waterhouse et al. v. Comer, *Federal Reporter* 55 (1893): 149–59.

33. Arthur et al. v. Oakes et al., *Federal Reporter* 63 (1894): 310–29.

34. Ames et al. v. Union Pacific Ry. et al., *Federal Reporter* 64 (1894): 14–15.

35. Quoted in G. Edward White, *Justice Oliver Wendell Holmes: Law and the Inner
Self* (New York: Oxford University Press, 1993), 288.

36. Quoted in Charles L. Zeldin, *Justice Lies in the District: The U.S. District Court,
Southern District of Texas, 1902–1960* (College Station: Texas A&M Press, 1993), 84.

37. Mitchell et al. v. Hitchman Coal and Coke Co., *Federal Reporter* 214 (1914):
699, 715.

38. House Judiciary Committee, *Receivership of Northern Pacific Railway Company,*
53d Cong., 2d sess., House Report 4147, 1887, 17–19.

39. Eggert, *Richard Olney,* 161–64.

40. *Congressional Record,* 54th Cong., 2d sess., 1897, 2387–90; *Congressional Record,*
55th Cong., 2d sess., 1898, 4640.

41. Industrial Commission, *Final Report of the Industrial Commission,* 57th Cong.,
1st sess., House Document 380, 1902, 801–2.

42. Ibid., 813–17. For the role played by social scientists in pushing the Industrial Commission toward recognition of trade unionism and union security, see
Wunderlin, *Visions of New Industrial Order,* 21–71; and Furner, "Knowing Capitalism," 241–86.

43. Industrial Commission, *Final Report of the Industrial Commission,* 951.

44. Ibid., 953. For an excellent study that reveals how popular protest rose
against antilabor and conservative judicial rulings only to recede in the teeth of
implicit reverence for judicial autonomy and authority, see William G. Ross, *A
Muted Fury: Populists, Progressives, and Labor Unions Confront the Courts, 1890–1937*
(Princeton, N.J.: Princeton University Press, 1994).

45. American Steel and Wire Co. v. Wire Drawers' and Die Makers' Unions Nos.
1 and 3 et al., *Federal Reporter* 90 (1898): 612–13.

7

The Crisis of 1894 and the Legacies of Producerism

Shelton Stromquist

THE BITTER LABOR CONFLICT of the late nineteenth century posed for many Americans the question of whether classes could be reconciled and on what terms. For members of the "producing class" who saw the world sharply divided into classes social harmony would come only from their own empowerment, the recognition of their just claims to the fruits of their labor, and the eventual unfolding of a cooperative commonwealth. For trade unionists, at least those whose views were represented in the leadership of the AFL, harmony between classes would result from mutual recognition of the distinct interests of labor and capital within the bounds of a corporate capitalist order. Liberal reformers believed a reconciliation of labor and capital could be achieved only if each accepted the higher claims and shared responsibilities of citizenship in a refurbished republic whose democratic processes were cleansed of corruption.

This essay examines the ways in which different heirs of nineteenth-century republicanism refashioned their legacies to meet the new circumstances brought on by the Pullman boycott and the crisis of 1894. Each drew from a common stock of republican language to define distinctive means of achieving social harmony between classes, but in the midst of the crisis their differences were not always clear-cut or precisely understood.

Within the space of several weeks during the spring of 1894 Eugene Debs, for instance, articulated quite distinct conceptions of the role general unions, such as the American Railway Union (ARU), might play in achieving social peace between classes.[1] Speaking to an enthusiastic gathering of townspeople on his return to Terre Haute from St. Paul, Minnesota, Debs reflected on the outcome of the Great Northern strike. His tone was conciliatory, and he framed the union's objectives modestly. "An era of close relationship between capital and labor, I believe, is dawning, one which I feel will place organized labor on a higher standard. [Only] when employer and employee can thoroughly respect each other, I believe, will strikes be a thing of the past. . . . It is said the chasm between capital and labor is widening, but I do not believe it. If anything, it is narrowing and I hope to see the day when there will be none," he remarked.[2] Just a few weeks later, however, at the first annual convention of the ARU, Debs echoed an old Knights of Labor principle and called on all railroad workers to "unite forces for the protection of all." The outcome he foresaw was still labor peace and an end to class warfare, but it would be achieved by different means. Invincible organization would make class warfare a thing of the past: "Such an army would be impregnable. No corporation would assail it. The reign of justice would be inaugurated. The strike would be remanded to the relic chamber of the past. And an era of peace and good will would dawn."[3] Debs embraced the ideal of social harmony in each of his statements, but like many reform-minded Americans, he revealed conflicting conceptions of the path to be pursued.

The social crisis of 1894, at the heart of which stood the meteoric rise of the ARU and the Pullman boycott, crystallized alternative prescriptions for how harmony between classes might be restored and contending interests conciliated. Those prescriptions would be central to the discourse of trade unionists, liberal reformers, and the socialist heirs of working-class producerism over the next twenty years. Although the ground had been well prepared by nearly two decades of intensifying labor conflict, the events of 1894 sharpened their differences.

Producers

The crisis of 1894 revived and then shattered a tradition of working-class producerism whose roots lay in the artisan republican revulsion toward early industrial capitalism. For American workers still attracted to the appeal of general unionism that had fired the imaginations of members of the Knights of Labor the previous decade, the crisis of the mid-1890s confirmed their view that society was divided into two broad classes whose interests were antagonistic. As Debs argued at the ARU convention, the path to social harmony lay in the thorough, invincible organization of a class of producers capable of asserting its interest as the general interest of society. Such an organization would have the capacity, as Debs told the U.S. Strike Commission, to "stop the whole machinery . . . by abolishing the wage system."[4]

The producers movement appropriated and refashioned the republican tradition by envisioning a role for the state in curtailing the power of aggregated capital.[5] As Leon Fink has masterfully demonstrated, the Knights of Labor combined a "labor theory of value" of mongrel republican origins with commitments to independence and the responsibilities of citizenship. The Knights of Labor clothed these commitments in what David Montgomery termed a mutualist "moral universality," tellingly captured in the simple dictum "an injury to one is the concern of all."[6] According to Fink, "The Knights wished to encumber the liberal marketplace with a limitation of hours, recognition of union shops, and a host of legislative reforms, including abolition of the banking system and nationalization of the monopoly power. Asserting a direct link between civic virtue, political democracy, and the economic welfare of the laboring classes, the Knights fashioned a social democratic vision—albeit one without the accoutrement of the administrative state."[7]

After Pullman the shattered remnants of producerism were translated, on the one hand, into a social democratic program that appealed to a narrower, mostly skilled stratum of the working class and, on the other, into a syndicalist movement deeply suspicious of political reform and ameliorative state action.[8]

Trade Unionists

Trade unionists in the AFL allied with Samuel Gompers articulated a different perspective on the meaning of producerism and the shifting class relations of the mid-1890s.[9] They viewed with deepening concern the field of social battle in those crisis years. Fearing the destruction of trade unions and chastened by the powerful role of the state, repeatedly demonstrated in the strikes of the previous years, they conceived society as composed of distinct and organized interests but not inevitably contending classes. They saw themselves bounded, on the one hand, by a new immigrant working class incapable of defending itself and prone to precipitous and irresponsible action and, on the other, by antiunion employers who could use the power of the state to destroy responsible unions. They looked for allied interests and found them in an emerging network of middle-class social reformers and among groups of farsighted employers.

Gompers's language was resolutely ambiguous during the early 1890s.

As the foremost interpreter of what Bruce Laurie has termed "prudential unionism," he occasionally used a republican rhetoric of producerism.[10] When he spoke to the Labor Congress at the World's Columbian Exposition in 1893, he described the division of society into classes as resulting from the abuse of political authority. "Capitalists gained their industrial monopoly" not, as the political economists suggested, through the natural laws of the marketplace but "by the infamous abuse of arbitrary power on the part of royal and federal potentates."[11] On numerous occasions he referred to the "final emancipation" of labor and seemed to regard the future of the "wages system" as contingent. His vision was more moderate and incremental than that of the producers. The key instrument for social improvement was always the "trade union . . . the only hope of civilization." Trade union methods, despite "the malevolent and unjust spirit with which they have had to contend," are "conservative, their steps evolutionary," and "seeking justice, they have not permitted their movement to become acrid by the desire for revenge."[12] Even as he spoke of the prospects for labor's "emancipation" through a campaign for the eight-hour day, he stressed that the shorter workday would be "beneficial to all concerned." While making toilers "more independent and manly," it "tends to raise the standard of excellence of all, nor does it destroy the business interest of the employers."[13]

Gompers and his AFL allies refashioned the class language of producerism to fit a more moderate vision of contending interests in a capitalist marketplace. If he accepted the "business interest of employers," he also envisioned the evolutionary improvement of labor's condition toward "more."[14]

Liberal Reformers

A diverse contingent of civic and social reformers joined some prominent businessmen to propound a different rhetoric of social harmony. They coalesced during the early 1890s through a variety of new organizations and reform networks to assert the necessity for reconciling the interests of labor and capital as part of a more general campaign to cleanse and refurbish democracy. Inserting themselves at strategic points in the crisis, most notably in and around Chicago, they conceived a society dominated by a broad middle in which the interests of labor and capital were harmonized and the corrupting influences on both ends of the social scale controlled.[15] They would in time form the ideological core of a "progressive movement."

At two moments separated by a year middle-class reformers and their business allies articulated with notable clarity their conception of class relations and the program of reform it implied. One of the participants in the Labor Congress at the World's Columbian Exposition in Chicago during August and September 1893 was the British editor and Christian reformer W. T. Stead. Stead remained in Chicago during the fall of 1893 to explore the city's darker side. Disturbed by his findings, he proposed a public meeting that would bring the rich and powerful together "with representatives of all who suffer."[16] In an interview he intimated his objective: to constitute "an organization that would represent all the better elements in the town . . . a spiritual counterpart to the City Council" and to see to it that "the whole moral affairs of the community were thrown in the way of good government and against rogues." This reconfiguring of classes into "the better elements in the town" and the "rogues" was a construction the reform community would regularly reaffirm.[17]

The Stead meeting lay the organizational basis for the Civic Federation of Chicago. In a spirit of cooperation that transcended narrow class interests the Civic Federation would seek "to serve as a medium of sympathy and acquaintance between persons and societies who pursue various and differing vocations and objects, who differ in nationality, creed, and surrounding, who are unknown to each other, but who, nevertheless, have similar interests in the well-being of Chicago, and who agree in the desire to promote the greater welfare of the people of this city."[18] It emphasized the fight against the corruption of civic morality and, alongside an abortive effort to arbitrate a peaceful end to the Pullman boycott, pursued a campaign against "boodlers" and local political corruption.

A year later—a momentous year—the Industrial Committee of the Civic Federation of Chicago, shadowed by the Pullman strike and its aftermath, held the Congress on Industrial Conciliation and Arbitration, to which it invited a cross section of businessmen, reformers, and trade unionists. The Chicago banker and civic leader Lyman Gage called the congress "a forward step in the movement of our industrial and social life," beyond the "mutual suspicions and misunderstandings, growing out of apparently opposing interests," that "have led the way to bitterness, hostility, human suffering, and social disasters."[19] When Joseph Weeks, the editor of the *American Manufacturer and Iron World*, called for the formation of "strong unions" of employers and employees to settle their disputes, the *Outlook* suggested that with such views on the part of employers "there seems less danger than before that the two classes of our citizens should drift hope-lessly apart."[20] Jane Addams, however, most forcefully articulated the reconception of class relations such views implied. Speaking against the "class distinctions" that divide the world into "capitalists and laboring men," she asserted that the progress of human society made it "too late" for such distinctions: "We are all bound together in a solidarity . . . which shall enfranchise all of us and give all of us our place in the national ex-istence." Arbitration would "accelerate that liberation."[21]

Producers, trade unionists, and liberal reformers saw on the industrial battlefield in 1894 the outlines of different class alignments and different paths to social peace. They redeployed a common stock of republican lan-guage in new and varied ways. As the smoke of class warfare cleared, they pursued new alliances.[22]

The Crisis of 1894

The year 1894 seemed to hold both fertile possibilities and great haz-ards for American working people. Another calamitous depression had visited the economy, bringing with it new hardships. Even as trade unions girded themselves against unemployment and employer offensives, new, broader organizing efforts that promised more effective defense, notably among railroad workers, were underway.

Following the closing of the World's Columbian Exposition, Samuel Gompers invited Henry Demarest Lloyd, the organizer of the Labor Con-gress, to address the annual convention of the American Federation of Labor in December 1893. Lloyd was an affable presence in the reform community. He had been welcomed by W. T. Stead just the month before to a place of honor on the stage of the Central Music Hall gathering that had seen the formation of the Civic Federation of Chicago. He spoke on occasion at the exclusive Sunset Club of reform-minded business in the city. His home was a regular gathering place for a heterogeneous collec-tion of civic and social reformers.[23]

The topic suggested to Lloyd by the AFL for his convention address was "The Safety of the Future Lies in Organized Labour." He used his speech to challenge the trade union leadership in distinctly producerist language: "Workingmen have the undoubted right of organization. The question of the day is: What are they going to do with it?"[24] In a line of argument

paralleling the soon-to-be-debated "Political Programme" Lloyd paid trib-
ute to the "unceasing agitation of organized labour" in England and to the
broad goals it pursued. Playing off the AFL's own rhetoric, he noted that
British workers, "too, want more." At recent trade union congresses they
had demanded nationalization of land and mines and most recently had
pledged themselves "'to the principle of the collective ownership and
control of all the means of production and distribution.'" In a pointed
lesson he noted, "Our English brothers could not have done this without
their trade-unions, but they could not have done it with their trade-unions
alone. They used their power of organized labour as a stepping-stone to
the greater power of organized citizenship."[25] Lloyd then returned to this
side of the Atlantic, noting that by virtue of the current conditions of starvation and unemployment, "panics, riots, overproduction and undercon-
sumption, our present aristocratic and monarchical government of industry stands self-confessed a failure." He at once embraced and expanded
the focus of labor's campaign for shorter hours: "It is by the people who
do the work that the hours of labour, the conditions of employment, the
division of the produce is to be determined. It is by them the captains of
industry are to be chosen. It is for the welfare of all that the coordinated
labour of all must be directed. Industry, like government, exists only by
the cooperation of all, and like government, it must guarantee equal protection to all." Toward the end of his speech Lloyd encouraged the AFL
to take the leadership in preparing the ground for "that next emancipation . . . that enlarged democracy." Challenging trade unionists and, implicitly, middle-class reformers, he argued that political freedom was
merely a step toward economic freedom: "The trade-union, even the federation, is but the initial step in the organization of labour. Shall we go
on?"[26]

Lloyd by all accounts struck a responsive chord at the convention. He
was warmly congratulated by the Chicago socialist and machinist Thomas
J. Morgan. The *Eight-Hour Herald*, a labor newspaper, agreed to print two
thousand copies of the speech to be sold under the auspices of the AFL.
Even Gompers in the early months of 1894 expressed eagerness to publish "anything you care to write."[27] More concretely, the convention turned
its attention to consideration of the Political Programme, explicitly crafted
along the lines of that passed by the British trade unions, to which Lloyd
had referred.

The 1893 convention can hardly be viewed as a moment of personal triumph for Gompers. He weathered a serious challenge to his presidency

by John McBride, president of the United Mine Workers of America. The Political Programme introduced by Thomas J. Morgan on behalf of the Resolutions Committee was approved for a referendum of the affiliated unions during the coming year, though Gompers was able, again by a small margin, to delete "favorable" from the official recommendation for its consideration. Gompers put the best face on the convention's actions, asserting that "the present industrial depression will have the effect of turning the thoughts of the workingmen of America toward independent political action. . . . Personally, I approve of nearly everything in the platform . . . and I believe it will be adopted by the organizations."[28] Finally, the convention supported the proposal from James R. Sovereign, newly elected grand master workman of the Knights of Labor, for a general unity conference of trade unions to be held early in 1894.

In such an atmosphere the labor movement opened the year 1894. Despite the desperate conditions faced by unemployed workers across the land and the defensive posture assumed by many trade unions reeling from the depression's effects, other evidence suggested that the legions of labor were mobilizing along new lines. The Knights of Labor, after years of decline and internal strife under Terence Powderly's leadership, seemed to have acquired a new lease on life along with its new leadership. Once again the hand of cooperation was extended across the organizational gulf that the AFL and Knights had maintained. Railroad workers, affiliated with neither of the great federations, flocked in remarkable numbers to the newly formed American Railway Union. Local unions, particularly in western railroad centers, mushroomed overnight, much in the manner of the Knights' growth during the early months of 1886.[29] Western hard rock miners and coal miners showed renewed organizational zeal. With Jacob Coxey's call for "a petition in boots" finding a powerful echo among unemployed workers in the early spring and the ARU successfully testing its mettle against James J. Hill, the president of the Great Northern Railroad, an atmosphere reminiscent of the mid-1880s took shape. Added to this simmering pot were the AFL's referendum on independent political action and the Populists' efforts to make good on the Omaha platform's promise of a farmer-labor alliance.

Three developments shattered the gathering momentum of a revitalized producers movement. Each in its own way repolarized the debate over relations between the classes and the prospects for social harmony in fin de siècle America. First, the miners lost a bitter national strike in the bituminous fields that left their ranks disastrously thinned and the viability of their national union in jeopardy. The United Mine Workers of America (UMWA) had led the opposition to Gompers in the AFL and had provided key support for the 1893 Political Programme. Second, the Pullman boycott, despite an impressive beginning, fell victim to the combined forces of state intervention (both military and judicial) and a renewed corporate collectivism.[30] Even as the tide in the boycott turned, AFL and ARU leaders met at Briggs House in Chicago to consider a call for a general strike. The outcome had profound effects on the future of the labor movement. Third, despite a generally favorable reception at the hands of the AFL's affiliated unions, the Political Programme was picked apart at the December 1894 convention, and the national momentum for independent political action was lost. In these circumstances Gompers and his allies moved aggressively to reconfigure the producerism of the labor movement and to construct alliances with a diverse community of reformers, who accepted, even welcomed, the AFL leaders as reliable partners in the quest for social harmony.

The Bituminous Miners' Strike

We lack an adequate historical account of the impact of the bituminous miners' strike of 1894 on the UMWA's development, let alone its effects on the wider labor movement. The strike did shatter for the time being a union that was a necessary bulwark to the construction of any broader alliance of industrial unions. Tied closely to workers on the railroads and in the iron and steel industry, the miners' union played a critical leadership role.

The UMWA in the early 1890s was a fragile coalition of former Knights of Labor miners and remnants of local miners' unions in search of a viable national organization.[31] A call for a general strike to enforce the eight-hour day in the coal fields on May 1, 1891 (following the successful campaign of the carpenters the year before) had been aborted, because the leadership feared the union would be unable to survive the campaign. Only Iowa miners followed the call, and their experience seemed to confirm the national leadership's fears.[32]

The onset of the depression in 1893 further eroded the strength of the miners' union. By the spring of 1894 the membership had dwindled from 50,000 to roughly 20,000, and the union's president, John McBride, declared to the fifth annual convention, "There is a limit to human endurance and you have reached that limit." The strike against further wage cuts was called for April 21. Nearly half of the 250,000 miners in the country responded to the call with what one historian called "a welcome men reserve for audacity."[33] The solidarity evidenced by the miners, most of whom were not officially members of the UMWA, reflected the growth of strike activity since the mid-1880s and the appeal of national organization. The previous nine years had seen sharp increases in strikes over "productive relations" and against absentee-owned mines; the strikes lasted longer and consistently involved a higher proportion of workers, indicating the spreading influence of organization.[34]

The 1894 strike, marked by violent confrontations between strikers and state militia, was officially called off on June 12 based on a feeble operator promise to pursue no further rate reductions. In some mines the strike continued into August. Its strength, if not its militancy, depleted, the leadership of the UMWA nonetheless issued a call for independent political action, and at a conference of trade unionists in Columbus, Ohio, on August 16 it endorsed the Populists' Omaha platform and the AFL's proposed Political Programme, including its "collectivist" plank 10. Although the miners fielded a large contingent of delegates for the December 1894 AFL convention in Denver and managed to see their president unseat Gompers as the AFL's president, the UMWA by 1895 had reached its lowest membership and showed only the faintest signs of life.[35] As a significant influence for general unionism and independent political action, the miners' union had for the time being effectively disappeared.

Although Gompers continued to harbor resentments toward the miners' leadership for its failure to carry through with the AFL's campaign for the eight-hour day in 1891, he put the best face on the 1894 bituminous strike, calling it "a notice served upon capital that the whole world of organized labor had determined to take a stand, to face about. . . ."[36] As that momentous summer turned to fall, however, he expressed considerable uneasiness about the AFL forces gathering under the banner of independent political action, whose challenge to his leadership had nearly succeeded the previous year. He suggested that the impending local defeat of labor's political slates was "not an unmixed evil . . . It may save the general movement from being dragged in the throes of a political squabble."[37] Despite the miners' defeat Gompers remained concerned about the opposition within the ranks of the AFL: "The men who worship other gods and simply use the trade union house of worship are summoning their forces, and the trade union movement will indeed pass through its most crucial test at Denver. There it will not be so much the question of a man or an officer as it will be the root and fundamental principles of the organization."[38] Battered by its defeat in the bituminous fields, the UMWA nonetheless mustered its diminished strength alongside other general unionists to contest Gompers for the legacy of producerism within the AFL.

The Pullman Boycott and the Briggs House Conference

The Pullman boycott heightened the anxiety of the AFL leadership. The American Railway Union had succeeded beyond all expectations, making itself in the short space of a year a dynamic alternative to the narrower trade unionism of the AFL leadership. Despite a long tradition of organizational elitism significant segments of the railroad operating trades had joined with the less skilled hands in the shops, in the yards, and on the tracks to create a vibrant industrial union of railroad workers.[39] With a membership variously estimated at between 100,000 and 200,000, the ARU had won a spectacular victory in the spring against the Great Northern Railroad, forcing James J. Hill to rescind a wage reduction that promised to be the first of a series on the western transcontinentals. The ARU leadership captured the imagination of workers and the public with a vision that drew inspiration from the wellspring of working-class republicanism.

The onset of the Pullman boycott catapulted Eugene V. Debs and the ARU into still greater prominence. The ARU found itself on a collision course with corporate and state power that posed an acute problem for Gompers and the trade union movement. The problem came to a head at Briggs House in Chicago during a series of meetings in early July, just days after the federal government's massive intervention on behalf of the railroads.

Calls for a general strike in support of the ARU had multiplied as the scale of federal intervention grew. On July 8 the Chicago Trades and Labor Assembly, some of whose unions had already struck in sympathy, drafted a telegram to Gompers requesting his presence in Chicago to consider broader concerted action in support of the ARU. Gompers responded by asking all members of the AFL executive council to join him, along with the executive officers of fifteen to twenty national unions. Between the initial call on July 8 and the meeting on July 12 the sympathy strike had spread. In addition to the Chicago trade unions, the Knights of Labor, responding to James R. Sovereign's call for sympathy strikes, had joined the fray. Gompers received wires informing him that large numbers of unionists in Missouri, Ohio, and Colorado awaited a call to action.[40]

The Briggs House gathering was remarkable for the attendance it drew. All of the major unions affiliated with the AFL were represented by their presidents. The general officers of the Brotherhood of Railroad Trainmen and the Brotherhood of Locomotive Firemen, the executive council of the AFL (four vice presidents, the secretary, the treasurer, and Gompers), and for part of the meeting Debs and George W. Howard, first vice president of the ARU, also attended. The conference heard from representatives of the local committee whose invitation had prompted the gathering. They urged the conference to "either order a general strike or recommend one." The request prompted a decision to ask the president of the United States "to use some of his influence for an amicable adjustment of the differences existing in this great struggle."[41] Delegates drafted and sent a telegram to that effect to the president. The conference then invited Debs and Howard to be heard. Debs, by all accounts, gave a brief overview of the strike, its origins and current status. He hesitated to tell the conference what it should do but laid before Gompers a resolution from the directors of the ARU proposing the settlement of the strike on the simple basis of reinstatement of the strikers. He suggested that Gompers and two or three of his colleagues "act in the capacity of peacemaker" and present the proposal to the General Managers' Association. After Debs and Howard retired the conference deliberated into the early morning hours. In the end they agreed to carry forward the proposition for ending the strike only if Debs accompanied them. This Debs was unwilling to do, knowing that because he was so "offensive" to the managers, "no good could possibly come from any action in which I would have a part."[42]

Clearly, however, more than mediation was on the table during the meeting and debates of July 12 and the day following. At some point in the deliberations Gompers asked Debs what he would do if he were in his place. Debs replied in classical producerist fashion: "I would make an injury to one in the cause of labor the concern of all. My theory has always been and is now that labor ought to stand by labor, and if I were you, in your place and you in mine, I would muster all the forces of labor in a peaceable effort to secure a satisfactory adjustment of our grievances, even if we had to involve all the industries of the country." That call for a general strike, with its allusions to the principles of the Knights of Labor, garnered some support in the debate that followed Debs's departure. Others expressed a variety of reservations about the management of the strike, Debs's arrogance, and the contractual obligations of their members.[43]

In the end the conference voted to give $500 to Debs's defense fund and passed a resolution that expressed general support for the strikers but specifically disavowed a sympathy strike. The AFL officials took pains to stress their deliberateness, their responsibility, and the conservatism of their demands. In particular they objected to the way the press had misrepresented matters such that "in the public mind the working classes are now arrayed in open hostility to Federal authority." They professed to be "as patriotic and law abiding as any other class of citizens," and they disavowed a general strike, despite their sympathy with "the manly purposes and sturdy struggle of the American Railway Union," because "the present contest has become surrounded and beset with complications so grave in their nature that we can not consistently advise a course which would but add to the general confusion."[44]

The document, so carefully hedged and worded, is nonetheless bejeweled with producerist rhetoric. After outlining the deliberate means by which organizations affiliated with the AFL enter into strikes—"only as a last resort, and after all peaceful adjustment of grievances have failed"— the resolution briefly described the origins of the "trade union movement." That movement "stands as the protector of those who see the wrongs and injustice resultant of our present industrial system," and "in the ever-present contest of the wealth producers to conquer their rights from the wealth absorbers," it works out "through evolutionary methods the final emancipation of labor." The conference declared that in view of "the responsibility resting on us" a general strike was "inexpedient, unwise, and contrary to the best interests of the working people."[45]

The Briggs House resolutions turned producerist language into a defense of trade union principles. Even the document's final, ringing call for workers to "go to the ballot box and cast our votes as American Freemen" was presented as an alternative to the "folly" of calling "men out on general or local strike in these days of stagnant trade and commercial depression." The heart of the strategy looked to trade union organization. It expressed, however, respect for the American Railway Union's "impulsive, vigorous protest against the gathering, growing forces of plutocratic power and corporation rule."[46] Years later Gompers would claim that the AFL's refusal to call a general strike on behalf of the ARU was "the biggest service that could have been performed to maintain the integrity of the Railroad

Brotherhoods. Large numbers of their members had left their organizations and joined the ARU. It meant, if not disruption, weakening to a very serious extent."[47]

In the moment of crisis Gompers framed his defense of trade unionism and his justification for the decision not to call for sympathetic industrial action on behalf of the ARU in the language of a producerist attack on "wealth absorbers" and simultaneously as a judicious act of self-restraint by trade unionists who were "as patriotic and law-abiding as any other class of citizens."

The Debate over the Political Programme

In the months preceding the December 1894 AFL convention Gompers urged trade unionists to distance themselves from the movement for independent political action. The arguments were well rehearsed by the time convention debate on the Political Programme opened. Apart from procedural maneuvering and the personal animus certain delegates expressed toward their opponents, the debate centered on two issues. The first concerned the preamble, which interpreted recent developments in the British labor movement as steering a course toward independent political action and called for the American labor movement to follow suit. The trade unionist faction successfully moved to strike the preamble and any reference to "independent labor politics" as an "auxiliary" to "economic action."[48]

The delegates then proceeded to adopt seriatim all of the planks of the program, including municipalization of utilities and nationalization of telegraphs, telephones, railroads, and mines. That left the controversial plank 10: "The collective ownership by the people of all means of production and distribution."[49] Plank 10 became the second major issue in the debate and brought out deep philosophical differences among the delegates about the relationship between workers and the state, the direction of social progress, individual rights to property, and the centrality of the land monopoly. P. J. McGuire put the matter simply and directly for the trade unionists (in remarks directed explicitly at Thomas J. Morgan's failure to build his machinists' union): "I say better go on with your work of organization. Organization precedes education . . . and after our unions' doors are closed we are citizens as well as workers. . . . Stick to your union, build it up and don't go after political will-o'-the-wisps."[50] Philip Penna from the UMWA belittled the exaggerated fears of the "trade unionists" over the disruption that passage of plank 10 would bring to the labor movement: "Now we are told . . . that we have adopted planks 8 and 9, and if we . . . adopt plank 10 why it is going to disrupt everything, the whole course of nature . . . you will discover the sun will rise in the West and set in the East, streams are going to run up hill and all nature turned upside down. What foolishness! . . . It is a libel on our wage earners. They say they are bound to cut apart the union and will desert labor organizations. They will not do it." Penna and supporters of the Political Programme believed that no fundamental division separated trade unionism and labor politics. "We are trade unionists first, last and all the time, but we believe that trades unionism should progress into open and adequate fields," Penna argued. "There is one class of privations we can remove by trades unionism. There is another class that can only be removed by political action."[51]

The defeat of plank 10 and the motion to refer the program to the affiliated unions for further discussion left the approval of virtually the entire program in place. However, with the defeat of W. C. Pomeroy's motion to adopt the whole program as amended, only August McCraith's move to postpone further consideration of the matter indefinitely could gain the support needed to close off debate. There, in a heap of confusion, the matter rested.

The defeat of the Political Programme, despite the broad support it appeared to have garnered during the previous year among members of unions affiliated with the AFL, was symptomatic of the shifting ideological sands in the crisis of the mid-1890s. Over the course of 1894 Gompers and his AFL allies recast and appropriated the language of producerism to the defense of "pure and simple" trade unionism. They did so despite spirited challenges from the ranks of general unionists in the United Mine Workers of America and the American Railway Union and from among remnants of the Knights of Labor absorbed into other AFL unions. Tarring their ideological opponents with the brush of "state socialism" and the divisive tactics that had come to be the stock-in-trade of Daniel DeLeon's Socialist Labor party, the trade unionists reconfigured producerist principles to serve their ends. Prowess on the linguistic field of battle did not determine their success, although Gompers was certainly a master rhetorician. The decisive ingredients were the collapse of general unionism, particularly the UMWA and the ARU, and the demonstrated power of the state to intervene on behalf of beleaguered corporations by means of injunctions, imprisonment, and military repression.

New Alliances/New Languages of Reform

Even as the trade unionist leadership of the AFL jettisoned sympathy strikes and political alignment with a broad producerist coalition, it groped toward new alliances that promised needed support. Henry Lloyd, a delegate from the Boston Central Labor Union, expressed in the debate his fears that plank 10 would make it nearly impossible to recruit "native Yankees" into the unions because they already saw them as "a foreign institution." He also feared isolation from the "better classes." "Not only that but in every university there are professors, such as Ely, Bailey, Bemis and others that can scarcely hold their jobs. You put the tenth plank in and advocate trade unionism and we will not have a professor in the colleges. There never was a time when we could so readily get the attention of the so-called 'better classes.' To-day on my way home I am billed to speak at Cornell, and I have also been invited to speak at Chicago."[52]

Gompers, too, repositioned himself and the AFL to buttress the institutional stability of the trade union movement through new alliances. With the embers of the Pullman boycott still hot in late July, Henry Demarest Lloyd had written to Gompers from his summer retreat on Cape Cod suggesting immediate action and a meeting of reformers: "This crisis is greater than that of 1776 and 1861. You have in your place at the head of the workingmen the key to the immediate future. You can write your name by the side of our greatest patriots. What is done needs to be done quickly."[53] Gompers responded nearly ten days later, with apologies for the delay. He wanted to lay the proposal before the executive council, which was just then meeting. While approving in a very general way the idea of a conference, he suggested that a parallel effort was already underway: "I presume you are aware however, that some such call has already gone forth from an organization of men in Chicago. I think among the number is the Civic Federation. . . . If such a movement is on foot it would certainly be unwise to call any other conference which instead of concentrating our efforts would only diffuse them and show the enemy the divisions which exist." He agreed that the times were "certainly propitious for aggressive action," and he believed that the advantage should be seized "to score a good point for labor."[54] Lloyd responded immediately. Clearly he perceived the alternative Gompers proposed as inadequate, but Lloyd failed to measure the degree to which his proposition clashed ideologically with Gompers's own. "I will say to you, privately," Lloyd wrote, "that while I have no knowledge of the proposed convention about which you enquire, I still am confidant that if it is under the auspices of the Civic Federation it will in no way fulfil the purposes for which a convention of the elements you could assemble would be useful."[55]

Lloyd envisioned instead a delegate assembly of all the reform elements "to give immediate direction and concentration to the acts of the people in the coming election." Clearly misgauging Gompers, he hoped that such a convention would accomplish purposes parallel to those of the Springfield conference of Illinois populists and socialists. There Lloyd had overcome the hesitations some populists and single-taxers had about the collectivism of plank 10. The AFL Political Programme had been appended to other platform planks by a carefully crafted amendment pledging members of the constituent organizations to vote for candidates of the People's party in the coming election, "who will pledge themselves to the principle of the collective ownership by the people of all such means of production and distribution as the people elect to operate for the commonwealth."[56] Lloyd hoped the convention he proposed to Gompers could "make terms for the workingmen with the Peoples' Party and the Socialist Labor Party and the Single Taxers that would be equal to the fruits of ten years of agitation . . . [and] we would revolutionise the politics of this country." Again he appealed to Gompers not to pass up the opportunity to lead such a movement: "No man in history has had a greater opportunity for usefulness and glory than now begs you to embrace it. The people are scattered, distracted, leaderless, waiting for just such guidance. And the opportunity will not recur."[57] Gompers chose not to reply. In the succeeding months, despite Lloyd's best efforts to revive and refurbish a producerist alliance, the campaign floundered.

As plans for the Civic Federation's Congress on Industrial Conciliation and Arbitration matured, Gompers responded favorably to Ralph Easley's invitation to participate. Gompers and P. J. McGuire spoke at the congress called by the Civic Federation in mid-November 1894. Gompers argued that successful organization of labor and employers was a precondition to the arbitration of differences.

His remarks defined a program in which the echoes of producerism were fainter and more circumspect. His participation in the congress and the AFL's representation on the newly created National Commission suggested a set of alliances different from those proposed by Henry Demarest Lloyd. The National Commission was "to give representation to all classes of society and various sections of the country." Thus began an enduring association between the AFL and the Civic Federation of Chicago and its successor, the National Civic Federation, that would last well into the twentieth century.[58]

Like the leadership of the AFL, the Civic Federation engaged in the construction of a new language, that of liberal reform, as it fought to define organizational space for its views. It called for claiming and using republican institutions for higher purposes and attacked greedy, selfish interests. The rhetoric of civic reformers displaced producers, as a class, with a wider democratic community of interest; a new "civic" morality usurped the "moral universality" of the producers' mutualist ethos.[59] The outlines of new alignments of interest and new conceptions of class that would flourish in the Progressive Era were already evident by the end of 1894. Liberal reformers and their trade unionist allies each claimed a share of the producerist legacy and refashioned it to suit their purposes.

After 1894 social and civic reformers maintained their faith that class harmony could be orchestrated and conflicting interests reconciled. John R. Commons placed his hope in a broad "public," whose overriding interest in social peace would transcend any residual tendencies toward class warfare among employers or laborers.[60] Such reformers as Paul Kellogg saw a program of "industrial eugenics" as crucial to preparing the worker for the duties of citizenship needed to protect American democracy from "the leeching and loafing elements in the community."[61] For trade unionists the new century seemed to confirm their confidence in trade union principles while making them more wary of entangling alliances. Battered by judicial attacks and a resurgent open-shop movement, they nonetheless persisted in their alliances with business leaders through the Civic Federation and with social reformers in a host of allied organizations, from the American Association for Labor Legislation to the National Child Labor Committee. Hemmed in by their narrow conception of the working class and its interest, they responded with foreboding to the reappearance of sentiment for general unionism evidenced by the influence of the Industrial Workers of the World and a more aggressive pursuit of labor's class interest.

The strike-torn railroad industry and the brotherhoods of operating employees led the way toward industrial peace. P. M. Arthur of the Brotherhood of Locomotive Engineers noted in 1900 that "of late years" they had received the "assistance and cooperation of the railroad companies" formerly denied them. Samuel Callaway, president of the New York Central Railroad, mused in testimony before the U.S. Industrial Commission at the turn of the century that unions, "originally intoxicated with their own strength and power," had attempted to regulate everything, but that in recent years "they have become more or less reasonable" in their demands, "largely organizations looking after their injured, sick and aged."[62]

The ideology of producerism had been rooted in a specific "movement culture" and organizational context. The withering of the Knights of Labor, the defeat of the American Railway Union and the United Mine Workers of America, the crisis of the depression for all organized trades, and the setbacks of labor-Populists eroded the organizational base of producerism. Although Henry Demarest Lloyd and proponents of the AFL Political Programme attempted to revive a more explicitly collectivist version of producerism, they failed. In the years immediately after 1894 liberal reformers and trade unionists used a discourse of social harmony to marginalize class-based ideologies. General unionism, so forcefully embodied in the ARU, found refuge in a few unions, primarily in the West, as the AFL enjoyed its most impressive period of growth, largely under the banner of craft exclusiveness.[63] The socialist movement over the course of the next decade reclaimed a share of the producerist legacy and reconstituted its own "movement culture," but except in a few localities it never enjoyed the mass following that nineteenth-century producerism had attracted.

In time a revolt of unskilled immigrant laborers and a revived general union movement, with support of socialist and radical allies, would make its own claims to the legacy of 1894. In a wave of mass strikes beginning at McKees Rocks in 1909 and cresting in the Paterson silk shops and the Colorado coal fields in 1913–14, a new immigrant working class constituted itself and in so doing asserted a class perspective that echoed the producerism of the Pullman strike and belied the reformers' dreams of social harmony.[64]

Notes

1. The term *general unionism* is used to describe a variety of forms of labor organization that were nonexclusive and encompassed all grades of workers. They included industrial unions, such as the United Mine Workers of America and the Brewery Workers, but also organizations that cut across industries and trades, such as the Knights of Labor and later the Industrial Workers of the World (IWW). The American Railway Union welcomed as members all workers employed by railroads or in the manufacture of railroad equipment. In practice this meant some miners, quarrymen, construction workers, and factory operatives.

The term is used in England to describe a species of noncraft-based unions that appeared in the 1880s and 1890s. See Eric J. Hobsbawm, "General Labour Unions in Britain, 1889–1914," in *Labouring Men: Studies in the History of Labour* (New York: Doubleday, 1967), 211–40.

2. Eugene V. Debs, *Debs: His Life, Writings and Speeches*, 10–12, quoted in Nick Salvatore, *Eugene V. Debs: Citizen and Socialist* (Urbana: University of Illinois Press, 1982), 124.

3. *Address of Eugene V. Debs at the Convention of the American Railway Union at Chicago, Illinois, June 12, 1894* (Terre Haute, Ind.: American Railway Union, 1894), 11.

4. United States Strike Commission, *Report on the Chicago Strike of June–July, 1894* (Washington, D.C.: Government Printing Office, 1895), 172.

5. As far back as the Revolution the suspicion of the state was deeply embedded in at least one strand of republicanism. See, for instance, Tom Paine's juxtaposition of state and society in *Common Sense:* "Society is produced by our wants and government by our wickedness; the former promotes our happiness *positively* by uniting our affections, the latter *negatively* by restraining our vices. The one encourages intercourse, the other creates distinctions; The first is a patron, the last a punisher. Society is in every state a blessing, but government, even in its best state, is but a necessary evil." Quoted in Eric Foner, *Tom Paine and Revolutionary America* (New York: Oxford University Press, 1976), 92.

6. Leon Fink, "The New Labor History and the Powers of Historical Pessimism: Consensus, Hegemony, and the Case of the Knights of Labor," *Journal of American History* 75 (June 1988): 119; David Montgomery, "Labor and the Republic in Industrializing America, 1860–1920," *Le Mouvement Social*, no. 111 (April–June 1980): 211.

7. Fink, "New Labor History and the Powers of Historical Pessimism," 119.

8. On alternative socialist conceptions of the working class, see Salvatore, *Eugene V. Debs*, 195–97, 200–212; and Ira Kipnis, *The American Socialist Movement, 1897–1915* (New York: Columbia University Press, 1952). On Milwaukee socialists in particular, see Marvin Wachman, *History of the Social-Democratic Party of Milwaukee, 1897–1910* (Urbana: University of Illinois Press, 1945); Frederick I. Olson, "The Milwaukee Socialists, 1897–1941" (Ph.D. diss., Harvard University, 1952); and Sally M. Miller, *Victor Berger and the Promise of Constructive Socialism, 1910–1920* (Westport, Conn.: Greenwood, 1973). The views of Max Hayes and the Cleveland socialists are most fully detailed in the *Cleveland Citizen*. On the syndicalists' hostility to socialists' parliamentary strategy, see Melvyn Dubofsky, *We Shall Be All: A History of the Industrial Workers of the World* (Chicago: Quadrangle, 1969); and Testimony of William D. Haywood, in U.S. Commission on Industrial Relations, *Final Report and Testimony*, 64th Cong., 1st sess., Document No. 415, vol. 11 (Washington, D.C., 1916), 10581–89, reprinted in *American Labor: The Twentieth Century*, ed. Jerold S. Auerbach (Indianapolis: Bobbs-Merrill, 1969), 87–99. A particularly good example of this syndicalist view is the pamphlet by William John Pinkerton,

a former ARU member and brakeman, *Debs Treachery to the Working Class* (Chicago: William John Pinkerton, 1911).

9. The AFL in the 1890s and the early twentieth century remained highly contested organizational terrain. While Gompers's views dominated the executive council and the overall direction of the AFL, they were contested. For a useful account, see Julie Greene, *Pure and Simple Politics: The American Federation of Labor and Political Activism, 1881–1917* (New York: Cambridge University Press, 1998). Socialist opposition to Gompers within the AFL is well documented in Kipnis, *American Socialist Movement, 1897–1915*.

10. Bruce Laurie, *Artisans into Workers: Labor in Nineteenth-Century America* (New York: Hill and Wang, 1989).

11. Samuel Gompers, "What Does Labor Want?" (Paper read before the International Labor Congress, Chicago, August, 1893), 6, American Federation of Labor, 1893, Chicago Historical Society.

12. Ibid.

13. On the emancipatory effects of the eight-hour day, see "Excerpts from a News Account of an Address in Seattle," March 23, 1891, *Seattle Post-Intelligencer*, in *The Samuel Gompers Papers*, vol. 3, *Unrest and Depression: 1891–94*, ed. Stuart B. Kaufman and Peter J. Albert (Urbana: University of Illinois Press, 1989), 53–54; on its ameliorative uses, see Samuel Gompers to Tom Mann, September 2, 1891, ibid., 94.

14. Gompers famous call for "more" came as part of his speech "What Does Labor Want?" at the World's Columbian Exposition in September 1893: "We want more school houses and less jails; more learning and less vice; more constant work and less crime; more leisure and less greed; more justice and less revenge; in fact, more of the opportunities to cultivate our better natures, to make manhood more noble, womanhood more beautiful and childhood more happy and bright" (4–5).

15. This view is nicely reflected in John R. Commons, "Is Class Conflict in America Growing and Is It Inevitable?" *American Journal of Sociology* 13 (May 1908): 756–83. See also Albion W. Small, "The Civic Federation of Chicago: A Study in Social Dynamics," *American Journal of Sociology* 1 (July 1895): 88–89. For a general account of the progressive movement that stresses its commitment to social harmony, see Shelton Stromquist, *Reinventing a 'People': The Progressive Movement and the Class Question* (forthcoming).

16. *Chicago Tribune*, November 11, 1893. Stead's visit is briefly discussed in Ray Ginger, *Altgeld's America: The Lincoln Ideal versus Changing Realities* (New York: New Viewpoints, 1958). See also Frederic Whyte, *The Life of W. T. Stead* (New York: Houghton Mifflin, 1926), 42–49; and Graham Taylor, *Pioneering on Social Frontiers* (Chicago: University of Chicago Press, 1930), 28–34.

17. *Chicago Tribune*, November 11, 1893.

18. Civic Federation of Chicago, *First Annual Report of the Central Council* (Chicago: R. R. Donnelley and Sons, 1895), 7.

19. Quoted in *Chicago Tribune*, November 14, 1894, 5.

20. *Outlook,* December 1, 1894, 896.

21. *Congress on Industrial Conciliation and Arbitration Arranged under the Auspices of the Industrial Committee of the Civic Federation of Chicago Held at Chicago, Tuesday and Wednesday, November 13 and 14, 1894* (Chicago: Civic Federation of Chicago, 1895), 48–49.

22. In what ways the crises of the mid-1890s also mark an important fault line in the material development of the American working class and the receptivity of different segments of workers to new conceptions of class relations is a crucial question but one that is impossible to address adequately in the space available. Any such consideration should examine the changes in the mix of skills and wage levels, the impact of immigration and internal migration, the changing boundaries of race and gender, the patterns of strike activity, the evolution of labor organization, and the character of working-class political mobilization. For a preliminary accounting, see Shelton Stromquist, "Looking Both Ways: Ideological Crisis and Working-Class Recomposition in the 1890s" (Paper presented at the conference, "The Future of American Labor History: Toward a Synthesis," Northern Illinois University, October 1984).

23. *Chicago Tribune,* November 13, 1893, 2; Sunset Club of Chicago, "Strikes and Injunctions," in *Report of the Seventy-fifth Meeting* (Chicago: Sunset Club of Chicago, October 25, 1894), 3–8; Chester M. Destler, *Henry Demarest Lloyd and the Empire of Reform* (Philadelphia: University of Pennsylvania Press, 1963), 214–16, 244–45.

24. Samuel Gompers to Henry D. Lloyd, November 1, 1893, Henry Demarest Lloyd Papers, State Historical Society of Wisconsin, Madison; H. D. Lloyd, "The Safety of the Future Lies in Organized Labour," in Henry D. Lloyd, *Men, the Workers* (New York: Doubleday, Page, 1909), 77.

25. Lloyd, "Safety of the Future Lies in Organized Labour," 87–88.

26. Ibid., 90–91.

27. T. J. Morgan to Henry D. Lloyd, December 19, 1893; Henry D. Lloyd to Samuel Gompers, February 2, 1894; Samuel Gompers to Henry D. Lloyd, April 5, 1894, all in Henry Demarest Lloyd Papers.

28. *Chicago Inter-Ocean,* December 19, 1893; Samuel Gompers to James Sovereign and John Hayes, January 4, 1894; *New York Herald,* January 7, 1894, all in *Samuel Gompers Papers,* ed. Kaufman and Albert, 435–40, 441–42, 444 (quote).

29. On the growth of ARU locals in the early months of 1894, see *Railway Times,* January 1, 1894, July 2, 1894.

30. See Shelton Stromquist, *A Generation of Boomers: The Pattern of Railroad Labor Conflict in Nineteenth-Century America* (Urbana: University of Illinois Press, 1987), 249–66; for the role of the federal government as midwife to a new framework of labor-capital cooperation on the railroads, see Gerald G. Eggert, *Railroad Labor Disputes: The Beginnings of Federal Strike Policy* (Ann Arbor: University of Michigan Press, 1967), 194–202.

31. For a review of the attempts at forming a national union of coal miners in

the 1880s, see Nellie K. Kremenak, "Urban Workers in the Agricultural Middle West, 1856–1893: With a Case Study of Fort Dodge and Webster County, Iowa" (Ph.D. diss., University of Iowa, 1995), 202–39.

32. Bill R. Douglas, "'Fighting against Hope': Iowa Coal Miners and the 1891 Strike for the Eight-Hour Day," typescript, 1977, Labor Collection, State Historical Society of Iowa, Iowa City, Iowa.

33. Quoted in Elsie Gluck, *John Mitchell, Miner: Labor's Bargain with the Gilded Age* (New York: John Day, 1929), 22–23. See also John H. Laslett, *Labor and the Left: A Study of Socialist and Radical Influences in the American Labor Movement, 1881–1924* (New York: Basic Books, 1970), 197–98; Michael Nash, *Conflict and Accommodation: Coal Miners, Steel Workers, and Socialism, 1890–1920* (Westport, Conn.: Greenwood, 1982), 48–54; Frank J. Warne, *The Coal-Mine Workers: A Study in Labor Organization* (New York: Longmans, Green, 1905); David J. McDonald and Edward J. Lynch, *Coal and Unionism: A History of the American Coal Miners' Unions* (Indianapolis: Cornelius Printing, 1939); Andrew Roy, *A History of the Coal Miners of the United States: From the Development of the Mines to the Close of the Anthracite Strike of 1902* (Westport Conn.: Greenwood, 1970); and Chris Evans, *A History of the United Mine Workers of America, 1860–1900* (Indianapolis: Cornelius, 1939).

34. Stephen B. Brier, "'The Most Persistent Unionists': Class Formation and Class Conflict in the Coal Fields and the Emergence of Interracial and Interethnic Unionism, 1880–1904" (Ph.D. diss., University of California at Los Angeles, 1992), 55–64.

35. Laslett, *Labor and the Left*, 200–201; Nash, *Conflict and Accommodation*, 52–53; Gluck, *John Mitchell*, 24–25.

36. Quoted in W. T. Stead, "A Talk with Mr. Gompers," *Review of Reviews*, July, 1894, 27–29, in *Samuel Gompers Papers*, ed. Kaufman and Albert, 544.

37. Samuel Gompers to Joseph Labadie, September 13, 1894, in *Samuel Gompers Papers*, ed. Kaufman and Albert, 585.

38. Samuel Gompers to Frank Foster, November 19, 1894, ibid., 606.

39. See Stromquist, *Generation of Boomers*, 48–99, for a discussion of the organizational cultures of railroad workers and the AFL and the Knights of Labor foundations on which the ARU built.

40. Samuel Gompers, testimony, in United States Strike Commission, *Report*, 189–90.

41. Ibid., 190.

42. George W. Howard, testimony, and Eugene V. Debs, testimony, ibid., 28–29, 146–47.

43. Eugene V. Debs, testimony, ibid., 155 (quote); *Rocky Mountain News*, July 13, 1894, in *Samuel Gompers Papers*, ed. Kaufman and Albert, 533–55.

44. "A Statement Issued by the Conference of Representatives of Labor Organizations Meeting at Briggs House, Chicago," July 13, 1894, in *Samuel Gompers Papers*, ed. Kaufman and Albert, 536.

45. Ibid., 537.

46. Ibid., 538.

47. Samuel Gompers, *Seventy Years of Life and Labor: An Autobiography* (New York: E. P. Dutton, 1925), 223.

48. *A Verbatum Report of the Discussion on the Political Programme, at the Denver Convention of the American Federation of Labor, December 14, 15, 1894* (Indianapolis: American Federationist, 1895), 8–13.

49. Ibid., 1–3.

50. Ibid., 45.

51. Ibid., 53.

52. Ibid., 59.

53. Henry D. Lloyd to Samuel Gompers, July 30, 1894, Henry Demarest Lloyd Papers.

54. Samuel Gompers to Henry D. Lloyd, August 9, 1894, in *Samuel Gompers Papers*, ed. Kaufman and Albert, 552–53.

55. H. D. Lloyd to Samuel Gompers, August 14, 1894, ibid., 561–62.

56. *Eight-Hour Herald*, July 10, 1894, quoted in Chester McArthur Destler, *American Radicalism, 1865–1901: Essays and Documents* (Chicago: Quadrangle Books, 1966), 173, which remains the best account of Illinois labor populism.

57. H. D. Lloyd to Samuel Gompers, August 14, 1894, in *Samuel Gompers Papers*, ed. Kaufman and Albert, 562.

58. The National Commission appointed by the Congress on Industrial Conciliation and Arbitration included such figures as the Chicago banker Lyman Gage; P. M. Arthur from the Brotherhood of Locomotive Engineers; P. J. McGuire; T. V. Powderly, the new commissioner of immigration; Jane Addams; Henry C. Adams; Edward Bemis; Albion Small; Charles Francis Adams; Mrs. Potter Palmer; Carroll D. Wright; Washington Gladden; N. O. Nelson; and others. Civic Federation of Chicago, *First Annual Report of the Central Council*, 76–78. On the National Civic Federation, see James Weinstein, *The Corporate Ideal of the Liberal State, 1900–1918* (Boston: Beacon, 1968); Marguerite Green, *The National Civic Federation and the American Labor Movement, 1900–1925* (Washington, D.C., Catholic University of America Press, 1956); and David Montgomery, *The Fall of the House of Labor: The Workplace, the State, and American Labor Activism, 1865–1925* (New York: Cambridge University Press, 1987), esp. 275–81.

59. Mary Furner distinguishes the liberalism of "corporate liberals," such as those in the Civic Federation of Chicago, from an alternative liberalism, a "democratic, statist collectivism," that comes close to the position of Henry Demarest Lloyd in the crisis of 1894. The distinction for Lloyd and others was not always so clearly drawn. See Mary O. Furner, "The Republican Tradition and the New Liberalism: Social Investigation, State Building, and Social Learning in the Gilded Age," in *The State and Social Investigation in Britain and the United States*, ed. Michael

J. Lacey and Mary O. Furner (Cambridge: Cambridge University Press, 1993), 175–76. See also Montgomery, "Labor and the Republic in Industrializing America."

60. Commons, "Is Class Conflict in America Growing and Is It Inevitable?" 756–83.

61. Paul U. Kellogg, "Occupational Standards," in *Proceedings of the National Conference on Charities and Corrections* (Fort Wayne, Ind.: Archer Printing, 1910), 386, 390.

62. Testimony of P. M. Arthur and Samuel Callaway, in U.S. Industrial Commission, *Report of the Industrial Commission on Transportation*, vol. 4 (Washington, D.C.: Government Printing Office, 1900), 327, 222. See also Stromquist, *Generation of Boomers*, 264–65.

63. The enormous growth of unionism among Chicago's packinghouse workers, teamsters, and machinists in 1903–4 (and similar patterns in some other cities) must qualify this generalization. See James R. Barrett, *Work and Community in the Jungle: Chicago's Packinghouse Workers, 1894–1922* (Urbana: University of Illinois Press, 1987).

64. The best discussion of the "revolt of the laborers" is in Montgomery, *Fall of the House of Labor*, 288–89, 310–29. See also Dubofsky, *We Shall Be All;* Ardis Cameron, *Radicals of the Worst Sort: Laboring Women in Lawrence, Massachusetts, 1860–1912* (Urbana: University of Illinois Press, 1993); Steve Golin, *The Fragile Bridge: Paterson Silk Strike, 1913* (Philadelphia: Temple University Press, 1988); Steven Fraser, *Labor Will Rule: Sidney Hillman and the Rise of American Labor* (New York: Free Press, 1991), 40–77; and Shelton Stromquist, "Class Wars: Frank Walsh, the Reformers, and the Crisis of Progressivism," in *Labor Histories: Class, Politics, and the Working-Class Experience*, ed. Eric Arneson, Julie Greene, and Bruce Laurie (Urbana: University of Illinois Press, 1998), 97–124.

8

Labor and the New Liberalism in the Wake of the Pullman Strike

Richard Schneirov

The Chicago strike is epochal in its influence as a subordinate phase of a silent revolution—a revolution probably in the interest of the public welfare.

> Carroll D. Wright, U.S. commissioner of labor,
> October 1894

Whatever else may remain for the future to determine, it must now be regarded as substantially settled that the mass of wage-earners can no longer be dealt with by capital as so many isolated units. . . . Organized labor now confronts organized capital . . . and the burning question of modern times is how shall the ever-recurring controversies between them be adjusted and terminated.

> Richard Olney, U.S. attorney general,
> October 1894

IN ASSESSING THE LARGER significance of the Pullman strike, many labor historians in recent years have interpreted 1890s American political history as a period in which large numbers of workers outside the elite craft unions, along with insurgent farmers in the South and West, sought to fashion a distinctive political and organizational culture independent of the major party politics of the time. They contend that this culture, embodying a producers republicanism, might have served as an alternative to a purportedly undemocratic liberalism that flourished by the turn of the century. They argue that highly contingent political events, notably those resulting from the political failure of the Populist insurgency and the ability of the employers, with the help of the courts, to defeat the strikes of industrial employees, especially at Homestead and Pullman, foreclosed a more democratic and more emancipatory set of historical circumstances in twentieth-century America.[1]

This new interpretation makes it difficult to understand late nineteenth- and early twentieth-century American history insofar as it ignores or marginalizes the actual record of change and development of working-class politics of the time. It might be well to recall Selig Perlman's contention that "perhaps the main achievement of the nineties" was the labor movement's acceptance of the "trade agreement" as its central goal over the less fruitful alternatives of insurrectionary strikes and independent politics. Perlman entitled his chapter on labor in the 1888–97 period "Stabilization," and his chapter on the 1898–1914 period "Partial Recognition and New Difficulties," an optimistic, prodevelopmental portrayal of labor history clearly at odds with the fin de siècle note of decay and declension that dominates many recent accounts.[2] The current dominant interpretation also either ignores or misunderstands the actual transformation of American democratic liberal thought and practice, a process that workers themselves helped initiate and develop.

Without resuming an outworn celebration of consensus or denying the importance of recognizing alternatives foregone, this essay focuses on the growing strength of trade unions in Chicago and relates their response to the Pullman strike to the rise of what has been called "new liberalism." It argues that new liberalism and the progressive movement, of which it was a part, were not necessarily antilabor or antidemocratic residues of labor-Populist defeat but instead constituted a synthetic and inclusive movement and mode of thought that drew in significant ways on the democratic upsurge of the period and recognized the presence of organized labor and socialism. This thesis is given substance by three subsidiary arguments. First, an important segment of the Chicago labor movement, led by unions enjoying trade agreements, became increasingly receptive to a new liberal politics that predisposed it to act in concert with progressives of other social strata. Second, from the post-Haymarket period to the immediate post-Pullman strike period new liberals of different stripes sought to appeal to the concerns of Chicago labor. Third, by creating and helping to mobilize a reform-oriented middle class, progressives reshaped Chicago's political terrain in the 1890s, thereby making possible a new reform configuration less hospitable to an independent labor party based on labor populism and more congenial to labor progressivism.

New liberalism in this essay overlaps significantly with what historians have termed *corporate liberalism, modern liberalism,* or *urban liberalism*.[3] New liberalism broke from the nineteenth-century assumption of a beneficent proprietary individualism regulated by a self-adjusting competitive market—an ideological theme that was interwoven in both elite mugwump reform and producer reform during the Gilded Age. By contrast new liberals recognized that unregulated competition in industries plagued by high fixed costs resulted in "cut-throat" competition, endemic overproduction, industrial chaos, recurring depressions, and threatened standards of living for the masses. Under such circumstances organized groups or "combinations" of employers and workers were necessary and legitimate means of regulating and administering—hence stabilizing—market relations.[4] As Franklin MacVeagh, a prominent Chicago new liberal businessman put it in 1897, "It is practically certain that combination in some form and measure is a permanent factor of modern industrial life. . . . Competition has not only to be moderated for the protection of capital; but it has to be moderated for the protection of labor."[5] The political corollary of new liberalism was that the public good was best achieved by the conciliation of functional and other interest groups in such larger bodies as the Civic Federation of Chicago (and later the National Civic Federation) and government commissions, outside party or governmental channels.[6]

The degree of support for new liberalism should be carefully qualified. In the mid-1890s the acceptance of group activity in competitive markets, including labor markets, as necessary and legitimate was grudging and hesitant and emanated less from the ranks of employers than from intellectuals, editors, jurists, bankers, and leading merchants. Nor should new liberalism be confused with a corporatism or statism. Few new liberals thought group action would or should completely supersede voluntary individual action, hence the extended debate in the Progressive Era over the application of the Sherman Anti-Trust Act to business combination and the uneasiness of most new liberals over the union closed shop and secondary boycott. The same suspicion of corporatism was evident in new liberals' belief that when groups took on rights and responsibilities once accruing to individual proprietors, some degree of state oversight was necessary to prevent abuses and preserve the public interest. But ststism—a centralized, bureaucratized state commanding society—should not be confused with government regulation. Over time new liberals increasingly recognized the need for expert-staffed government commissions but bridled at most forms of state command or statism. The result was a flexible mix of organizational regulation and positive government that affirmed, while updating, the liberal principle of the superiority of society over the state.[7]

New liberalism in Chicago grew in close concert with the belief that class conflict and organized labor were ineradicable. The watershed year for that recognition was 1887, the year following the Haymarket affair and the eight-hour-day strikes. Three critical events marked these years: (1) the public trauma associated with the Haymarket bombing and the repression of anarchist and socialist activity, culminating in the execution of four anarchists on November 11; (2) local capital's counterattack on labor's gains in 1886, capped by a lockout of the packinghouse workers and an open-shop movement directed against labor's strongest bastion, the construction trades; and (3) a momentarily successful challenge to the two major parties in the form of the United Labor party's mayoral campaign.

In response to these developments three key new liberal figures emerged to attempt a restoration of class peace in the city—though not on the old terms—and to begin willy-nilly a rethinking of older forms of liberalism. The first of these was Lyman Gage. President of the First National Bank of Chicago and later William McKinley's secretary of treasury, Gage was one of the first to recognize that the modern economy was producing surplus capital. In 1887 he came close to getting Chicago business leaders to agree to a request that the governor commute the sentences of the convicted anarchists. The next year he pioneered a series of public conferences that brought together business leaders, radical reformers, and labor leaders to discuss controversial social issues and reform solutions. Also in 1887 labor leaders asked the respected federal judge Murray F. Tuley to intervene as arbitrator in the open-shop conflict in the building trades. His solution, accepted by both the mason contractors and the bricklayers' union, took the form of a series of yearly collective bargaining conferences, with arbitration by a neutral third party as the final resort. The third figure, Franklin MacVeagh, a wholesale grocer and clothing manufacturer who later became an executive board member of the National Civic Federation and William Taft's secretary of treasury, had gained prominence as the first president of the mugwump Citizens Association. Because of his participation in Gage's conferences and the Sunset Club meetings that succeeded them, however, he became a prominent advocate in the Democratic party for the recognition of labor unions, so much so that a local labor party asked him to run on its ticket for mayor in 1891.

Within four years of the 1886 upheaval liberal reformers had brokered another major success for local labor. Lyman Gage, who had by then replaced Marshall Field as the city's most respected business leader, was selected to head the building of the World's Columbian Exposition. Gage used his influence to govern the construction according to the principles of arbitration and the eight-hour day. Though many unions were unhappy that the World's Fair did not mandate a standard minimum wage and the closed shop for union labor, the actions of the World's Fair directorate set an important precedent in partially legitimating unions and collective bargaining.[8]

In the meantime organized craftworkers had jettisoned their affiliation with the Knights of Labor and adopted the strategic and organizational innovations associated with what has been called "the new unionism," "business unionism," or "pure and simple unionism." Organizationally the new unions tried to regulate the competitive labor market and make rights portable for mobile workers within a craft jurisdiction. Normally they strove for closed-shop control over employment through hiring halls, union label and licensing arrangements, and exclusive agreements with their employers and the manufacturers of the materials on which they worked. Without abandoning strikes they increasingly took joint responsibility with their employers for the prosperity of the industry, which often included regulating cutthroat competition in the product market.[9]

The new unions cannot be easily characterized ideologically. They creatively combined an acceptance of class conflict with practical support for ongoing cooperation with their employers. They also mixed the argument that unions could be paying "business" propositions capable of raising workers' standard of living with the bold promise of some version of industrial democracy. A prominent Chicago labor editor predicted in 1890 that "within a life time 'the strike' will change its character, and instead of being merely a demand for wages will consist in discharging the 'boss' and undertaking the job under contract."[10]

By the early 1890s Chicago labor's organizational culture was durable and effective. By 1893 well over 100,000 workers were organized in over 150 unions that employed dozens of full-time, paid "walking delegates." Many of the new unions, notably those in the building, printing, machinery, and culinary industries, were "amalgamated" in trades councils. Approximating industrial associations of crafts, these councils allowed labor activists to use sympathy strikes and the union label boycott to enforce trade agreements. By 1892 twelve local unions used the union label.[11] Employers' increasing use of court injunctions against boycotts and strikes led many labor leaders to rely on the "arbitration" of labor disputes, by which they meant an early form of collective bargaining. In 1893 labor leaders boasted that they met their employers "on a common plane to adjust matters for the common weal." One indication of the effectiveness of the new labor organizations was an 1892 report by the British consulate in Chicago that "labor organizations have had a powerful influence in keeping up the rate of pay . . . and in some employments wages have even risen despite falling prices."[12]

This emerging competency of organized labor provided a crucial impetus to the formation of new liberal thinking. Perhaps the most important public body manifesting the break with past political practice was the Civic Federation of Chicago, whose first president was Lyman Gage. Unlike the older Citizens Association, which was founded on the mugwump idea of society as a moral hierarchy of individuals topped by the best men, the Civic Federation implicitly defined the polity as composed of organized groups representing classes, interests, and reform causes. Accordingly it was the first civic reform association in the city's history to include labor in its membership. Fully one-sixth of the Civic Federation's first members were associated with unions. The Civic Federation sought to serve as a "medium of sympathy" among diverse groups and classes in the city and to reconcile their interests in a deliberative and lobbying reform body outside the channels of electoral politics and government. In this way it hoped to moderate social conflict in the city and to serve as an alternative to the corrupt practices of party machines.[13]

During the Pullman strike, but before the American Railway Union (ARU) boycott, the Civic Federation formed a fifteen-member board of conciliation composed of employers, labor leaders, and reform intellectuals, notably Bertha Honore Palmer and Jane Addams. Though they consulted both sides almost daily to resolve the strike, they were rebuffed by Pullman, thus making inevitable the boycott of railways carrying Pullman sleeping cars and the railroad managers' subsequent resort to a federal court injunction declaring that boycott illegal.[14]

As Melvyn Dubofsky, among others, has pointed out, the reasoning behind the antilabor federal injunction was hardly a legal innovation; it rested on the classical jurisprudential premise that a public interest existed in protecting the right of free contract within an untrammeled competitive market. One of the most important outcomes of the Pullman strike was the more intensive questioning of this doctrine. The political atmosphere following the Pullman strike reverberated with calls for alternatives to the use of the federal injunction to abate labor disputes. In the next few years a new liberal jurisprudence would emerge that would accord legal recognition to labor combinations and collective actions, such as the secondary boycotts and strikes for closed shops, to regulate market competition.[15] But in 1894 the legal view that in the new political economy group action could supersede individual action in these areas was in a decided minority. Reformers and trade unionists were forced to turn to legislative alternatives. Socialists, populists, ARU leaders, and a handful of new liberals endorsed some form of government ownership of the railroads. By far the most common reform approach, however, was the advocacy of some form of government-facilitated collective bargaining.

On July 19, 1894, the Civic Federation's Industrial Committee, which was chaired by M. J. Carroll, decided to call a national conference of capital and labor to propose state and national means for the conciliation and arbitration of labor disputes. On July 20, frustrated by its failure to me-diate the strike, the Industrial Committee, including many of the city's most prominent labor leaders as well as Bertha Palmer and Jane Addams, issued the call for the conference. A few days later President Grover Cleve-land established the U.S. Strike Commission to investigate the strike's causes and also recommend means for adjusting labor disputes.[16]

Arbitration as an alternative to strikes, the major solution both the Civic Federation and the U.S. Strike Commission prescribed, was not a novel reform. Mugwump liberals, Knights of Labor reformers, and, to a lesser extent, union leaders had championed it as a panacea since the 1860s. In its early postbellum interpretation the meaning of arbitration was gov-erned by the desire to create an alternative to group conflict. Mary Furner has pointed out that between the U.S. House of Representatives' hearings in 1877–78 and the Senate's 1883–85 hearings the language of labor had been reconstructed. Instead of including all producers (free labor), the word *labor* now referred to one of many organized social bodies composing society. The meaning of arbitration also began to change, from a means of restoring harmony in the commonweal to a voluntary mechanism for adjusting the differences between two contending organized groups. Under the new definition Samuel Gompers and other labor leaders could accept arbitration because it validated the principle of collective bargain-ing between equals and gave labor access to respectable new liberal allies. Particularly in the immediate aftermath of the Pullman strike, when "sen-timent for arbitration reached its peak," labor's national leaders normally endorsed arbitration, although carefully distinguishing voluntary from compulsory versions.[17]

The federal commission investigating the Pullman strike drew on this emerging consensus and issued a report in mid-November that was a ring-ing manifesto of the new liberalism. Strongly influenced by its chair, U.S. Commissioner of Labor Carroll D. Wright, the report declared that the fixing by the railroad's General Managers' Association of prices, wages, and labor practices had "destroyed the theory" that competition would protect the public and had proven laissez-faire obsolete. Vigorously endorsing the principle of union recognition, it called for collective bargaining under the auspices of a permanent federal strike commission with powers of conciliation and arbitration enforced by the courts. It even recommended that the public seriously consider government ownership of the railroads.[18]

During the same week that the strike commission's report was released the Civic Federation held its national conference on conciliation and arbitration. Retreating from the advocacy of compulsory state arbitration that had been popular in the weeks following the strike, most speakers favored collective bargaining and voluntary arbitration as an alternative to strikes. One of the few advocates of compulsory arbitration was Judge Murray F. Tuley, the local federal judge who was already something of a local labor hero for his judicial decisions in behalf of free speech for anarchists and his support for collective bargaining in the mason trade. Tuley attacked the federal court's reliance on labor injunctions and proposed a legislative remedy based on his experience in the mason trade. Tuley called for workers and employers to enroll in publicly licensed bodies that would be compelled to bargain collectively.[19]

After the conference leading craft unionists in the Civic Federation drafted a bill creating an arbitration board, though without compulsory powers, and submitted it to the state legislature. Chief among the advocates of arbitration were M. J. Carroll, editor of the *Eight-Hour Herald,* and officers of the bricklayers' union. Arbitration also drew support from other craft unionists enjoying regularized collective bargaining relationships with their employers.[20] During the debate on arbitration ARU leaders, socialist-leaning unionists, and such radical social reformers as Henry Demarest Lloyd and Clarence Darrow pinned their hopes on the success of the People's (or Populist) party and government ownership of the railroads. They took no part in the discussion leading to the arbitration bill and were unable to tip the scales in the direction of compulsory arbitration, which they favored. Labor leaders subsequently lobbied vigorously for the bill, which was passed in July 1895.[21]

Arbitration was only one of a variety of popular reform causes the Civic Federation and local progressive reformers promoted in the mid-1890s. Some reforms hearkened back to the mugwump movements of the 1870s and 1880s. The Civic Federation's first issues were the suppression of vice and gambling and the passage of a civil service law to replace bad men in local government with the "best men." Yet, just as with the changing meaning of the term *arbitration,* there was something new even about these old issues. Instead of being linked with the anti-anarchist hysteria and the repression of labor, they were associated with a host of popular reform issues relating to the establishment of democratic election proce- dures and were backed by a new mass politics advertised by the press.[22] Two such issues with potential for mass mobilization were the franchises that were being given away to municipal corporations and the tax assess- ment practices that allowed wealthy citizens to escape paying their fair share of taxes. These issues implied a new analysis of municipal corrup- tion: that businessmen, not bad men or even partisan, undemocratic elec- toral procedures, corrupted local politics.[23]

In the period between the Pullman strike and the November 1894 elec- tion progressive reform did not dominate the urban agenda, however. Issues of class conflict, fueled by the 1893 panic and subsequent demon- strations of the unemployed, workers' outrage at the crushing of the Pull- man boycott and Illinois coal strike, and the existence of an insurgent national alternative to the two old parties in the form of the People's party, overshadowed cross-class issues. For a year, beginning in December 1893, the salience of class issues, coming amidst a national economic and po- litical crisis, opened up a window of opportunity for advocates of inde- pendent labor political action. That month the AFL began to canvass its members about whether to conduct an independent campaign based on a program advocating collective ownership of the means of production (plank 10) similar to that of the Independent Labour party in Britain.

In Illinois the road to a labor party ran through the Populist camp. At the Illinois State Federation of Labor convention in July 1894 Henry Demarest Lloyd effected a historic compromise between state Populists, socialists, single-taxers, and labor advocates of independent political ac- tion. Lloyd's populist-socialist compromise involved an alternative to plank 10 that affirmed the principle of collective ownership but applied it only in cases where a popular majority could be mustered. The social- ist collectivism of the modified plank 10, however, rested in an uneasy balance with an older antimonopolism derived from republicanism in both its labor and populist versions. Lloyd's recently published book, *Wealth against Commonwealth,* had argued that giantism and concentra- tion of capital resulted not from an evolutionary process inherent in the logic of market society undergoing industrialization but from fraud and political favoritism, that is, from class legislation corrupting the republic. Lloyd championed what he called a "counterrevolution of the people" against corporate combinations and other trusts, and he appealed to workers to regain ownership and control of the product of their labor through a cooperative commonwealth.[24] Such an analysis was not compatible with the socialism of plank 10, which called for surplus capital to be socialized through government ownership of large-scale private property rather than turned back to the discretion of producers. It was also incompatible with a political economy of capital accumulation on which both the corporations and the new liberalism were premised.[25]

The new People's party found the bulk of its support in Chicago. There Lloyd's historic compromise allowed the city's leading English-speaking socialist, Thomas J. Morgan, to persuade German-speaking socialists to break with Daniel DeLeon, the leader of the Socialist Labor party, and merge their identity with the People's party. It also enabled local single-taxers to enter into coalition with the socialists, which required a break with their national leader, Henry George. Finally, the compromise persuaded a majority of local unionists to repudiate Samuel Gompers's opposition to third parties. The result was a precarious coalition on the local level, vulnerable to the pressures from national leaderships based in New York City.[26]

Chicago's unions dominated the new People's party, making it virtually a labor party, though a group led by the Populist Henry S. Taylor played an important minority role. The party enjoyed the support of an impressive array of newspapers, including two labor papers, the *Railway Times* and the *Chicago Workman*, and a Populist paper, the *Searchlight*, edited by Henry Vincent. The party's most important media friend was the *Chicago Times*, which boasted the city's largest circulation because it had supported the ARU during the Pullman strike.[27]

Since the number of organized workers was at least as large as that of the Haymarket period, party leaders were optimistic, expecting to poll at least 50,000 votes in November. They were sorely disappointed. The 30,000 votes the Populist candidates received left the party with 12 percent of the vote, far below the 31 percent the United Labor party had received in 1887, and cast a pall over the hopes of Lloyd and his allies that they would be able to parlay local success into a national labor-Populist alliance on the model of Britain's Independent Labour party.[28]

Party leaders and activists publicly wrung their hands and debated the reasons for the failure of labor voters to turn out for the People's party. Even in retrospect the reasons for the party's failure are not at all clear.

One possible reason for labor's unexpected weakness may have been the effect of unemployment on union membership. With unemployment in the city's large firms employing 38 percent of its work force at over 40 percent, one local union leader estimated that of 110,000 members claimed by the unions in 1893 not more than 50,000 remained in 1894. A year and a half later T. J. Morgan wrote that "economically the industrial class is on the rocks." Historically, however, unemployment and trade union weakness had been inversely proportional to the strength of labor protest at the polls. Both the Socialist Labor party in 1877–79 and United Labor party in 1886–87 emerged as rivals to the two major parties during times of high unemployment or union strike defeats or both.[29]

A different explanation for labor-Populist failure centers on the deep and persistent rift between socialists and nonsocialists in the labor movement and among potential labor voters. Although the principle and sentiment of socialism had grown in popularity and the topic had become an acceptable one in respectable circles, opposition to socialist *ideology* remained unalterable among the small property owners and middle-class professionals, who were potential allies of the party, and among Catholic workers, who constituted perhaps half of the city's work force. When Chester McArthur Destler researched his seminal history of Chicago labor-Populists in the 1930s, Clarence Darrow and an ex-Knights leader told him that the party was hurt by "the reluctance of Catholic wage-earners to support an independent movement in which Socialism figured so prominently."[30]

Ideological tensions within the People's party over socialism were evident as early as October 1894, when Henry George, speaking in Chicago, repudiated the local Single Tax Club's alliance with the Socialist Labor party. This encouraged single-taxers to support opposition leader William C. Pomeroy's successful attempt to seize control of the Illinois State Federation of Labor and replace Lloyd's modified plank 10 with a single-tax plank. In November the defeat of the People's party compounded these internal strains and led Lloyd and like-minded reformers to create a Fabian socialist forum, the Radical Club, independent from the party apparatus. When the December convention of the AFL repudiated plank 10 and independent political action, Chicago unions supporting the People's party withdrew from the Trades and Labor Assembly and formed the Chicago Labor Congress. Dominated by German-speaking socialists, the Labor Congress endorsed democratic reforms and affirmed the cooperative commonwealth.[31]

Although dissent over socialism clearly divided members of the local labor-Populist coalition, it is far from clear that it was decisive in limiting the Populist vote in the electorate. Beginning in the late 1870s and early 1880s Democratic Mayor Carter Harrison I openly wooed and included socialists in the Democratic party without jeopardizing its majority status. When the socialist-led United Labor party of 1886–87 eventually split, the secession of nonsocialists from socialists did nothing to free up a nonsocialist, prolabor party voting bloc among workers in Chicago (or in New York for that matter). Likewise, the nonsocialists' eventual takeover of the local People's party in 1895 did not enable the party to pick up any additional votes. In fact, deprived of its socialist voting bloc, the party's electoral strength quickly evaporated, just as in 1887–88.

Three factors emerge as more crucial than the issue of socialism in explaining the defeat of the People's party. First, many stable and powerful craft unions received important political benefits from the major parties, including immunity from police interference during strikes and the offer of government offices for trade union leaders. In virtually every union that supported the People's party strong factions were opposed to an independent labor party. According to Henry Demarest Lloyd writing in 1895, the "capitalistic parties" bolstered their hold on working people by having police "favor" unions during strikes, thus making it "impossible for the employers to introduce 'scabs.'" When "independent political action is broached in the lodges of a union which has thus been favored," he continued, those members who have government positions "are quick to point out that the union cannot expect police favors in the next strike if they wander from the old political fold." Though difficult to prove conclusively, there is considerable anecdotal evidence that trade unionists did not deliver a strong labor vote for the People's party. Henry Vincent of the *Searchlight* observed that wards with a heavy union membership did not poll more Populist votes than did wards with few unionists. In a *Searchlight* forum union leaders agreed, admitting that members who wanted revenge on President Cleveland probably supported Republican rather than Populist candidates. Such an explanation is made more persuasive by the fact that 1894 was a national election year in which voters tended to ignore third parties and to choose between the two major parties. To make matters worse, by running candidates against Democrats for local offices, the Populist party assured itself of determined Democratic opposition.[32]

Two other factors combined to limit the party's attractiveness: the growing strength of nonpartisan social reform, which made it impossible for the labor-Populists to monopolize the reform mantle, and the willing-ness of major political and civic leaders to stand against federal antilabor repression, which minimized the incentive to look for protection outside the existing parties. These two developments occurred *outside* the labor movement and constituted labor's political opportunity structure. Lloyd caught sight of this in January 1895, when he was interviewed in Boston. Lloyd admitted his grave disappointment with Chicago workers for fail-ing to support the party in November: "It is amazing that workingmen are not more radical than they are. In Chicago the workingmen are mysti-fied, troubled, apprehensive, and scarcely know which way to turn." Standing in contrast to working-class disarray was middle-class vigor. According to Lloyd, "The most striking effect [of recent events and deci-sions of the courts] is the spread of radicalism among the middle classes." Here Lloyd referred to "the demand for municipal or state control of pub-lic functions," which he viewed as "but an intermediate step toward public ownership."[33]

Lloyd then took steps to bring the People's party into line with his up-dated evaluation of the middle class. In his February 22 draft program for the spring mayoral campaign Lloyd revised the party's emphasis on im-mediate municipal ownership, instead stating that as a step toward that goal no further franchises should be granted unless the city secured "an adequate portion of the annual gross earnings and that the franchise re-vert absolutely to the city after twenty years." Rather than attack the Civic Federation's reform efforts, as had been done in the first campaign, Lloyd commended them. The convention then nominated the physician Bayard Holmes, an obvious appeal to reform-oriented native-born urban profes-sionals. During the mayoral campaign Lloyd, Darrow, and others dropped their rhetorical advocacy of the cooperative commonwealth in favor of focusing on the link between city corruption and franchise steals, a popu-lar cross-class issue.[34]

Underlying Lloyd's reworking of the Populist program in the direction of cross-class progressivism was a profound transformation of the political terrain in the city from the mid-1880s. Since 1887, especially since the 1889 annexation of surrounding suburbs, the city included many reform vot-ers not only hostile to corrupt machines but also sensitive to such social issues as inequitable taxation, the regulation of sweatshops, Charles Yerkes's monopoly of public transportation, and the arbitration of labor disputes.[35] During the 1880s the independent labor vote composed of German socialists, Irish nationalists, and trade unionists had been the swing vote between the two regular parties. But beginning in 1889 a much larger independent reform vote held the potential balance of power in the city. The strength of the independent reform vote was evident in 1897, when John Maynard Harlan, a Municipal Voters' League reformer, ran as an independent for mayor against Democratic and Republican candidates. Harlan received 69,730 votes, or 22.5 percent of the total, but 30.5 percent of the vote in the newly annexed suburban Twenty-fifth through Thirty-fourth wards. By contrast, at the height of the People's party strength in 1894, the labor vote for sheriff produced 30,724 votes, or 12 percent of the total, and 12 percent in the suburban wards. These changed electoral conditions implied that the labor vote could have clout only as part of a reform coalition with the middle class rather than as part of the Democratic party or as an independent party.

Two other political developments further strengthened the reform vote and inhibited labor-Populist prospects: press sensationalism and the growing openness of some business leaders to reform. Like the "educational" politics of the old liberals, press sensationalism was above partisanship and issue-oriented, but in contrast to mugwump elitism the new press campaigns sought to mobilize a mass constituency. In the mid- to late 1890s Chicago's newspapers united in a nonpartisan reform campaign full of sensational exposés of the vote-buying machinations of the traction magnate Charles Yerkes. In this way the press further popularized a new politics that condemned business for corrupting municipal government. Doing so enabled new liberals to link two of the three major issues of Gilded Age urban politics—eliminating party corruption and righting the injustices suffered by labor (dropping the issue of temperance reform)—to create a new political agenda.[36]

By the mid-1890s Chicago's downtown businesspeople had turned against such franchise buccaneers as Yerkes and were becoming open to issues with mass appeal, such as tax reform. At the same time they were adamantly opposed to the People's party subtreasury program and free silver, both of which obstructed the kind of banking reform advocated by such local and national leaders as Chicago's Lyman Gage, the leading new liberal heading up the Civic Federation. Chicago differed from other midwestern cities where the upper class was split over the issue of silver, thus opening a fissure through which urban populism might flow. In Chicago key business leaders lent their support to middle-class municipal reform at the very time they stiffened opposition to the local People's party for its national stands.[37]

The continuing vigor of labor's ties to the Democratic party, the growing support among respectable voters for a new liberal political agenda
sponsored by the press, and the united opposition of business leaders to
populism all contributed to the faltering of the local People's party at a
time when progressive reform was gaining momentum. These factors
were strongly present in the spring mayoral campaign. Popular wrath was
aroused by a press exposé of nine blatant franchise giveaways by the city
council, notably one to Ogden Gas Company. When Mayor John Hopkins,
who secretly owned shares in Ogden Gas, signed the ordinance, voters
were outraged. Seeking to punish the Democrats, they gave the Republican George B. Swift a landslide victory. The Populist Holmes received less
than 5 percent of the vote, which was a final crushing blow for the labor-
Populist alliance. Just before the election Henry S. Taylor had executed an
antisocialist coup in the People's party. After the election the socialists
reconstituted themselves as an independent body and returned to De-
Leon's Socialist Labor party and his revolutionary strategy, which involved
formation of a dual union federation, the Socialist Trade and Labor Alliance. Simultaneously Henry Vincent adopted an antisocialist and
prosilver policy for the *Searchlight*. Nationally the defeat emboldened
prosilver forces in the People's party, foreshadowing their success in fusing with the Bryan-led Democrats in 1896. As a result, Lloyd's and Morgan's ardent hope that the old antimonopolist-socialist-trade unionist
coalition dating from the late 1870s could be used to fashion an American labor party under the auspices of the People's party was effectively
dashed.[38]

Labor-Populist disintegration was only the start of a remarkable
flowering of nonpartisan municipal reform under the wing of the Municipal Voters' League (MVL). Early accounts of the MVL accepted at face
value its rhetoric that it was putting reputable professionals and businessmen in office in place of disreputable ward politicians. Revisionist scholars on progressivism seized on this rhetoric to brand MVL leaders anti-
immigrant, anti-working-class elitists. Whatever the accuracy of this
characterization for other urban centers, it was not the case in mid-1890s
Chicago. The MVL was not run by the city's leading business magnates
but by their sons and by much less substantial businessmen, notably
George Cole. The MVL did not seek to remove power from working-class
wards by sponsoring at-large elections or commission government. The
MVL activists Cole, William Kent, Walter Fischer, Charles Merriam, and
Ralph Easley of the Civic Federation had faith in a popular public opin-

ion educated and directed by reformers and the press. The reform journalist Lincoln Steffens distinguished Chicago's reform movement from
"reform waves that wash the 'best people' into office to make fools of
themselves and subside leaving the machine stronger than ever." MVL
reform, Steffens stated, was "slow, sure, political democratic reform, by
the people, for the people."[39]

Viewed in historical perspective, the MVL's official program and its
criteria for endorsing candidates were quite distinct from those of the old
mugwumps. The MVL's stated goal was "to wrest the city away from the
clutches of men who brazenly barter away the people's rights to corporations." It called for utility franchises that would expire in twenty years and
"provide for the opportunity of public ownership on fair and reasonable
terms." The goal of possible municipal ownership and franchise reform
as a means of remedying political corruption was close to the goal in the
draft program Lloyd had crafted for the People's party a year earlier to
appeal to the reform middle class. The MVL's acceptance of this goal
helped legitimize public ownership and place it first on the public agenda
during the next decade.[40]

The MVL also courted support from the labor movement, which resulted in partial reciprocation from a segment of labor leadership. Though
many Chicago unions were either too discouraged by the dissolution of
the People's party or too suspicious of its business leadership to be actively
involved in progressive reform, the MVL won avid support from the bricklayers' union, which had close ties with Judge Tuley. John J. McGrath, ex-
president of the bricklayers' union and the Trades and Labor Assembly,
was heavily involved in the Civic Federation and the MVL. Other active
labor leaders included J. J. Ryan (gasfitters), J. Elderkin (seamen), P. J.
Minter (bricklayers), J. J. Linehan (carpenters), and V. B. Williams (paint-
ers). M. J. Carroll, a longtime leader of the typographers' union, was
labor's most forceful spokesman for an alliance with progressive reformers and employers. As editor-proprietor of the *Eight-Hour Herald*, funded
by the bricklayers' union, he supported Gompers's opposition to third
parties and published biting attacks on "faddists, rainbow chasers," and
advocates of a cooperative commonwealth. Carroll distinguished trusts
or monopolies from corporations, which he saw as valuable and impossible to eradicate. He consistently favored arbitration and endorsed the
idea that the building trades should pull back from sympathy strikes to
facilitate stable agreements with employers. Carroll served on the Civic
Federation's executive board and the MVL's Committee of 15. During the

spring campaign he was tapped by Cole to be on the Committee of 7 that governed the daily activities of the MVL.[41]

An analysis of the sources of MVL voting strength reveals its ability to draw on both the labor-Populist and progressive reform constituencies. When an MVL-type reformer ran as an independent mayoral candidate in 1897, six of his top ten wards (in absolute vote) had also been among the top ten wards of the People's party in 1894. Every one of these wards ranked among the top ten in the percentage of German-born registered voters. In subsequent years these German wards continued to provide support for the MVL.[42]

Notwithstanding the proclivities of the Germans, labor-Populist leaders refused to participate in a labor-reform alliance. The *Union Workman*, the paper of the Chicago Labor Congress, championed immediate municipal ownership and sought to unmask Mayor Swift, the Civic Federation, and the MVL as probusiness, antilabor reformers. The paper ridiculed the idea of a "businessmen's council" because businessmen were the source of municipal corruption. The *Union Workman* was distressed that Jane Addams, prolabor ministers, and women's unions based at Hull-House cooperated actively with the MVL, and it attacked labor leaders who at MVL meetings endorsed reforms that often had been decided in advance.[43]

There was some truth to these criticisms. Most respectable reformers were ambivalent about whether electing good men was enough to clean up municipal government. Moreover, with the exceptions of Carroll and McGrath, labor leaders were followers rather than leaders in the progressive reform of the mid-1890s. Yet it is hard to argue that the MVL's program endorsing tax reform and the principle of municipal ownership differed fundamentally from Lloyd's in 1895. Alzina Stevens, leader of the women's labor movement based at Hull-House, seemed to recognize that cross-class reform was the only viable movement in Chicago when she wrote Lloyd, "We see reason for tolerating the Civic Federation, while we must regret that the opposition [to Yerkes] was not initiated by a really representative, clean-handed body of citizens."[44]

Business progressives, far from being shills for business interests, were far in advance of most city employers. When Lincoln Steffens arrived in the city in 1903, he found that all but one of the great business leaders he interviewed were opposed to the MVL. "They rose up, purple in the face," wrote Steffens, "and cursed reform. They said it had hurt business; it had hurt the town."[45] The gulf between reform leaders and employers was nowhere more evident than when it came to engaging in collective bargaining. During the MVL's campaign in 1896 a major strike of garment workers put the labor question on the front burner of reform for the first time since the Pullman strike. The strike began with a lockout of 900 union clothing cutters by large garment employers. When the Civic Federation asked employers to accept state arbitration, they refused, just as Pullman had done a year and a half earlier. Like the Pullman sympathy boycott, the strike soon expanded when 20,000 unskilled and sweated tailors walked out, both in sympathy with the cutters and for recognition of their own union. At the behest of Addams, Civic Federation leaders signed a letter supporting union recognition and sought to arbitrate the strike. In their meeting with clothing employers the Civic Federation's new president, the Board of Trade chief William T. Baker, pointed out "that all through the building trades, the printing trades, iron trades in almost every line of skilled labor, trades unions were recognized without any demoralization of business." Baker's statement indicated that the term *arbitration* was becoming almost synonymous with voluntary collective bargaining without a third-party arbiter, a practice that would later be sanctioned by the National Civic Federation. Still, garment employers were intransigent, forcing the strike's defeat.[46]

The defeat pointed up flaws in the state's new system of voluntary arbitration, and it underlined the gap between the collective bargaining that progressive reformers supported and the antiunion practices of employers facing a weak group of workers in a fiercely competitive market.[47] Reformers' inability to deliver meaningful collective bargaining beyond such trades as construction explained, as much as anything else, the continued resistance and apathy among the broader ranks of labor to cooperation with the Civic Federation and the MVL.

Until the November 1896 election the differences between the leaders of the Trades and Labor Assembly and the Labor Congress persisted and even worsened. The two factions held separate Labor Day parades and carried on a rancorous exchange in their respective papers over trade union philosophy and support for progressive reform initiatives. The political gulf deepened when the Labor Congress, along with most Chicago union leaders and rank-and-file Democrats, endorsed free silver, while the Trades and Labor Assembly criticized it. The election of November 3 was a disaster for the silver forces in Chicago. Bryan suffered a 57 to 41 percent thumping. Of 20 wards "inhabited almost exclusively by workingmen," according to M. J. Carroll, "only 8 returned free silver majorities."[48]

It was also a watershed for the late nineteenth-century labor movement in Chicago. Disillusioned with independent politics, the Labor Congress finally merged with the Trades and Labor Assembly on November 10 to form the Chicago Federation of Labor (CFL). The CFL acceded to the wishes of the Labor Congress to bar those not working at their trade, a slap at William C. Pomeroy and his corrupt cronies who had dominated the Trades and Labor Assembly during the early 1890s. But it also adopted a provision preventing it from endorsing any political party, a slap at the Labor Congress and the silverites. The program was hardly pure and simple trade unionist, for like the Trades and Labor Assembly, the CFL expressly repudiated free silver, but it favored federal ownership of the railroads and telegraphs and municipal ownership of all utilities, as the Labor Congress did. The CFL was, in fact, the start of a new political synthesis for Chicago labor, though one that would not be consolidated until 1905, with the advent of John Fitzpatrick as CFL president.[49]

Chicago labor's support for reform was part of a new tide of cross-class urban progressivism that began to restir the political waters of Chicago during the late nineteenth century. In the spring of 1897 the city's reform forces united to oppose the Humphrey bill in the state legislature, which would have extended the Yerkes streetcar franchises for ninety-nine years, eliminating any possibility for municipal ownership. The CFL joined the coalition, but labor's commitment to antiparty reform was far from sure. In the 1897 election Carter Harrison II, the young son of the five-time mayor, gathered up the old coalition of ethnic groups and organized labor to win the mayoralty in a landslide. Harrison's triumph was not a simple restoration of the old machine, though. Just as voters had turned en masse to the Republicans when the Democrats nominated an antireform candidate in 1895, they turned to the Democrats in 1897, when the Republicans threw sand in the face of reformers by nominating their own machine candidate. Harrison was quite aware that he owed his job to the reform vote. Though the new mayor deferred to his ethnic base of support by openly tolerating gambling, he soon demonstrated his reform credentials by assuming leadership of the successful reform fight in the state legislature against the Allen bill, a revised version of the Humphrey bill, thereby winning the MVL's endorsement. Moreover, Harrison continued the Democratic machine's policy of police neutrality during strikes and one-upped progressive reformers' support of arbitration by endorsing the closed shop for the building trades, something most new liberals would not do. According to one observer in 1904 Harrison had assembled his own version of a progressive coalition consisting of "the regular Democratic machine; the more or less independent Democrats, whose public consciences had been soothed by gradual improvements in the city hall; the regular radicals, whose social consciences had been soothed by insinuations about municipal ownership, and the reformers, who, possessing consciences of both the public and the social kind, halted between two opinions, but finally inclined to the latter." Harrison's new politics demonstrated that if old mugwump reformers could become new progressives, machine politicians could keep pace with the new agenda just as well.[50]

Much can be inferred from the many astonishing events and developments that shook Chicago politics between 1894 and 1899. Labor populism and progressivism do not appear in this story as mutually exclusive alternatives, the former radical and insurgent and the latter antidemocratic and hegemonic. In Chicago progressivism drew on, superseded, and included labor populism as well as opposing and containing it. The Pullman strike, the emergence of strong unions with a presence in local politics, the nationwide Populist insurgency, and the urban socialist movement, together with the newly mobilized middle class and a new liberal business leadership, helped create the shape and determine the content of progressive municipal reform. As Karl Polanyi argued long ago, what we have called new liberalism was part of a reaction within and among all classes beginning in the late nineteenth century against the self-regulating market system. Martin J. Sklar has recently redefined corporate liberalism in a similar way, as not simply a creation and imposition of corporate leaders but a cross-class construction that synthesized elements of socialism, labor republicanism (including its Populist version), and liberalism, with the requirements and—just as important—the potentialities of an emerging corporate capitalism.[51]

Perhaps it is time to question the interpretation that views the nineteenth-century labor movement as culminating in the mid-1890s in a tragic defeat of a labor republicanism committed to a cooperative commonwealth. Instead of drawing a sharp distinction between republicanism and liberalism and dwelling on the decline of labor populism and the recurring failures of independent labor parties, labor historians might carry the story further and chart the flow of elements of that movement into the Municipal Voters' League and other turn-of-the-century progressive movements in which labor would play an important role. In this way they would better take into account the real political developments in the working class and other classes and strata. They would also be truer to the dialectic of continuity and change that characterizes all historical transitions, a dialectic in which nothing is ever completely lost or completely new.

Notes

Portions of this essay were published in Richard Schneirov, *Labor and Urban Politics: Class Conflict and the Origins of Modern Liberalism in Chicago, 1864–97* (Urbana: University of Illinois Press, 1998).

1. Notwithstanding important differences among the following works, they have all contributed to the new interpretation: Leon Fink, "The New Labor History and the Powers of Historical Pessimism: Consensus, Hegemony, and the Case of the Knights of Labor," *Journal of American History* 75 (June 1988): 115–36; Gregory S. Kealey and Bryan D. Palmer, *Dreaming of What Might Be: The Knights of Labor in Ontario, 1880–1900* (New York: Cambridge University Press, 1982), chap. 8; Gerald Friedman, "The State and the Making of the Working Class: France and the United States, 1880–1914," *Theory and Society* 17 (May 1988): 403–30; Kim Voss, *The Making of American Exceptionalism: The Knights of Labor and Class Formation in the Nineteenth Century* (Ithaca, N.Y.: Cornell University Press, 1993); and American Social History Project, *Who Built America?* vol. 2 (New York: Pantheon Books, 1992). Two historians of labor law have taken a similar perspective: William Forbath, *Law and the Shaping of the American Labor Movement* (Cambridge, Mass.: Harvard University Press, 1991); and Victoria Hattam, *Labor Visions and State Power: The Origins of Business Unionism in the United States* (Princeton, N.J.: Princeton University Press, 1993). For a survey, see Larry G. Gerber, "Shifting Perspectives on American Exceptionalism: Recent Literature on American Labor Relations and Labor Politics," *Journal of American Studies* 31 (August 1997): 253–74. Especially for Chicago this interpretation finds a basis in Chester McArthur Destler, *American Radicalism, 1865–1901: Essays and Documents* (New London: Connecticut College, 1946), which drew on the historical experience of Henry Demarest Lloyd, the architect of the labor-Populist coalition.

2. Selig Perlman, *A History of Trade Unionism in the United States* (New York: Macmillan, 1923), 130, 145, 163.

3. For my understanding of corporate liberalism I have relied primarily on Martin J. Sklar, *The Corporate Reconstruction of American Capitalism, 1890–1916: The Market, the Law, and Politics* (New York: Cambridge University Press, 1988), esp. chaps. 1 and 5–7; Martin J. Sklar, *The United States as a Developing Country: Studies in U.S. History in the Progressive Era and the 1920s* (New York: Cambridge University Press, 1992), chaps. 1, 2, and 7; Mary O. Furner, "The Republican Tradition

and the New Liberalism: Social Investigation, State Building, and Social Learn-ing in the Gilded Age," in *The State and Social Investigation in Britain and the United States*, ed. Michael J. Lacey and Mary O. Furner (Cambridge: Cambridge Univer-sity Press, 1993); and Daniel R. Ernst, *Lawyers against Labor: From Individual Rights to Corporate Liberalism* (Urbana: University of Illinois Press, 1995). Earlier inter-pretations of modern U.S. liberalism building on but differing substantially from the Hofstadter interpretation are to be found in William Appleman Williams, *Contours of American History* (Chicago: Quadrangle Books, 1961), which views modern liberalism as arising from an "industrial gentry and social reformers"; James Weinstein, *The Corporate Ideal in the Liberal State, 1900–1918* (Boston: Bea-con, 1968); and James Livingston, *Origins of the Federal Reserve System: Money, Class, and Corporate Capitalism, 1890–1913* (Ithaca, N.Y.: Cornell University Press, 1986), which view it as deriving from a rising corporate capitalist class. On urban or modern liberalism, see John D. Buenker, *Urban Liberalism and Progressive Reform* (New York: W. W. Norton, 1973).

4. The classic text on the self-adjusting market is Karl Polanyi, *The Great Trans-formation: The Political and Economic Origins of Our Times* (1944; reprint, Boston: Beacon, 1967); on the nineteenth-century identity between classical political economy and American law, see Herbert Hovenkamp, *Enterprise and American Law, 1836–1937* (Cambridge, Mass.: Harvard University Press, 1991. For the pro-mar-ket, antimonopoly assumptions underlying producer reform, see Richard Schneirov, *Labor and Urban Politics: Class Conflict and the Origins of Modern Liberal-ism, 1864–97* (Urbana: University of Illinois Press, 1998), 9–10, 173–79, 185–88, 230, 237–40, 298–304; James L. Huston, "The American Revolutionaries, the Political Economy of Aristocracy, and the American Concept of the Distribution of Wealth, 1865–1900," *American Historical Review* 98 (October 1993): 1079–1105; and Thom-as Goebel, "The Political Economy of American Populism from Jackson to the New Deal," *Studies in American Political Development* 11 (Spring 1997): 109–48. Growing recognition during the late nineteenth century of "market failure" is discussed in Carl P. Parrini and Martin J. Sklar, "New Thinking about the Mar-ket, 1896–1914: Some American Economists on Investment and the Theory of Surplus Capital," *Journal of Economic History* 43 (September 1983): 559–78; Furner, "Republican Tradition and the New Liberalism"; and Hovenkamp, *Enterprise and American Law*, parts 2–4.

5. Franklin MacVeagh, *The Values of Certain Social and Economic Facts: Address before the Chicago and Cook County High School Association, Mar. 6, 1897* (Chicago: Chicago and Cook County High School Association, 1899), 16.

6. Though interest or pressure groups existed during the "party period" in the nineteenth century, they began to be recognized in the late Gilded Age and espe-cially during the Progressive Era as ineradicable and increasingly legitimate forms of public representation existing independently of party apparatuses. See Ernst, *Lawyers against Labor*, 155–64; Richard L. McCormick, *The Party Period and Public*

Policy (New York: Oxford University Press, 1986), 223–27; Arthur S. Link and Richard L. McCormick, *Progressivism* (Arlington Heights, Ill.: Harlan Davidson, 1983), 48, 56–59, 66; David P. Thelen, *The New Citizenship: Origins of Progressivism in Wisconsin, 1885–1900* (Columbia: University of Missouri Press, 1972), chaps. 1 and 2; Philip J. Ethington, *The Public City: The Political Construction of Urban Life in San Francisco, 1850–1900* (Cambridge: Cambridge University Press, 1994), 299–308, 319–26; 408–11; and Ballard Campbell, *Representative Democracy: Public Policy and Midwestern Legislatures in the Late Nineteenth Century* (Cambridge, Mass.: Harvard University Press, 1980), 150–57. On the regulative function of organizations, especially corporations, see Alfred D. Chandler, *The Visible Hand: The Managerial Revolution in American Business* (Cambridge, Mass.: Harvard University Press, 1977); and Louis Galambos, "Technology, Political Economy, and Professionalization: Central Themes of the Organizational Synthesis," *Business History Review* 57 (Winter 1983): 471–93. On the role of interests and government commissions, see Stephen Skowronek, *Building a New American State: The Expansion of National Administrative Capacities, 1877–1920* (New York: Cambridge University Press, 1982); and William R. Brock, *Investigation and Responsibility: Public Responsibility in the United States, 1865–1900* (Cambridge: Cambridge University Press, 1984).

7. Sklar, *Corporate Reconstruction of American Capitalism*, passim, esp. 437–38; Ernst, *Lawyers against Labor*, 108–9, 178, 212–13, 228–29, 234–35; Sidney Fine, *Laissez-Faire and the General-Welfare State: A Study of Conflict in American Thought, 1865–1901* (Ann Arbor: University of Michigan Press, 1964), 167–68, 335, 376. On corporatism or statism, see Furner, "Republican Tradition and the New Liberalism"; and Clarence E. Wunderlin Jr., *Visions of a New Industrial Order: Social Science and Labor Theory in America's Progressive Era* (New York: Columbia University Press, 1992).

8. For an in-depth discussion of the role these figures played during this period, see Richard Schneirov, "Rethinking the Relation of Labor to the Politics of Urban Social Reform in Late Nineteenth-Century America: The Case of Chicago," *International Labor and Working Class History* 46 (Fall 1994): 93–108; and Schneirov, *Labor and Urban Politics*, chap. 11; for Chicago labor leaders' expression of their appreciation for Gage, see *Times-Herald*, January 25, 1897.

9. Schneirov, *Labor and Urban Politics*, chap. 12; Dorothy Sue Cobble, "Organizing the Postindustrial Work Force: Lessons from the History of Waitress Unionism," *Industrial and Labor Relations Review* 44 (April 1991): 419–36, esp. 424–25; Robert Max Jackson, *The Formation of Craft Labor Markets* (Orlando, Fla.: Academic, 1984); Michael J. Piore and Charles F. Sabel, *The Second Industrial Divide* (New York: Basic Books, 1984), 115–20; Marc Jeffrey Stern, *The Pottery Industry of Trenton: A Skilled Trade in Transition, 1850–1929* (New Brunswick: N.J.: Rutgers University Press, 1994).

10. *Rights of Labor,* April 26, 1890. See also Dyer Lum, *Philosophy of Trade Unions* (New York: American Federation of Labor, 1892); Charles B. Spahr, *America's Working People* (New York: Longmans, 1900), 189–90; and Mark Erlich, "Peter J. McGuire's Trade Unionism: Socialism of a Trade Union Kind," *Labor History* 24 (Spring 1983): 165–97.

11. *Chicago Tribune,* April 27, 1891, August 30, 1891; *Eight-Hour Herald,* December 7, 1895, June 25, 1896, August 27, 1896, May 25, 1897.

12. *Chicago Tribune,* August 30, 1891, September 4, 1893; *Chicago Record,* September 4, 1893 ("common plane" quote); *Eight-Hour Herald,* November 3, 1897; *Report on the Earnings of Labour and Cost of Living in the Consular District of Chicago,* Misc. Series No. 235 (London: British Foreign Office, 1892) ("powerful influence" quote).

13. Civic Federation of Chicago, *First Annual Report of the Central Council* (Chicago: R. R. Donnelley and Sons, 1895), 7–14; Ralph Easley, *The Civic Federation of Chicago: What It Has Accomplished* (Chicago: Hollister Brothers, 1899), 14.

14. United States Strike Commission, *Report on the Chicago Strike of June–July, 1894* (Washington, D.C.: Government Printing Office, 1894), 645–48; *Congress on Industrial Conciliation and Arbitration Arranged under the Auspices of the Industrial Committee of the Civic Federation of Chicago Held at Chicago, Tuesday and Wednesday, November 13 and 14, 1894* (Chicago: Civic Federation of Chicago, 1895), 94; Albion W. Small, "The Civic Federation of Chicago: A Study in Social Dynamics," *American Journal of Sociology* 1 (July 1895): 85.

15. Melvyn Dubofsky, "The Federal Judiciary, Free Labor, and Equal Rights," in this volume; Melvyn Dubofsky, *The State and Labor in Modern America* (Chapel Hill: University of North Carolina Press, 1994), 26–27, 31, 44–48; Ernst, *Lawyers against Labor;* Hovenkamp, *Enterprise and American Law,* chap. 18; Michael Les Benedict, "Laissez-Faire and Liberty: A Re-evaluation of the Meaning and Origins of Laissez-Faire Constitutionalism," *Law and History Review* 3 (Fall 1985): 293–331. For a different view, see Forbath, *Law and the Shaping of the American Labor Movement.*

16. Civic Federation of Chicago, *First Annual Report of the Central Council,* 75–81; *United States Strike Commission, Report,* xv–xvi. On the importance of Bertha Palmer, see Graham Taylor, *Pioneering on Social Frontiers* (Chicago: University of Chicago Press, 1930), 41. For a survey and analysis of the various political and literary responses to the Pullman strike, see Carl Smith, *Urban Disorder and the Shape of Belief: The Great Chicago Fire, the Haymarket Bomb, and the Model Town of Pullman* (Chicago: University of Chicago Press, 1995), chaps. 10 and 11.

17. Furner, "Republican Tradition and the New Liberalism," 198–205; Perlman, *History of Trade Unionism in the United States,* 144–45; "A News Account of an Address in Denver," February 10, 1888, in *The Samuel Gompers Papers,* vol. 2, ed. Stuart B. Kaufman (Urbana: University of Illinois Press), 87–88; "Compulsory Arbitra-

tion," *American Federationist* 1 (September 1894): 147–49; William E. Akin, "Arbitration and Labor Conflict: The Middle-Class Panacea, 1886–1900," *Historian* 29 (August 1967): 565–83 (quote on 575).

18. United States Strike Commission, *Report*, xxxi, xlvi–liv (quote on xlvii). Additional editorial declarations of support for the principle of collective bargaining were made by the *Chicago Tribune,* July 21, 1894, and the *Chicago Daily News,* November 15, 1894.

19. *Congress on Industrial Conciliation and Arbitration; Chicago Times,* November 11, 1894, November 14, 1894.

20. That the arbitration bill enjoyed wide support among Chicago trade union leaders is evident from interviews in the *Chicago Times-Herald,* August 3, 1895. Like other reformers in this period, labor leaders affirmed the power of voluntary association and an educated public opinion to shape political behavior with minimal state administrative intervention. See Alexander Yard, "Coercive Government within a Minimal State: The Idea of Public Opinion in Gilded Age Labor Reform Culture," *Labor History* 34 (Fall 1993): 443–56.

21. *Chicago Times-Herald,* May 20, 1895, June 29, 1895, August 3, 1895; Earl Beckner, *A History of Labor Legislation in Illinois* (Chicago: University of Chicago Press, 1929), 77–79.

22. David Paul Nord, *Newspapers and New Politics: Midwestern Municipal Reform, 1890–1900* (Ann Arbor: University of Michigan Press, 1981). For a more critical view of the same development on a national level, see Michael McGerr, *The Decline of Popular Politics: The American North, 1865–1928* (New York: Oxford University Press, 1986), 138–83, which identifies the mid-1890s as the watershed for a new "advertising" political style that gradually replaced partisan party mobilization of northern voters.

23. Richard L. McCormick, "The Discovery That Business Corrupts Politics: A Reappraisal of the Origins of Progressivism," *American Historical Review* 85 (April 1981): 247–74, views this new analysis as the core of progressivism in the first decade of the twentieth century.

24. Henry Demarest Lloyd, *Wealth against Commonwealth* (New York: Harper and Brothers, 1894). Lloyd explicitly argued against the idea that trusts were an organic, unavoidable development in a review of Ernest Von Halle's *Trusts and Industrial Combinations in the United States* published in the *Chicago Times-Herald,* April 14, 1895. On the attitude of populists toward trusts, see Goebel, "Political Economy of American Populism."

25. For a discussion of the Populist program's incompatibility with a modern political economy and the pivotal role this conflict played in the politics of the mid-1890s, see Livingston, *Origins of the Federal Reserve System,* 55n11 and 71–102, esp. 90–96. For Karl Marx's critique of the nineteenth-century idea, prevalent in Germany as well as in the United States, that the producer should receive "the undiminished proceeds of his labor," see *Critique of the Gotha Programme* (1891; reprint, New York:

International, 1966), 7–9. Similar American criticisms can be found in, for example, George Gunton, *Wealth and Progress: A Critical Examination of the Labor Problem* (New York: D. Appleton, 1887); and Thorstein Veblen, *The Theory of Business Enterprise* (1904; reprint, New York: Mentor Books, 1963), 144–76.

26. Destler, *American Radicalism*, 200, 224–25.

27. *Chicago Times*, August 19, 1894, August 20, 1894, August 26, 1894; *Union Workman*, February 1, 1896; Destler, *American Radicalism*, 190–209.

28. *Chicago Times*, November 6, 1894, November 8, 1894; *Searchlight*, January 9, 1895.

29. *Chicago Tribune*, December 18, 1893; *Searchlight*, January 9, 1895; T. J. Morgan to Henry D. Lloyd, February 2, 1896, Henry Demarest Lloyd Papers, State Historical Society of Wisconsin, Madison. *The Report of the Bureau of Labor Statistics in the State of Illinois, 1902* (Springfield: Phillips Brothers, 1904) listed 44,193 unionists in Chicago in 1897.

30. The words are Destler's in *American Radicalism*, 190.

31. *Chicago Times-Herald*, February 18, 1895; Destler, *American Radicalism*, 200–204. Issues of the *Union Workman* contain platforms of affiliated unions and officers of the Labor Congress.

32. Henry D. Lloyd, "The American Labour Movement," *Labour Leader*, November 5, 1895, Reel 23, Henry Demarest Lloyd Papers (quote); *Searchlight*, January 9, 1895. Terence J. McDonald, *The Parameters of Urban Fiscal Policy: Socioeconomic Change and Political Culture in San Francisco, 1860–1910* (Berkeley: University of California Press, 1986), found that when municipal elections were held separately from national and state elections, significantly higher numbers of voters voted independent.

33. *Searchlight*, January 17, 1895.

34. Ibid., February 28, 1895. That the winter and spring of 1895 represented a turning of Lloyd and the People's party toward the middle classes and the political center is argued cogently by Destler, *American Radicalism*, 236–51. Yet because Destler did not sufficiently emphasize developments external to the working class, he gives the impression that the defeat of labor populism was due largely to internal dissension.

35. Michael P. McCarthy, "The New Metropolis: Chicago, the Annexation Movement, and Progressive Reform," in *The Age of Reform: New Perspectives on the Progressive Era*, ed. Michael H. Ebner and Eugene M. Tobin (Port Washington, N.Y.: Kennikat, 1977); Michael P. McCarthy, "On Bosses, Reformers, and Urban Growth: Some Suggestions for a Political Typology of American Cities," *Journal of Urban History* 4 (November 1977): 29–38.

36. David Paul Nord, "The Politics of Urban Agenda Setting in Late Nineteenth-Century Cites," *Journalism Quarterly* 58 (Winter 1981): 565–74; Nord, *Newspapers and New Politics*, 16–18 and passim. Compare McGerr, *Decline of Popular Politics*, 107–83.

37. The strength of antisilver forces in the respectable wing of the Democratic party is evident in the struggle for the presidency of the Iroquois Club. See *Chicago Times-Herald*, April 18, 20, and 24, 1895. In St. Louis the controversy over silver overwhelmed municipal reform, while in Chicago the unity over municipal reform in the middle and upper classes was reinforced by unity over the silver question. See Nord, *Newspapers and New Politics*, 81–82, 98–100.

38. Destler, *American Radicalism*, 251–53. Local socialists invited DeLeon to speak in Chicago to promote his dual union. See *Chicago Record*, May 1, 1896; and Thomas J. Morgan to Lloyd, June 9, 1896, Henry Demarest Lloyd Papers.

39. Lincoln Steffens, *The Shame of the Cities* (1903; reprint, New York: Hill and Wang, 1992), 164, 184. For an early account, see Sidney I. Roberts, "The Municipal Voters' League and Chicago's Boodlers," *Journal of the Illinois State Historical Society* 53 (Summer 1960): 117–48. Revisionist scholars include Samuel P. Hays, "Political Parties and the Community-Society Continuum," in *The American Party System: Stages in Political Development*, ed. William Nisbet Chambers and Walter Dean Burnham (New York: Oxford University Press, 1975); and the much-cited Joan S. Miller, "The Politics of Municipal Reform in Chicago during the Progressive Era" (M.A. thesis, Roosevelt University, 1966). For different views, see Michael Patrick McCarthy, "Businessmen and Professionals in Municipal Reform: The Chicago Experience, 1887–1920" (Ph.D. diss., Northwestern University, 1970), 34–39; and Nord, *Newspapers and the New Politics*, 115. In the case of Ralph Easley, it should be noted that his transformation from journalist for the *Chicago Inter-Ocean* to a professional reformer was a direct result of the Pullman strike. See Gordon Maurice Jensen, "The National Civic Federation: American Business in an Age of Social Change and Social Reform, 1900–1910" (Ph.D. diss., Princeton University, 1956), 24–25.

40. *Chicago Times-Herald*, February 26, 1896 (first quote), March 5, 1896 (second quote); Roberts, "Municipal Voters' League and Chicago's Boodlers," 139. The final set of principles adopted by the People's party for the mayoral campaign was an amalgam of progressive reform and socialism. Its first four principles favored "Good government and civil service reform; Non-partisan administration of the city government; Municipal control of the city railways, gas works, natural monopolies and municipal construction; ownership and control of the down-town loop; Franchises not to be squandered, but controlled for the benefit of the municipality." See *Principles Advocated by the Peoples Party of the Twenty-Sixth Ward for the Municipal Campaign*, Henry Demarest Lloyd Papers.

41. *Eight-Hour Herald*, October 26, 1892 (quote), November 2, 1895, November 9, 1895, May 21, 1896, August 6, 1896, September 4, 1896. For a list of labor leaders active in the Civic Federation, see *Union Workman*, January 18, 1896.

42. *Chicago Daily New Almanac and Political Register* (Chicago: Chicago Daily News, 1895 and 1898); McCarthy, "New Metropolis."

43. *Union Workman*, December 28, 1895, January 4, 1896, January 18, 1896, Janu-

ary 25, 1896, April 25, 1896. See also Morgan's attack on the Civic Federation, *Chicago Times-Herald,* December 15, 1895.

44. Alzina Stevens to Henry D. Lloyd, March 15, 1897, Henry Demarest Lloyd Papers.

45. Steffens, *Shame of the Cities,* 188–89. Chicago businessmen, led by Marshall Field, still preferred "government by purchase," according to the MVL leader William Kent. Quoted in Robert L. Woodbury, "William Kent: Progressive Gadfly, 1864–1928" (Ph.D. diss., Yale University, 1967), 118.

46. *Chicago Times-Herald,* February 20, 1896, February 23, 1896, March 9, 1896, March 14, 1896, March 22, 1896 (Baker quote).

47. Overall, however, the state arbitration board was far from being a complete failure. See Beckner, *History of Labor Legislation in Illinois,* 79–101.

48. *Eight-Hour Herald,* August 6, 1896, August 26, 1896, September 3, 1896, November 10, 1896 (quote).

49. *Chicago Times-Herald,* November 11, 1896, November 23, 1896; *Eight-Hour Herald,* November 10, 1896, November 24, 1896; Barbara Warne Newell, *Chicago and the Labor Movement: Metropolitan Unionism in the 1930s* (Urbana: University of Illinois Press, 1961), 24–26, 252–53.

50. *Chicago Times-Herald,* April 7, 1897, April 8, 1897, May 23, 1897, August 15, 1897; *Independent,* April 14, 1904 (quote); Buenker, *Urban Liberalism and Progressive Reform,* 27–31.

51. Polanyi, *Great Transformation,* esp. 151–62; Sklar, *Corporate Reconstruction of American Capitalism,* 36–40, 434–41; Sklar, *United States as a Developing Country,* 71–77.

Epilogue:
The Pullman Boycott and the Making
of Modern America

David Montgomery

A HUNDRED YEARS AGO the United States, along with the rest of the industrialized world, was in the grip of an economic crisis so profound that it provoked an intense social and political reaction against the regime of free market liberalism by which it was then governed. The Pullman boycott epitomized that conflict. On one side the American Railway Union had organized the collective power of railway workers of all grades over the vast geographic terrain from the northern Appalachian Mountains to the Pacific Coast. Its members imposed an effective boycott across the western portion of the country in a concerted effort to assist the men and women whose incomes had been gutted by the Pullman Company. On the other side were the railway executives (who had bound themselves together in the General Managers' Association), the justices of the highest courts, and President Grover Cleveland.

Cleveland stood like Horatio at the Bridge, prepared to sacrifice his presidency and his party's control of Washington and to endure in secret a painful operation, so that he might slash government expenditures, pare down the tariff, and save the gold standard—to his mind and to his admirers, the ultimate emblem of Euro-American civilization and unfettered global commerce. As the rapid flow of gold out of the United States in 1893 made starkly evident, pegging national currencies to gold imposed a tight discipline on the budgets of every industrialized country. Gunboats and marines were soon to be deployed to impose similar budgetary discipline on less developed countries (or, to use the language of Theodore Roosevelt, those who were less "civilized").[1]

The personalities and ethics of the 1890s have receded so far into the past that it is hard to imagine a Gene Debs or a Grover Cleveland among us today. Debs had been but a child and Cleveland a young man when a bloody civil war secured the future of the United States as a unified capitalist republic, in which people related to each other through contractual relationships—marriage, sales, and wages. Both of them had served political apprenticeships as Democrats—devoted to the integrity of the nation and to a government that rested lightly on the self-regulating economic activity and exuberant religious and cultural diversity of civil society. No prominent individual in our current political scene closely resembles either one of them. Yet their dramatic confrontation in the summer of 1894 framed issues involving the most desirable relationship between organized society and what is called the "free market" that haunt our current discussion of the Pullman boycott, not like ghosts of Christmas past but like ghosts of Christmas yet to come.

The issues at stake were concisely formulated by Karl Polanyi in 1943, trying to explain what had produced the bloodiest war that human beings had ever experienced. Polanyi wrote in his book *The Great Transformation* that "the fount and matrix" of nineteenth-century civilization was "the self-regulating market." But, he observed, "the idea of a self-adjusting market implied a stark utopia. Such an institution could not exist for any length of time without annihilating the human and natural substance of society. . . . Inevitably, society took measures to protect itself, but whatever measures it took impaired the self-regulation of the market, disorganized industrial life, and thus endangered society in yet another way."[2]

Looking back at the Pullman boycott over the span of a century of soaring hopes, embattled accomplishments, and crushing defeats for working people may help us assess the promise and the perils of both the free market and society's attempts to protect itself from the social and environmental ravages market freedom has inflicted on us.

By the time of the Pullman boycott the United States added more value to its national income by manufacturing than did any other nation of the world. It also exported unequaled quantities of agricultural products. The American economy had undergone prodigious expansion since the 1850s, but that growth had been spasmodic and vexed by a protracted decline in the selling prices of both manufactured and agricultural wares since the early 1870s. The depression of the 1890s began in mining and commercial agriculture, the major shippers for the vast railway network. The railroads' loss of revenues precipitated the spring 1893 crisis of major investment banks, and that in turn contracted sales, abruptly pitched already deflated prices to levels that precluded profits, and paralyzed manufacturing.

For twenty years before the outbreak of that depression, despite remarkable technological improvements in some industries, the nation's manufacturing output had grown primarily as a result of ever greater inputs of labor—especially the arrival of 6,825,000 immigrants since 1881 (one-quarter of them from Germany, but an ever-increasing proportion from the rural outskirts of European capitalism). Output per worker continued to increase steadily, but it did not grow at the spectacular rates that had been evident between 1840 and 1870. The endemic decline in selling prices pushed down the average rate of return to investors in manufacturing, which produced a relentless battle over production costs—and in the 1870s and 1880s that usually meant efforts by employers to hold down wages and especially to reduce piece rates. The great Pullman works in Chicago had been the scene of a running war over piece rates for more than a decade before the conflict exploded in the strike of 1894.[3]

Real incomes of workers had risen considerably since 1850, though the wide gap between the highest and lowest earnings of workers, the insecurity of every worker's income, and fierce competition for jobs and survival made deprivation and want the fighting themes of workers' rhetoric. Those themes appeared not only in the famous speech of Reverend William Carwardine of the town of Pullman to the 1894 convention of the American Railway Union but also in Samuel Gompers's denunciation of "the barbarity of capitalism" the same year.[4]

By the 1880s workers had developed powers of resistance to their employers' wage-cutting efforts that drew strength from familial, gender, ethnic, and community loyalties and especially from the decisive role of craft-workers in the existing relations of production. The contest so pervaded social life that the ideology of acquisitive individualism, which explained and justified a society regulated by market mechanisms and propelled by the accumulation of capital, was challenged by an ideology of mutualism, rooted in working-class bondings and struggles. Contests over pennies on or off existing piece rates had ignited controversies over the nature and purpose of the Republic itself. On one side of that ideological divide stood President Cleveland and Attorney General Richard Olney. On the other stood Debs and the delegates to the ARU's historic convention.

The ARU embodied something new in the labor movement: a style of trade unionism that embraced all grades of workers, that often covered large geographic regions, and that openly opposed the free market economy. The great 1894 strike of bituminous coal miners, which stretched from Ohio to Illinois, exemplified this trend. So did the strike of textile workers in Lawrence, Massachusetts, that summer—a general stoppage of 2,500 workers in all the city's mills, which was the climax of decades of small strikes by groups of textile workers (as well as a futile effort by the Knights of Labor to improve wages through arbitration). Only two years earlier in New Orleans a demand for the closed shop by laborers who handled sugar and molasses products had ultimately brought out on strike forty-two unions with more than 20,000 white and black members—all the city's unions, with the noteworthy exception of the powerful waterfront cotton-handling trades. The New Orleans struggle not only enjoyed the vigorous support of the American Federation of Labor (AFL), which hoped it might open the way to unionization of the South, but also inspired the AFL to devote close attention to the unionization of southern black workers for a few years. Until 1895 it barred the International Association of Machinists (IAM) from affiliating because the IAM allowed only Caucasians in its ranks.[5]

All these industrial strikes had foundered on the heavy unemployment produced by the economic crisis. All of them had also triggered the mobilization of military power by state governors to enable scabs to pass through the strikers' lines. Moreover, the Workingmen's Amalgamated Council of New Orleans, which had organized that city's general strike, was successfully prosecuted under the new Sherman Anti-Trust Act. The crime of the New Orleans workers, wrote the district judge, consisted of this: "The combination setting out to secure and compel the employment of none but union men in a given business, as a means to enforce this compulsion, finally enforced a discontinuance of labor in all kinds of business, including the business of transportation of goods and merchandise which were in transit through the city of New Orleans, from state to state, and to and from foreign countries."[6]

Both the enlarged role of the state and the consolidation of organization in the business world, which were evident in the strikes of the early 1890s, deserve our close attention. It is important to keep in mind that although free market policies sharply restricted the scope of governmental activity, leaving major decisions about priorities in social development to private economic and social entities, the free market (and above all the reduction of labor to an unprotected commodity) could never have matured without significant strengthening of the coercive authority of the government. Policing the everyday behavior of working men and women and enlarging the geographic domain encompassed by the industrializing economy—not to mention preserving the United States against secession, destroying chattel slavery, and incorporating rural and urban freed people into the nexus of wage labor—had all contributed to the appearance of uniformed municipal police forces, professional (rather than personal) prosecution of crimes, and draconic legislation against tramps and vagrants (the "wandering unemployed") as well as incessant attempts to regulate popular drinking and public conduct.[7]

In a word, the political order that celebrated freedom of contract as its basic principle had become one in which what the eminent typographer Andrew Cameron called "the cruel law of supply and demand" determined not only the level of people's incomes but even whether they had any income at all. Whatever reciprocal obligations had once bound masters and servants had given way to the commodification of labor, a safety net of abstemious relief for the so-called worthy poor, and police repression of idleness and dissipation. A learned commentary on criminal law written by Joel Bishop in 1892 made the point clear: "There is, in just principle, nothing which a government has more clearly the right to do than to compel the lazy to work; and there is nothing more absolutely beyond its jurisdiction than to fix the price of labor."[8]

The growing coercive power of government was also evident in the development of a small but effective standing army, which had a highly professionalized officer corps, and a National Guard, which placed an elaborate network of volunteer companies and armories at the disposal of governors in every state of the Union. Between 1886 and 1893 state governors called out their units of the National Guard 328 times. In one-third of the mobilizations the adjutant generals officially reported the cause as "labor troubles." Numerous other disturbances also arose out of workplace disputes. For example, soldiers were dispatched to return convicts whom miners had set free in Tennessee. General Coxey's Commonweal of Christ and the related Industrial Army of the Far West on their marches to Washington in 1894 were constantly dogged by the National Guard, which was called out nine times against them. No fewer than 91 other guard actions had been caused by lynchings or outbreaks officially described as "race troubles (negroes and whites)." That description usually referred to the suppression of some collective action by African Americans, but it could include anything from evicting black squatters to enforcing laws against gathering oysters.[9]

"Government by injunction," which the Democratic platform of 1896 denounced as "a new and highly dangerous form of oppression," had been born of the marriage of court orders and enforcement by bodies of armed men drilled for action against urban crowds. Precedents for the court orders had two major sources. One was the growing use of injunctions against railroad strikes during the 1880s, a development that has received careful attention in this volume.[10] The other was court orders against boycotts.

The citywide boycott, by which all residents were mobilized to "leave severely alone" a particular firm that persecuted or defied its workers, had developed by the mid-1880s into the most effective weapon of the Knights of Labor. While workers defended their hundreds of local boycotts as the sort of private arrangement to promote the common welfare that was favored by America's Jeffersonian legacy, courts prohibited them precisely because their motivation was not self-interested but sympathetic. By introducing community moral standards into economic behavior, boycotts represented a particularly flagrant intrusion by society into the hallowed preserve of the market. Judges made and enforced the law by which community boycotts, which Virginia's judges called "combinations of irresponsible cabals or cliques," were proclaimed criminal acts.[11]

The ARU's boycott of Pullman cars was national in scope, and it focused on the railroad system. In response, as William Forbath has written, "Federal judges . . . turned their courtrooms into police courts by issuing roughly one hundred decrees prohibiting the ARU and other unions from threatening, combining, or conspiring to quit in any fashion that would embarrass the railways' operations. They also enjoined refusals to handle the cars of other struck lines."[12]

This escalating confrontation between capitalism and popular liberties sounded alarm bells in the organizations of workers and farmers alike. Although the conference of twenty-four officials of national unions held in Chicago's Briggs House shortly after Debs's arrest on conspiracy charges declined to call a general strike in support of a demand for reinstating all ARU strikers, its official communique saluted the boycott as "an impulsive, vigorous protest against the gathering, growing forces of plutocratic power and corporation rule." Its concluding lines summoned workers to strengthen their unions and prepare to "go to the ballot-box and cast our votes as American freemen, united and determined to redeem this country from its present political and industrial misrule, to take it from the hands of the plutocratic wreckers and place it in the hands of the common people."[13]

A very different interpretation was offered by John Bates Clark, then president of the American Economics Association. Clark, too, saw the decade's social conflict as the birth pangs of a new social and political order, but in his 1894 address to the association he described the current merger movement in industry as the precondition of both greater stability in the business world and a new upsurge of productivity, from which all members of society would benefit. "What productive energies will this process unchain!" Clark exclaimed. Electricity not only would provide cheap "motive power" for machinery everywhere but also would call unimagined "forms of utility and beauty . . . out of non-existence at the touch of a button!" Clark prophesied that those the trade unionists had denounced as "plutocratic wreckers" would not destroy democracy but would renew and reconstruct it: "The crowning gain of it all is the irrepressible democracy of it. By the processes that others control, and by wealth that others own, the laborer will get, in the end, the most valuable personal gains. Mastership and plutocracy, in a good sense, yield by natural law a democratic result; for it is by the wealth that these ensure that the productive power of man must rise."[14]

As Clark had written six years earlier, "The new era has, in fact, begun, but it has not brought socialism."[15] On the contrary the new era was presaged by the railway executives who sat on the General Managers' Association. Although the largest factories before the 1890s were owned by individuals or partnerships, such as those of Pullman and Carnegie, their major customers were railroads. The consolidated railroad systems themselves were owned by corporations and directed by elaborate managerial bureaucracies. The expanding use of the corporate form of organization in manufacturing and commerce and the widespread formation of holding companies during the waves of business mergers immediately before and after the depression of 1893–97 greatly enlarged the capacity of business executives to administer the markets in which they bought materials and sold finished products, while both the judiciary and Congress concluded a protracted and intense debate over the legality of corporate economic power by ultimately authorizing its exercise, provided the marketing practices pursued by corporations were "reasonable." As Martin J. Sklar has argued persuasively, the public controversy over governmental regulation of corporate activity, which dominated political discussion during the two decades before 1914, was also the process by which corporate control of economic life was legitimated.[16]

That very process, however, was also part of the development Polanyi had in mind when he wrote that "society took measures to protect itself" against the destructive impact of "the self-regulating market."[17] The era of the trust did not end with "the *nation*" taking "*possession* of the *trusts*," as the Socialist Victor Berger had desired. Nor did antitrust laws fragment economic activity into units governed by market forces beyond their individual capacities to shape. On the contrary a few large enterprises came to dominate most industries and also provide young men and women new careers as employees. Such regulatory measures as local, state, and federal governments undertook in this turn-of-the-century reshaping of market activities were increasingly entrusted to commissions of professional experts rather than to elected members of legislative bodies.[18]

The gold standard *was* retained until the Great Depression of the 1930s. Business leaders, with the noteworthy exception of owners of silver mines, rallied vigorously to its defense with a massive campaign of public education between 1893 and 1896, spearheaded by the Reform Club of New York. As James Livingston has observed, the Reform Club feared that expansion of the currency, through free silver or greenbacks, would reinvigorate small competitors to the emerging corporations and further destabilize the economy. To defenders of the gold standard money was more than a medium of exchange; it was the instrument of expanded production through accumulation and credit—its acquisition the reason for engaging in production. Control of the money supply was a crucial instrument of economic regulation and consequently had to be entrusted to experts who understood its purpose.[19]

In brief neither the political and economic order Debs and Gompers championed nor the one Cleveland defended emerged intact from the depression of the 1890s. Even before the decade ended Cleveland's name had appeared, together with Gompers's, on a futile plea to the U.S. Senate not to annex the Philippines and Puerto Rico. The new business regime, which took shape in the major industrial countries with breathtaking speed during the decade and a half of erratic but vigorous economic expansion after the depression, was accompanied by mounting international tension and armament (especially naval construction in the United States), providing early evidence of Polanyi's point that the measures taken by society "to protect itself . . . endangered society in yet another way." For the labor movement neither the merger movement itself nor governmental demands for patriotic service and loyalty ended military repression of strikes, but they did present new opportunities and new perils.[20]

Although most manufacturing and construction firms remained relatively small and privately owned, the average worker in manufacturing now worked for one of the new giant enterprises. By 1909 fully 62.2 percent of all wage earners in manufacturing were employed by only 4.8 percent of the firms (all of them corporations).[21] These firms shaped the cutting edge of new technologies, scientific management, and sometimes company welfare experiments. Unsuccessful strikes in steel, meatpacking, and farm equipment had left large-scale industry overwhelmingly nonunion, even while the trade union movement increased its membership by more than three-and-a-half times between 1897 and 1904. Although workers still hungered for the improved earnings and control over their working lives that only collective action could bring, the new circumstances left their firm imprint on workers' organizations.

In his 1894 reflections on the Pullman boycott Samuel Gompers advocated cautious and deliberate action by working people to secure effective power in their occupations and to improve their own conditions step-by-step.[22] This course of action was heartily approved by the delegates to the AFL's 1895 convention. It emphasized the pursuit of trade agreements with employers or associations of employers to fix the terms of employment for union members. Sympathetic actions were curtailed, and general strikes were anathema to most national union leaders. During the economic upswing between 1897 and 1903 union membership expanded more rapidly than in any other comparable period of time in American history, and sympathy strikes were numerous. But few of those strikes were sanctioned by the international unions. Citywide general strikes that took place later—in Philadelphia in 1910; Springfield, Illinois, in 1917; Kansas City and Billings in 1918; and Seattle in 1919—were all basically sympathetic actions organized by local trade unionists in the face of vigorous opposition from the top officials of the AFL. In 1922, when AFL unions in the railroad shopcrafts waged a strike involving far more workers than had engaged in the Pullman boycott and reaching every corner of the land, national unions in the carrying and maintenance trades directed their members not to participate.[23]

Second, the efforts at political alliances between black and white workers and farmers, which had been widespread if hesitant during the decade and a half between Virginia's Readjusters and North Carolina's Populist-

Republican coalition, crumpled before a new wave of disfranchisement, segregation, and lynchings. The blood-drenched drive to racial segregation was a critically important lineament of the society that emerged from the 1890s, and it imposed its stamp decisively on the union movement and labor politics. It also framed the proposals Progressive Era reformers made for governmental regulation of social life and the market economy. The last attempts in the U.S. Congress to keep alive the possibility of interracial democracy in the South had appeared in 1890, with the demise of Senator Henry Blair's bill for federal aid to primary education and Senator Henry Cabot Lodge's proposal that federal election supervisors be dispatched to every congressional district where a hundred citizens petitioned for such help against electoral fraud and coercion. Both bills went down to defeat under the combined and vehement opposition of southern white congressmen, the Democratic party, and Republican friends of free silver. In the summer of the Pullman boycott the Democratic majority in Congress repealed the portions of the Enforcement Act of 1870 on which Lodge's proposals had been based. By 1896 the Republicans themselves had dropped from their national platform all mention of fair voting in the South.[24]

Segregation became institutionalized in the trade union movement itself, starting with the railroads, which had long been distinguished by elaborate racial hierarchies. The carrying trades were among the few sectors of employment in the country that were dominated by native-born whites. Brakemen drew their recruits largely from local farm youth. Repair shops and northern switchyards were the domain of northern European immigrants in some regions, native-born whites in others. Track laying varied with the region: Scandinavians in the Northwest, Chinese and Mexicans in the Southwest, African Americans in the Southeast. Union practice both reflected and reinforced those divisions. The brotherhoods had long excluded any but whites from membership. At its 1894 convention the ARU followed suit. The next year the AFL admitted the International Association of Machinists, whose members were pledged to propose only Caucasians for affiliation. That decision laid out the AFL's welcome mat to numerous other unions that barred black workers from their ranks.[25]

Finally, the socialist movement grew to far greater size, coherence, and influence than it had exhibited during the nineteenth century. The Socialist Party of America, whose resolutions and candidates for AFL offices mustered a third of the votes at federation conventions by 1910–12, called for collective ownership of industrial enterprise and the subordination of all economic activity to the democratically determined needs of working people. The Industrial Workers of the World (IWW) transformed the historic attempts of the Knights of Labor and the ARU to enroll all grades of workers into a campaign to organize both industrial and agricultural workers along lines that flouted historic craft divisions, dispensed with salaried officials (as well as with strike and benefit funds), and rejected the very idea of contractual relations with the bosses. Unlike the ARU, the IWW scorned all racial exclusions. Japanese, Mexicans, African Americans, and all other wage earners were summoned, as Arturo Giovannitti told the jurors in Salem, Massachusetts, to join "the heralds of a new civilization," to diffuse "in every known tongue, in every civilized language, in every dialect . . . this message of socialism, this message of brotherhood, this message of love."[26]

Toward the 1990s

Looking back over the hundred years since the Pullman boycott, Americans found that the measures society took to prevent the self-regulating market from "annihilating the human and natural substance of society" (to repeat Polanyi's words) turned out to have a life span of little more than three-quarters of a century. As the centennial of the historic conflict between the American Railway Union and the General Managers' Association was commemorated, the ascendant ideology once again celebrated "a free market economy," while the incremental improvement of workers' lot by trade unionism had been forced into retreat, the welfare state was under vigorous attack, and public advocacy of socialism had been virtually eclipsed. That paradox challenges us to assess carefully not only the causes of the confrontation of 1894 but also the remedies that it evoked.

John Bates Clark was right in believing that worker productivity would rise to previously unimagined heights. During the 1930s, when levels of unemployment remained brutal, the output of those who were at work continued to rise remarkably. After 1940, when the United States stood as the economic leader of the world, consistently rising productivity provided the glue that held the social order together and made possible a modus vivendi between business and a union movement that by the early 1950s embraced 42 percent of the workers in manufacturing, 87 percent of those in construction, and 76 percent of those on the railroads. Pattern bargaining made rising wage scales, seniority rights, grievance procedures, and company-provided insurance the accepted standards of a "good job," which corporations also sought to match for their nonunion employees. A revived international economy, in which the dollar had replaced Grover Cleveland's beloved gold standard as the common currency of world trade and international banking agencies disciplined government budgets and shaped global patterns of investment, allowed the structures of commerce and investment to be undergirded in all industrialized countries by government protection of major sectors of the population against injuries that the market system inflicted on them.[27]

The New Deal had completed the domestic institutional framework for this accomplishment. It had freed the federal budget for reform purposes by abandoning the gold standard and had instituted a limited but carefully gendered system of social security to shelter male earnings against unemployment and old age, while underwriting state systems of welfare payments to mothers with dependent children, which had their roots in the Progressive Era. It had also empowered workers to reshape industrial relations and incomes through collective bargaining, while it sought to channel the vigorous militancy of the times into paths compatible with a market-regulated economy. Political repression during the cold war years guaranteed that labor remained in that channel. One result was a resurgence of industrial unionism as a formidable and durable reform agency in American life, but it was shorn of the revolutionary edge it had carried in the first two decades of this century.[28]

When the economy was refashioned from what Martin Sklar has called its proprietary-competitive form into its twentieth-century corporate-administrative shape, the trade union movement found it difficult (and dangerous) to resist the advice of coal miners' leader John Mitchell that it could "make progress only by identifying itself with the State—by obeying its just laws and by upholding the military as well as the civil arm of the government."[29] For working men and women citizenship acquired a new meaning. Citizenship came to embody social entitlements. Working people expected government to secure their lives against the ravages of a market-driven economy. What workers owed in return was patriotic loyalty—a readiness to go to war and to combat those who had been identified as the country's enemies—abroad and at home.[30]

Between 1965 and 1975, in the wake of yet another of the century's wars, this formula came unstuck. The policies that had secured growth, social cohesiveness, and military prowess since 1940 now appeared to hobble the further expansion of capitalist production and accumulation. At first Richard Nixon's administration sought to combat the twin menace of stagnation and inflation by wielding the weapons of government intervention in the economy more draconically than any of his predecessors and by repudiating the world dollar standard, the way Franklin Roosevelt had earlier abandoned the gold standard.

By the end of the 1970s, however, the way out of stagflation had been found in a global restructuring of the economy, which decorated urban America with closed factories, and in a crusade to "unleash enterprise" from government intervention. A slash-and-burn policy was applied to the welfare state. Ironically the rhetoric in which the new free market mania was couched drew heavily on such popular struggles to liberate civil society from the heavy hand of the modern state as the antiwar movements of the 1960s and the popular risings of countries under Communist rule. What Karl Polanyi had called the "stark utopia" on which the cult of the self-adjusting market rested had returned in our times as the guiding doctrine of states and international investment agencies. With the collapse of regimes that had called themselves socialist the allegedly immutable law of the marketplace could now appear as the only realistic foundation on which to base social policy.[31]

Confronted with the profound social changes of the 1890s, President Cleveland had wielded the full coercive power of government to defend the self-adjusted market against the demands of workers and farmers, for whom it generated intolerable social distress, even while that ideal was bowing off the stage. The American Railway Union responded to such distress with a vision of a more humane social and economic life. Who will champion the "human and natural substance of society" in our time?

Notes

1. Horace Samuel Merrill, *Bourbon Leader: Grover Cleveland and the Democratic Party* (Boston: Little, Brown, 1957); Nick Salvatore, *Eugene V. Debs: Citizen and Socialist* (Urbana: University of Illinois Press, 1982); John Sproat, *"The Best Men": Liberal Reformers in the Gilded Age* (New York: Oxford University Press, 1968), 170–203; Theodore Roosevelt, "Fourth Annual Message . . . December 6, 1904," in *A Compilation of the Messages and Papers of the Presidents*, vol. 15 (New York: published by the authority of Congress, 1914), 7053–54.

2. Karl Polanyi, *The Great Transformation: The Political and Economic Origins of Our Time* (New York: Farrar and Rinehart, 1944), 3.

3. David Montgomery, *The Fall of the House of Labor: The Workplace, the State, and American Labor Activism, 1865–1925* (New York: Cambridge University Press, 1987), 44–57, 126–31, 148–54; James Livingston, "The Social Analysis of Economic History and Theory: Conjectures on Late Nineteenth-Century American Development," *American Historical Review* 92 (February 1987): 69–96.

4. Montgomery, *Fall of the House of Labor*, 69–70, 171–72; William Carwardine, *The Pullman Strike* (Chicago: Charles H. Kerr, 1894); Samuel Gompers, "The Strike and Its Lessons," in *A Momentus Question: The Respective Attitudes of Labor and Capital*, ed. John Swinton (Philadelphia and Chicago: Keller Publishing, 1895), 314. On workers' efforts to deal with insecurity, see S. J. Kleinberg, *The Shadow of the Mills: Working-Class Families in Pittsburgh, 1870–1907* (Pittsburgh: University of Pittsburgh Press, 1989); August Sartorius von Waltershausen, "Das Hilfkassenwesen in Nordamerika," *Jahrbücher für Nationalökonomie und Statistik*, Neue Folge, 10 (1885): 97–154; and Alexander Keyssar, *Out of Work: The First Century of Unemployment in Massachusetts* (New York: Cambridge University Press, 1986). For an argument that workers' incomes did decline relative to those of the upper classes between 1870 and 1900, see Jeffrey G. Williamson and Peter H. Lindert, *American Inequality: A Macroeconomic History* (New York: Academic, 1980), chaps. 10–11.

5. Montgomery, *Fall of the House of Labor*, 126–30, 154–70, 198–201; Maier B. Fox, *United We Stand: The United Mine Workers of America, 1890–1990* (n.p.: United Mine Workers of America, 1990), 44–47; Eric Arnesen, *Waterfront Workers of New Orleans: Race, Class, and Politics, 1863–1923* (New York: Oxford University Press, 1991), 114–18.

6. United States v. Workingmen's Amalgamated Council of New Orleans et al., 54 Fed. 994 (1893): 999.

7. David Montgomery, *Citizen Worker: The Experience of Workers in the United States with Democracy and the Free Market during the Nineteenth Century* (New York: Cambridge University Press, 1993), 52–114. New state constitutions of the 1870s had narrowed the range of state legislative powers over economic activity. See Morton Keller, *Affairs of State: Public Life in Late Nineteenth Century America* (Cambridge, Mass.: Belknap of Harvard University Press, 1977), 110–21.

8. Andrew Cameron, editorial in Workingman's Advocate, March 25, 1865; Joel Bishop, *New Commentaries on the Criminal Law*, vol. 1 (Chicago: T. H. Flood, 1892), 273–74.

9. Winthrop Alexander, "Ten Years of Riot Duty," *Journal of the Military Service Institution of the United States* 19 (July 1896): 1–62 (quote on 26); Henry Vincent, *The Story of the Commonweal* (Chicago: W. B. Conkey, 1894).

10. The Democratic Platform of 1896, in *National Party Platforms*, ed. Kirk H. Porter (New York: Macmillan, 1924), 185; Gerald G. Eggert, *Railroad Labor Disputes: The Beginning of Federal Strike Policy* (Ann Arbor: University of Michigan Press, 1967).

11. Norman J. Ware, *The Labor Movement in the United States, 1860–1895* (New

York: D. Appleton, 1929), 334–45; William E. Forbath, *Law and the Shaping of the American Labor Movement* (Cambridge, Mass.: Harvard University Press, 1991), 79–97; *Crump v. Commonwealth*, 84 Va., 927, 946 (1888), quoted in Forbath, *Law and the Shaping of the American Labor Movement*, 84.

12. Forbath, *Law and the Shaping of the American Labor Movement*, 75.

13. The Briggs House statement is reproduced in Swinton, *Momentus Question*, 308–13 (quotes on 312, 313). For a description of the conference, see Almont Lindsey, *The Pullman Strike: The Story of a Unique Experiment and of a Great Labor Upheaval* (Chicago: University of Chicago Press, 1942), 326–29.

14. John Bates Clark, "The Modern Appeal to Legal Forces in Economic Life," *Publications of the American Economic Association* 9 (October and December 1894): 501, quoted in Nancy Cohen, "The Problem of Democracy in the Age of Capital: Reconstructing American Liberalism, 1865–1890" (Ph.D. diss., Columbia University, 1995), 364–65.

15. John Bates Clark, *The Philosophy of Wealth* (Boston: Ginn, 1886), 291.

16. Alfred D. Chandler Jr., *The Railroads, The Nation's First Big Business: Sources and Readings* (New York: Harcourt, Brace and World, 1965); Alfred D. Chandler Jr., *The Visible Hand: The Managerial Revolution in American Business* (Cambridge, Mass.: Belknap of Harvard University Press, 1977); Naomi R. Lamoreaux, *The Great Merger Movement in American Business, 1895–1904* (New York, 1985); Martin J. Sklar, *The Corporate Reconstruction of American Capitalism, 1890–1916: The Market, the Law, and Politics* (New York: Cambridge University Press, 1988), 33–40.

17. Polanyi, *Great Transformation*, 3.

18. On Berger, see Sally M. Miller, *Victor Berger and the Promise of Constructive Socialism, 1910–1920* (Westport, Conn.: Greenwood, 1973), 26. On careers and expertise, see Sklar, *Corporate Reconstruction of American Capitalism*, 20–33; Dorothy Ross, *The Origins of American Social Science* (New York: Cambridge University Press, 1991), 219–56; and Ellis W. Hawley, "Herbert Hoover, the Commerce Secretariat, and the Vision of an 'Associative State,' 1921–1928," *Journal of American History* 61 (June 1974): 116–40. J. Morgan Kousser, *The Shaping of Southern Politics: Suffrage Restriction and the Establishment of the One-Party South, 1880–1910* (New Haven, Conn.: Yale University Press, 1974), 252–62, argues that deliberate and effective restriction of the size of the electorate was an important part of this process.

19. James Livingston, *Origins of the Federal Reserve System: Money, Class, and Corporate Capitalism, 1890–1913* (Ithaca, N.Y.: Cornell University Press, 1986), 83–99.

20. Philip S. Foner, *History of the Labor Movement in the United States*, vol. 2 (New York: International, 1955), 423–24; Howard K. Beale, *Theodore Roosevelt and the Rise of America to World Power* (Baltimore: Johns Hopkins University Press, 1956).

21. Livingston, *Origins of the Federal Reserve System*, 57–7. See also Daniel Nelson, *Managers and Workers: Origins of the New Factory System in the United States, 1880–1920* (Madison: University of Wisconsin Press, 1975), 3–10.

22. Gompers, "The Strike and Its Lessons," 306–14.

23. Montgomery, *Fall of the House of Labor*, 263–65, 371, 407–10; Fred S. Hall, *Sympathetic Strikes and Sympathetic Lockouts* (New York: Columbia University Press, 1898); Ken Fones-Wolf, *Trade Union Gospel: Christianity and Labor in Industrial Philadelphia, 1865–1915* (Philadelphia: Temple University Press, 1989), 167–70; Dana Frank, *Purchasing Power: Consumer Organizing, Gender, and the Seattle Labor Movement, 1919–1929* (New York: Cambridge University Press, 1994), 34–39; Colin J. Davis, *Power at Odds: The 1922 National Railroad Shopmen's Strike* (Urbana: University of Illinois Press, 1997).

24. Kousser, *Shaping of Southern Politics;* Luther P. Jackson, *Negro Office-Holders in Virginia, 1865–1895* (Norfolk: Guide Quality, 1945); James Tice Moore, *Two Paths to the New South: The Virginia Debt Controversy, 1870–1883* (Lexington: University Press of Kentucky, 1974). The abrupt and violent demise of political democracy in North Carolina is described vividly in Glenda Elizabeth Gilmore, *Gender and Jim Crow: Women and the Politics of White Supremacy in North Carolina, 1896–1920* (Chapel Hill: University of North Carolina Press, 1996), 1–146.

25. Montgomery, *Fall of the House of Labor*, 74–81, 198–201; Shelton Stromquist, *A Generation of Boomers: The Pattern of Railroad Labor Conflict in Nineteenth-Century America* (Urbana: University of Illinois Press, 1987), 48–80, 201–11.

26. John H. M. Laslett, *Labor and the Left: A Study of Socialist and Radical Influences in the American Labor Movement, 1881–1924* (New York: Basic Books, 1970); Ira Kipnis, *The American Socialist Movement, 1897–1912* (New York: Monthly Review Press, 1952); James Weinstein, *Decline of Socialism in America, 1912–1925* (New York: Monthly Review Press, 1967); Montgomery, *Fall of the House of Labor*, 281–329; Joyce L. Kornbluh, *Rebel Voices: An I.W.W. Anthology* (Ann Arbor: University of Michigan Press, 1968), 193–95 (Giovannitti's speech to the jury).

27. On productivity in the 1930s, see Richard C. Wilcox, "Industrial Management's Policies toward Unionism," in *Labor and the New Deal*, ed. Milton Derber and Edwin Young (Madison: University of Wisconsin Press, 1957); and Richard J. Jensen, "The Causes and Cures of Unemployment in the Great Depression," *Journal of Interdisciplinary History* 19 (Spring 1989): 553–83. On trade union membership, see Leo Troy, "The Rise and Fall of American Trade Unions: The Labor Movement from FDR to RR," in *Unions in Transition: Entering the Second Century*, ed. Seymour Martin Lipset (San Francisco: Institute for Contemporary Studies, 1986), 87. On productivity and welfare states, see Charles S. Maier, *In Search of Stability: Explorations in Historical Political Economy* (New York: Cambridge University Press, 1987); Thomas J. McCormick, *America's Half Century: United States Foreign Policy in the Cold War* (Baltimore: Johns Hopkins University, 1989); and Giovanni Arrighi, *The Long Twentieth Century: Money, Power, and the Origins of Our Times* (London: Verso, 1994).

28. Polanyi, *Great Transformation*, 14–23, 229–33; David Montgomery, "Labor and the Political Leadership of New Deal America," *International Review of Social*

History 39 (December 1994): 335–60; Steve Rosswurm, ed., *The CIO's Left-Led Unions* (New Brunswick, N.J.: Rutgers University Press, 1992).

29. John Mitchell, *Organized Labor,* quoted in Marc Karson, *American Labor Unions and Politics, 1900–1918* (Boston: Beacon, 1958), 90.

30. Maier, *In Search of Stability,* 121–52, has offered an especially insightful exploration of what he calls the "politics of productivity" in an international context.

31. Mike Davis, *Prisoners of the American Dream* (London: Verso, 1986), 157–255; William E. Simon, *A Time for Truth* (New York: McGraw-Hill, 1978); Charles S. Maier, "The Collapse of Communism: Approaches for a Future History," *History Workshop* 31 (Spring 1991): 34–59.

Contributors

VICTORIA BROWN is a member of the History Department at Grinnell College in Grinnell, Iowa. She has published essays on female socialization in Los Angeles at the turn of the century and on Jane Addams.

MELVYN DUBOFSKY is Distinguished Professor of History and Sociology at SUNY–Binghamton. His writings include *The State and Labor in Modern America* (1994); *Industrialism and the American Worker, 1865–1920,* 3d ed. (1996); and *Essays in Labor History* (forthcoming).

SUSAN E. HIRSCH is an associate professor of history at Loyola University of Chicago. Her work includes *Roots of the American Working Class: The Industrialization of Crafts in Newark, 1800–1860* (1978); *A City Comes of Age: Chicago in the 1890s* (with Robert Goler, 1991); and *The War in American Culture: Society and Consciousness during World War II* (coedited with Lewis Erenberg, 1996).

DAVID MONTGOMERY is Farnam Professor of History Emeritus at Yale University and president-elect of the Organization of American Historians. He is the author of, among other books, *The Fall of the House of Labor: The Workplace, the State, and American Labor Activism, 1865–1925* (1987) and *Citizen Worker: The Experience of Workers in the United States with Democracy and the Free Market during the Nineteenth Century* (1993). He is coeditor, with Marcel van der Linden, of *August Sartorius Von Waltershausen: The Workers' Movement in the United States, 1879–1885* (forthcoming).

LARRY PETERSON is managing editor of the *Journal of Comparative Politics*. He is the author of *German Communism, Workers' Protest, and Labor Unions: The Politics of the United Front in Rhineland Westphalia, 1920–1924* (1993) and numerous articles on German, American, and comparative labor history.

JANICE L. REIFF teaches social history, the history of modern America, and quantitative methods at UCLA. She is the author of *Structuring the Past: The Use of Computers in History* (1991) and is one of the coeditors (with James R. Grossman and Ann Durkin Keating) of the *Encyclopedia of Chicago History* (forthcoming)

NICK SALVATORE is a professor of history in the American Studies Program and the School of Industrial and Labor Relations at Cornell University. He is the author of *Eugene V. Debs: Citizen and Socialist* (1982) and *We All Got History: The Memory Books of Amos Webber* (1996).

RICHARD SCHNEIROV teaches the history of labor and social movements at Indiana State University. He is the author of *Union Brotherhood, Union Town: The History of the Carpenters' Union of Chicago, 1863–1987* (with Thomas J. Suhrbur, 1988); *Pride and Solidarity: A History of the Plumbers and Pipefitters of Columbus, Ohio, 1889–1989* (1992); and *Labor and Urban Politics: Class Conflict and the Origins of Modern Liberalism in Chicago, 1864–97* (1998).

SHELTON STROMQUIST teaches labor and social history at the University of Iowa. He is the author of *A Generation of Boomers: The Pattern of Railroad Labor Conflict in Nineteenth-Century America* (1987); *Solidarity and Survival: An Oral History of Iowa Labor in the Twentieth Century* (1993); and *Reinventing "the People": The Progressive Movement and the Class Question* (forthcoming).

ROBERT E. WEIR is an associate professor of liberal studies at Bay Path College in Longmeadow, Massachusetts. He is the author of *Beyond Labor's Veil: The Culture of the Knights of Labor* (1996) and has lectured and published widely on the Knights of Labor and Gilded Age social and cultural issues.

Index

The Working Class in American History

Work and Community in the Jungle: Chicago's Packinghouse
Workers, 1894–1922   *James R. Barrett*

Workers, Managers, and Welfare Capitalism: The Shoeworkers and
Tanners of Endicott Johnson, 1890–1950   *Gerald Zahavi*

Men, Women, and Work: Class, Gender, and Protest in the New
England Shoe Industry, 1780–1910   *Mary Blewett*

Workers on the Waterfront: Seamen, Longshoremen, and Unionism
in the 1930s   *Bruce Nelson*

German Workers in Chicago: A Documentary History of Working-
Class Culture from 1850 to World War I   *Edited by Hartmut Keil and
John B. Jentz*

On the Line: Essays in the History of Auto Work   *Edited by
Nelson Lichtenstein and Stephen Meyer III*

Upheaval in the Quiet Zone: A History of Hospital Workers' Union,
Local 1199   *Leon Fink and Brian Greenberg*

Labor's Flaming Youth: Telephone Operators and Worker Militancy,
1878–1923   *Stephen H. Norwood*

Another Civil War: Labor, Capital, and the State in the Anthracite
Regions of Pennsylvania, 1840–68   *Grace Palladino*

Coal, Class, and Color: Blacks in Southern West Virginia, 1915–32
Joe William Trotter, Jr.

For Democracy, Workers, and God: Labor Song-Poems and Labor
Protest, 1865–95   *Clark D. Halker*

Dishing It Out: Waitresses and Their Unions in the Twentieth
Century   *Dorothy Sue Cobble*

The Spirit of 1848: German Immigrants, Labor Conflict, and the
Coming of the Civil War   *Bruce Levine*

Working Women of Collar City: Gender, Class, and Community in
Troy, New York, 1864–86   *Carole Turbin*

Southern Labor and Black Civil Rights: Organizing Memphis
Workers   *Michael K. Honey*

Radicals of the Worst Sort: Laboring Women in Lawrence, Massachusetts, 1860–1912   *Ardis Cameron*

Producers, Proletarians, and Politicians: Workers and Party Politics in
Evansville and New Albany, Indiana, 1850–87   *Lawrence M. Lipin*

The New Left and Labor in the 1960s   *Peter B. Levy*

The Making of Western Labor Radicalism: Denver's Organized Workers, 1878–1905   *David Brundage*

In Search of the Working Class: Essays in American Labor History
and Political Culture   *Leon Fink*

Lawyers against Labor: From Individual Rights to Corporate
Liberalism   *Daniel R. Ernst*

Typeset in 10.5/13 Cycles
with Cycles display
Book design by Dennis Roberts
Composed by Jim Proefrock
at the University of Illinois Press
Manufactured by Cushing-Malloy, Inc.